For Surjit

Shamed

The honour killing that shocked Britain –
by the sister who fought for justice

SARBJIT KAUR ATHWAL

with Jeff Hudson

Foreword by DCI Clive Driscoll

10

First published in the United Kingdom in 2013 by Virgin Books,
an imprint of Ebury Publishing

A Random House Group Company

www.randomhouse.co.uk

Addresses for companies within The Random House Group Limited can be
found at **www.randomhouse.co.uk/offices.htm**

The Random House Group Limited Reg. No. 954009

A CIP catalogue record for this book is available from the British Library

Penguin Random House is committed to a sustainable future for
our business, our readers and our planet. This book is made from
Forest Stewardship Council® certified paper.

Designed and typeset by K DESIGN, Winscombe, Somerset
Plate section design: www.envydesign.co.uk
Printed and bound by Clays Ltd, St Ives plc

ISBN: 9780753541548

To buy books by your favourite authors and register for offers, visit
www.randomhouse.co.uk

CONTENTS

FOREWORD

In 1998, a young English girl left her home – and never returned.

Her only 'crime' was refusing to live the lifestyle imposed upon her by purveyors of extremist religious views. One could argue that these views were just a personal interpretation of what is, in fact, a gentle religion. I have always found it insulting that Sikhism is tarnished by the behaviour of some of its followers; the vast majority of religious people I have met of *all* denominations are kind and live a peaceful and good life.

Regrettably, in my time as a police officer, I have investigated criminals who have hidden behind the face of religion and used that religion to mask their criminal activity. I think it is essential that the police follow the integrity of the investigation at all times and search for the truth above all other considerations.

Make no mistake: Honour Based Violence (HBV) is a blight on society. For young people to be threatened or tricked into a path that they do not wish to follow offends their basic human rights. The act of murder carried out as punishment for not obeying another's religious principles must always be wrong and – in my opinion – a priority for any police force, no matter where they are in the world. And that stands even in this age of austerity, when all police services in the UK face severe financial restriction. Murder and other serious crime, and protection of the public, should be the priority.

For we know that the threat of detection and conviction remains a big deterrent in preventing these awful crimes.

My son is a Royal Marine Commando who fought in many recent campaigns, and lost many of his colleagues. The bravery these young men and women show, every day, is an inspiration to me. However, the courage that Sarbjit Kaur Athwal, the author of this book, showed by coming forward as a witness makes her equally as brave and inspirational to me as the very brave young men and women who serve this country. And that goes not just for Sarbjit, but also other witnesses who have placed truth and *real* honour first, coming forward to give evidence in HBV cases. To me, their courage matches that shown by troops in our armed forces, and by the young men and women who protect our streets while patrolling as police officers.

The pressure Sarbjit faced in the lead-up to the criminal trial cannot be underestimated: the intimidation she faced verbally and via her children, who were used as pawns against her. The methods employed were, in my view, similar to the intimidation techniques that criminal networks employ.

But she stood firm and did her Sikh duty.

I hope the readers of this book will accept from me that this witness, and one other who cannot be named for legal reasons, were absolutely pivotal in my investigation.

In addition, I would like to thank Mr Jagdeesh Singh and Surjit's mother and father for the help, support and encouragement they gave me during the investigation.

I would also like to thank personally all of the officers who worked on Operation Yewlands. There is little doubt the police performed some duties well, and some duties we wish we had done to higher standards. However, the dedication these officers showed culminated in the successful prosecution of Bachan Kaur Athwal and Sukhdave Singh Athwal.

It has been a privilege to act as a Senior Investigating Officer (SIO) on all of my murder cases and I thank the Metropolitan Police for allowing me this honour.

I also thank the publishers of *Shamed* for asking me to write this foreword.

DCI Clive Driscoll, 2013
(SIO Operation Yewlands)

IT'S DECIDED

It looked like just another family gathering. An ordinary lounge in an ordinary house on an ordinary street in west London. But there was nothing ordinary about what happened next.

Two brothers and a sister-in-law – me – waited, poised to hear why we'd been summoned. All eyes were on the elderly matriarch perched on the sofa, between her doting sons. Pious-looking and respectfully dressed for prayer, she stared proudly around the room, smiled at her boys, and then spoke.

'It's decided then,' the old lady announced. 'We have to get rid of her.'

My sister-in-law is going to die.

PART ONE
HONOUR

CHAPTER ONE

ALL VICTORIOUS

It's a feast of the senses. The air is filled with incense and the aromas of a busy kitchen. Brightly dressed women jostle for position with men wearing colourful turbans, their long beards trailing down their chests. The sound of their rapid-fire conversation is punctuated by frequent bursts of laughter between mouthfuls of chapatti and sips of chilled lassi. It's a typical day of celebration for the local Sikh community but despite Punjabi being the only language used, the gathering is a long way from Amritsar or Chandigarh. It's in Hounslow, west London. And they are there to welcome a new arrival.

The happy but exhausted young woman clutches the tiny, gurgling bundle to her chest and smiles. Again. She can't help it. Just seeing her baby's little face, hearing each quick intake of breath, sends new joy soaring through her. She can't imagine ever being unhappy again.

Around her a dozen friendly faces seem to agree. The small living room has never hosted so many people, never had so much laughter reverberate off its walls, but they've all come to see the new arrival and most of them want a hold as well.

The mother watches as her first-born is passed around the circle of admirers. The women cuddle and coo while their husbands pull faces or try to tickle the wide-eyed little infant. The mother is among her closest friends and family but she doesn't relax, doesn't take her eyes off her little treasure until the wriggling bundle is finally passed back to her.

As she hands the baby over, a woman smiles. 'Congratulations, Amarjit Kaur,' she says, touching the baby's soft cheek. 'But it should have been a boy.'

* * *

I was born on 6 November 1969, the first-born child of Sewa Singh and Amarjit Kaur Bath, of Hounslow, London. Being a girl in an Indian family is not the best way to start life. In many people's eyes, that was the first time I brought shame on my family.

Mum's parents had uprooted their whole family to settle in England via Singapore. By contrast, Dad was the first member of his family to move out of their village in the Punjab, India. When he did so, however, it was as a married man. Sewa Singh and Amarjit Kaur had been selected for each other by their families and were married in a ceremony in India having never set eyes on each other before.

Home for the newlyweds was a four-bedroomed house in Hounslow – or, at least, a fraction of it. My grandparents lived in one room, Mum's sister and her children had another room, her brother, his wife and children had the third. Which left the smallest room for Mum and Dad – and another brother! When I came along, they somehow squeezed a cot in, too.

Growing up in such a packed household had been normal for both Mum and Dad, and I never knew anything different. Whatever the word for 'privacy' was in Punjabi, I wouldn't need it for some time. Apart from when I answered a call of nature, I can't recall a time when there were ever fewer than two people around me.

On the plus side, being surrounded by relatives meant there was no shortage of people to tell me stories about the wonders of India. At bedtimes especially I would sit with my cousins, rapt, while my auntie wove another colourful tale. At the end I'd be bursting with questions.

'Does the sun really shine all day?'

'Do cows really just walk along roads like cars?'

It sounded like a magical place.

I wonder why Mum and Dad want to live here instead?

Living under the same roof as their extended families wasn't the only tradition that my parents brought from India. In fact, apart from the weather you'd never guess we were living in the shadow of Heathrow Airport and not the Punjab. Punjabi was the only language spoken in the house. It was the only language my grandparents knew and certainly the only one I was taught. When my father got a job working for British Airways at Heathrow, he was forced to learn English at a rate of knots. But it was never spoken inside the house. I wasn't aware it existed until I started school.

Sometimes I looked out of my bedroom window and noticed that the people walking past were dressed differently to me. Even the girls. Around the house and outside, I always wore the traditional Punjabi outfit of a *salwar* – loose-fitting trousers – and *kameez* – a kind of shirt. My mother and aunts and cousins had versions in many colours and I enjoyed dreaming of all the exotic shades I could one day wear. Most important of all, when I stepped through the front door, my head was covered by a kind of shawl called a *chunni* or *dapatta*. The girls outside my window didn't wear these but I never considered myself different. Everyone in my house dressed like me. Everyone I ever spoke to dressed in the same way. It was the only world I knew.

It's the girls outside my window who are different. Not me.

It wasn't just the women in our family who covered their heads. My father, grandfather and uncles all wore turbans. Historically in India, it was only the gentry who were permitted to wear such ostentatious headwear. But – my father told me – three hundred years ago a man called Gobind Singh decreed that no class should have superiority over others. Yet, I learned, Gobind Singh was no ordinary man himself. He was a 'Guru' – one of the ten founding fathers of Sikhism.

Like so many other things, I was not particularly aware I came from a religious family. It was just the way we were.

Doesn't every child live like this?

One of my earliest memories is going to a large yellow building not far from our house. This, my father explained, was the *gurdwara* – or 'temple'. All I really knew was that this place looked like a castle. I was mesmerised by the two beautiful white round domes perched at the top of the tall columns either side of the entrance. Inside there were no kings or queens. Just hundreds of people dressed exactly like us. I wasn't the only little girl who'd put on her Sunday best to go there and for a few moments I felt swamped by the variety of bright colours on show.

Even though I was wearing my prettiest shoes, I was told to take them off. I followed my family and saw hundreds of pairs of footwear lining the wall. Then, while my father, grandfather and uncles went one way, my mother and the women from our family turned another.

I'd never seen a room as large as the main hall of the temple. But at least I was used to being in a crowd, if not one divided into men and women. There were people everywhere, all silent, all seated cross-legged on the floor, all praying. This, I did know how to do. My grandmother had taught me from a very young age. It was, she said, my time to communicate with God. Not *our* God, or *my* God – Sikhs believe there is only one deity. Other religions may worship different names, but whatever they call Him, it's the same God we pray to.

If the scale of the room surprised me, its decoration completely caught me out. I looked up at the large paintings of men in turbans and white beards staring down and thought, *We have those pictures at home!*

With the familiar image of Guru Nanak Dev Ji, the founder of Sikhism, staring back, I couldn't have felt more comfortable.

I like it here.

***

There were several temples that my family used to visit. This one in Hounslow was closest but two others in Southall – one in Park Avenue and one on Havelock Road – seemed to be chosen for more important occasions. Sometimes there were sermons conducted by priests. Mainly, though, we were left to our own thoughts. After the noise and chatter at home, it was a relief to close my eyes and enjoy something close to silence.

Outside of the prayer room, however, the temples were incredibly social places. I remember once holding my mum's hand, staring up as she and her friends caught up on each other's news. Across the room I saw Dad and his friends putting the world to rights over a meal of chapatti and lentil soup.

Suddenly I was incredibly hungry myself.

'Can I have *langar* as well, Mum?' I asked.

My mother paused her conversation and squeezed my hand. 'Off you go,' she said. 'But come straight back.'

Every temple in the world offers *langar*, or vegetarian food and drink, to those who want it.

'You don't even have to be a Sikh!' Dad had explained. 'Anyone is welcome here.'

Volunteers arrive when the building opens at two in the morning and the large cooking pots, often still warm from the evening before, are fired up. The wonderful aromas of spices and oils were one of the first things that struck me as I entered Hounslow's *gurdwara* for the first time and they still do today.

Something else that reminds me of home.

There were other nods to my home life as well. Even as a young child, I'd heard so much about 'the community' but I'd never seen them. I never knew who 'they' were. That changed the moment I stepped foot inside Hounslow temple. Here they all were: the men, the women, religious leaders and friends. Some I'd seen before, at our house or theirs, but most were strangers to me. Still, as far as Mum and Dad were concerned, 'We're Sikhs. We're all part of one big family.'

* * *

I can appreciate that coming to Sikhism later in life would be a lot to take in. It's only years later, as an adult, that I realise how different some of our rules must seem. Even something as simple as a name carries a lot more weight in this religion. Like everything else, it's dictated by one of the gurus themselves.

Except this guru isn't a person at all.

When the Tenth Guru, Gobind Singh's time was coming to a close, he didn't name a person to follow him, as had been the tradition of his predecessors. Instead he chose a thing. A book. A bible. *The* bible. The word of God.

If you go into any Sikh temple or house today, you'll find a copy of the 'Eleventh' Guru Granth Sahib – or 'Holy Book' – mounted on a platform beneath a small roof or cover. We draw all our learning from its 1,430 passages. It shapes everything we do – even our names.

When I was born, my parents, like their parents before them, opened their copy of the Holy Book at a random page.

Then, in keeping with tradition, they took the first letter from the first word on that page – 'S' – and chose my name accordingly. There are only a few hundred given names in Sikh culture and they all have a religious or moral meaning. 'Sarbjit', for example, was selected by my proud father because it means 'all victorious'. As his first-born, he thought it seemed appropriate. Over the coming years, however, I would question the validity of that choice more than once.

To the uninitiated there is another aspect of Sikh names that stands out as different. I have a brother-in-law called Sarbjit but nobody in our community blinks an eye at that. He hasn't got a girl's name and I haven't got a boy's one. In fact, all Sikh names are non-gender-specific, so in theory you could choose the name before learning your baby's sex. The way you tell us apart on paper is by checking the middle name. If it's 'Singh' – meaning 'lion' – then the person is male; if it's 'Kaur' – 'princess' or 'lioness' – she's a woman. It does take a bit of getting used to but, like everything else in my childhood, I never questioned it because I never knew any different.

Because my father is Sewa Singh Bath, you know he's a man. Similarly, Amarjit Kaur has to be a woman. However, like most Sikhs, my true parents were called 'Honour' and 'Shame'. Everything a Sikh does is governed by one simple question: is this the right or the wrong thing to do? Or, to put it another way: will I bring honour or shame on my family? And where our faith is concerned, a family isn't just two or three other people …

There are only around 400,000 Sikhs living in the UK – but sometimes it can feel that they all have a say in your life! My parents not only had their close family to please, but also distant aunts and uncles, all their neighbours plus every member of their local temple got a say as well. The worst thing a Sikh could do, it seemed to me growing up, was lose the respect of the community.

But I was never going to do that. I'd brought shame on my family once by not being Sarbjit *Singh*, and I had no intention of doing it again.

* * *

To their credit, my parents were the ones who were the least bothered by me being a girl. They would have preferred a son, no doubt, but mainly because their community would have preferred one for them. And for Sikhs, the community is something to be ignored at your peril. But, as far as they were concerned, me not being a boy shouldn't mean I didn't have a role to play. On the contrary, from the moment I was old enough to carry a plate, I was made aware of my responsibilities. I was taught to clear a table, wash up and launder before my fifth birthday.

I knew from an early age that I was being groomed to become the equal of my mother. But there was one thing I had to tackle that she never had.

School.

As a girl in post-war India, it hadn't been a priority for Mum's family to get her an education. She didn't feel deprived. She was a woman. What use was an education to her? Twenty years later, it didn't seem very important for me either.

As a five-year-old I had chores to do around the house so it was almost begrudgingly that I was packed off to primary school. If it weren't for the law saying I had to go, I doubt my parents would have got me as far as the classroom. It didn't take me long to wish they hadn't bothered.

My first day at school was hard. Eye-opening, even. Everyone dressed the same – and nothing like I was used to. The girls wore long socks and short skirts. Blouses, ties, jumpers. All the same colour, all the same style and all very, very alien to me. My mother walked me through the crowded playground and found the line where my new classmates were gathering. My teacher smiled at me and assured my mother I would be OK. At least that's what I assumed she said.

I couldn't understand a word she was saying!

I can't imagine sending a child to school without any knowledge of that country's language. But that's what was happening to me, I realised. The teacher, the other children, the dinner ladies – they all spoke in a completely foreign tongue. I may as well have been deaf. How was I going to follow lessons if I couldn't understand something as simple as 'hello'?

The second my mother tried to leave me there I burst into tears. I wasn't the only one. But at least all the other new pupils could understand what was going on.

Day one was hell. Day two was hell. Day three was hell. I hated every minute of every day. Only as I began to pick up the language, thanks to some very intensive lessons at school, did I even start to feel comfortable being there. But I was convinced that I would never feel comfortable in the uniform. I somehow felt exposed and restricted at the same time. I was obviously my parents' daughter because as soon as I got home I was sent to my room to change. Not to protect my snow-white shirts but to wipe away any vestige of Western decadence. If I could have changed before I entered the house, I'm sure my parents wouldn't have stopped me.

After the hellish time at school I was actually glad to be back with my chores in the kitchen.

At least I understand them …

***

I don't know how well I would have done academically if I'd been able to speak the language when I arrived at school. At the end of my first academic year, however, it wasn't my language holding me back. Young children are tremendously sociable creatures and even someone as shy and awkward as me couldn't help mingling and laughing with some of my classmates some of the time. Even though I wasn't forming firm friendships, I wasn't being left out either.

One day after school finished I was delighted to be given an envelope from a girl in my class. I noticed a dozen or so others received one as well. Excitedly we all tore them open. The others whooped and squealed and the girl who'd handed it to me was the centre of attention as we put on our coats and made our way out of the building.

Slowly I picked over the words:

> Dear Sarbjit,
> You are invited to Claire's birthday party on …

It was an invitation to a party. Now *I* was excited, too.

I couldn't wait to show my mother. Even before I'd translated it, though, she started shaking her head.

'Mum, it's an invitation,' I said. 'To a party! Can I go? Please?'

'No,' she said eventually. 'That will not be possible.'

'Why not?'

'Because there will be boys there.'

Boys? I had no time for boys. Why was that an issue?

'But Mum,' I begged, 'everyone else is going.'

'We are not everyone else,' she said. 'That is my final answer.'

I was crushed, and would be again and again until eventually people stopped inviting me anywhere. Hearing my classmates talking excitedly about their forthcoming parties on a Friday then listening to them replaying the highlights the following week was torture. There were afternoons I cursed how much I could understand. I wasn't even allowed to play at friends' houses for an hour or two after school. I certainly couldn't invite anyone to ours, which struck me as odd given the inclusive stance I'd been taught Sikhism stood for, with everyone welcome, whatever their creed.

So much for the gurdwara being a haven for all.

Up until that point I never knew that I was missing out on anything. I still didn't know about English TV, so I couldn't miss that. I'd never had any real toys, but I didn't know anyone who had, so I didn't miss those either. But I was seeing the alternative to my own life every day and the more I saw, the more I craved it. Mum saw it too and stamped down. Hard.

'Just because you have to dress like everyone else, doesn't mean you have to be like them,' she explained.

***

When I was six we finally moved out of my grandparents' house. Dad's hard work at BA had paid off and he'd managed to scrape together a deposit for a house of his own. And just in time.

I was too young to remember much about my sister Karmjit being born in 1972, but by the time Mum became pregnant again in 1974 I was aware that the view of guests to the house – and therefore out there in the community – was that two girls in the family was enough. So it was a lot of pressure on number three, pressure her body resisted. Baby Kamaljit *Kaur* was born defiantly in 1975. I didn't care. What six-year-old girl doesn't want a baby sister to play with? I never got to spend time alone with my mother or father and I had no toys to speak of or books. So as far as I was concerned, the more siblings the better.

A year later, history repeated itself. Another sister, Inder, joined the family. But then, in 1979, a landmark event occurred. With very little ceremony – it was almost a regular occurrence by then – Mum went into labour once again and we all fell into our usual roles. She'd been through it all so many times before that everyone knew what they had to do to keep the house ticking in her absence. I looked after my sisters. Dad worked and Mum's parents looked after her. Life outside the maternity ward continued exactly as it normally did – apart from one thing.

This time Mum *didn't* emerge with a girl.

I don't know if I imagined the celebrations being more lavish than usual or the congratulations of friends and family seeming more heartfelt. All I really knew or cared about was looking forward to enjoying my baby brother. I was ten. The age difference was perfect. Unfortunately, a landmark event of my own soon put a stop to all thought of enjoyment with any of my siblings.

As usual I was helping in the kitchen when Dad came home from work. Chopping and cutting, washing and drying – if I wasn't at school or looking after my siblings, that was my life. After the customary hellos, Dad said something to Mum and the pair of them went into the living room. When they were comfortable, they called me in.

Seated beneath the portrait of Guru Nanak, Dad looked particularly austere. His beard was shorter and darker than the First Guru's, but as far as I was concerned, his word was to be just as respected. At least, that's what I thought until he told me what was on his mind.

'We are going to India.'

'India? Really?'

I realised I was smiling. The only holidays I ever experienced were breaks from school and even then nothing changed. We never went anywhere except to visit family at weekends. I was ten years old and I'd never left London – but now I was going to India.

India! Just the name conjured possibilities and dreams. All my aunts and uncles spoke of their home country so fondly and I still recalled the wonderful bedtime stories set there. As far as I could tell, it was paradise on earth – and we were going!

'Where will we stay?' I asked, ever the practical little girl.

It was Dad's turn to smile now. 'In my house, of course.'

That made sense. As a family we were by no means well off by European standards, but Dad's BA salary went a long way back in Chandigarh and when his own father had died, Dad had bought a house in Patti, on the Punjab border, for his mother and other relatives to live in. He'd also recently bought another smaller property to renovate. He visited Patti at least once or twice every year, courtesy of the cheap deals possible for BA staff. Jetting over to Delhi, Dad said, was like hopping on a bus for him.

My mind was racing. There was so much to take in. If Dad's house over there was anything like the one we lived in here, there wouldn't be a chair that didn't have a bottom sitting on it.

'Where will we all sleep?' I asked.

Dad contemplated the question. 'I suppose I shall have my brother's room,' he replied, 'and you will sleep with your aunt.'

In our culture, sharing a bed with family members of the same sex is common. In fact, it's considered an insult if you refuse. I didn't know my aunt but if she would have me in her room then I was honoured.

'OK, but where will Karmjit, Kamaljit and Inder sleep?' I asked. 'And what about the baby? Do they have a cot?'

At that point Dad stopped smiling. Had I asked too many questions? Then I looked at Mum and for the first time realised she hadn't yet said a word.

'Your brother and sisters won't need a bed,' Dad explained.

'Why not?'

Dad sighed. 'Because they're not coming.' He paused. 'Sarbjit, my daughter, it is just you and me.'

All trace of excitement vanished as suddenly as it had arrived – and with it went my bravado. I'd never felt smaller or more confused. This wasn't a holiday any more. I didn't know what it was – but I knew I didn't like the sound of it. And, for all the exotic lure of India, I was now adamant I never wanted to set foot there. Not like this. Not without my whole family.

My mind began whirring. Why me? What had I done wrong?

'Am I being punished?' I asked.

Now my mother spoke. 'No, no, Sarbjit, you've done nothing wrong.'

'So why are you sending me away?'

Mum looked at Dad, who shook his head at her then me. He wasn't angry but he hadn't expected so many questions. Not from me. I was his eldest but I was by far the meekest. Even my brother, at barely six months, was already showing more desire for independence than I ever had. What's more, he clearly expected me to be jumping for joy at the offer. The chance to visit the home of our religion? To see where the roots of our family originated? I should be honoured to go there. Instead, there I was, almost challenging him.

'I'm taking you to India to learn the ways of our country,' he said emphatically. 'Your grandmother and your aunts will teach you to be a woman. They will teach you how to look after a family, how to run a house, how to clean and how to cook the Indian way.'

To cook? We both knew I'd just come from the kitchen.

'I can learn here,' I said. 'I *am* learning here.'

So many thoughts – *questions* – flooded my head at once. What could be more 'Indian' than the way we already lived? Even our area in London was known as 'Little India'. Outside of school I never spoke to anyone of a different religion or race. And how long were they talking about? The word 'holiday' hadn't come up once. It didn't sound like something we could squeeze into the summer holidays.

And what was this talk of being a 'woman'? I was ten years old and I could already cook and clean. What more could there be to learn?

However they put it, I still felt like I was being punished.

I was so confused, so scared of being sent from my home to a family I had never even met. But nothing I said made a difference. Even as Mum tried to calm me, her air of resignation told me the decision was already made.

'You'll be back before you know it, my darling,' she said, adding, 'and don't even think about your chores here.'

My chores? They were the last thing on my mind. What about my brother and sisters? Playing with them was the only time I was truly happy. What if they thought I wanted to leave them?

What if they forget who I am?

***

As far as my parents were concerned, the matter of the trip was closed the moment they told me about it. From my point of view, I never gave up hope that it was a bad dream.

I couldn't wait to escape from the living room to tell my sisters. Maybe they'd say that Mum and Dad were joking. Or maybe they'd beg them to change their minds.

I found Karmjit and Inder in our room. I blurted out my news and a second later we were all crying. But something was wrong. This wasn't what I wanted.

I'd only been thinking of myself when I told them, but the moment I saw my sisters' tears, the stronger I became. I had to. In the space of minutes I went from wanting to scream 'It's not fair!' at my parents to defending their decision in front of the others. The last thing I wanted was to upset my little sisters. And I certainly didn't want them to think the day might come when they would be sent away, too.

Even if I knew it would.

No, it was my problem and I would have to deal with it. From that moment on, the only time I dared admit how unhappy I was, was to myself and God.

Several months passed between being informed of my journey and leaving. Every new day felt like the sword over my head could fall at any time.

Will it be today? Is today the day they tell me?

I didn't want to ask my father. In my childish logic I thought, *If I don't mention it, maybe he'll forget.* But when I noticed the passport application form in my name lying on the kitchen table, I knew it was only a matter of time. Eventually Dad told me he was trying to arrange for building work on his property to coincide with his visit back home. Once that was sorted, he'd buy the tickets and we'd be off.

In the meantime it was business as usual – but with one massive change. September 1980 arrived and I started my secondary education at Brentford School for Girls. If I'd thought my Hounslow junior school was hard to get used to, this place, at five times the size, was at least that much more intimidating. I wasn't the only Sikh in the school but my English still wasn't as good as most people's. Trying to settle in when you are struggling to keep up with the language can be overwhelming. It also makes you stand out.

I'd only been there one day when an older girl sneered at me and said: 'Go back to your own country.'

It was all I could do to hold back the tears. Not because of the racism behind her words, but the fact she'd hit a nerve. I was already in my own country, but I'd be going back to my parents' country very, very soon.

* * *

Between the name-calling and the struggle to learn I had the extra pressure of not being allowed to make friends with anyone. While my classmates went back to each other's houses after school to play, I had to go to school for no longer than legally required, then home, change out of the 'disgusting' uniform – as my grandfather called it – then get on with my peeling or tidying. There was no television, I had no hobbies, no friends and no choices.

And then one evening when I got home Mum was waiting for me. 'Dad bought your tickets today,' she said. 'It's time.'

India, here I come.

CHAPTER TWO

WELCOME TO INDIA

The heat was the first thing that hit me. Eleven summers in England had not prepared me for anything like the warm hug of the air on my skin as I followed Dad to the top of the aeroplane steps and prepared to disembark.

The colours were next. England has its fair share of blue skies but not like this. *And not so much of it.* Even with the smell of oil and the thunderous roar of engines competing with the shouting of mechanics and ground staff, all I could think about as I stepped on to Indian soil for the first time was how vast and pure the sky seemed. It wasn't quite the stuff of bedtime stories but it felt comforting. I couldn't help smiling.

Perhaps I will like it here.

Heathrow Airport is regarded as one of the busiest in the world and it had certainly seemed it as Dad and I had picked our way through the tourists and businessmen coming and going. But Delhi was something else. Everyone apart from me appeared to know where they were going – and to be in a hurry to get there. Staff and passengers flitted every which way like butterflies. There seemed to be at least three people competing for every square inch of pathway. And as for the noise – a school playground at home time would be drowned out here.

Part mesmerised, part in fear for my life, I held my father's hand tighter and looked up for reassurance.

'You'll get used to it,' he laughed. 'But,' he added, 'don't let go of my hand. And do not wander off.'

One of my father's relatives met us at the gate and led us to a dusty old car parked quite randomly, it seemed to me, among thousands of other apparently abandoned vehicles. We definitely weren't in England any more.

As much as I wanted to take in every inch of the views, I soon fell asleep in the car. When I woke, I was aware of the faces filling every window.

'Come on, sleepyhead,' Dad sad. 'Time to say hello to your family.'

**

For all my fears, Dad had tried to make the travelling fun. I'd had books and a doll to play with on the plane and he'd tried to take my mind off the intimidating flight experience by holding my hand and telling me stories about India. In fact, for a while I began to feel like it really was an adventure. But meeting my new family for the first time brought home the truth.

This isn't a holiday. It's a training camp.

In my mind I think I'd built up my Indian family as ogres. But they all looked normal. In fact, apart from some of the males wearing shorts and T-shirts, they acted and dressed the same as anyone from my family back home.

The old woman who hugged me the hardest was Dad's mum and my gran, Hernan Kaur. She was eighty years old but still had a lot of life in her. She also liked to talk. It seemed like she was trying to fill Dad in on every aspect of her life since he'd last visited a year earlier. Even though we only spoke Punjabi at home, it took a while to tune my ear

into her accent. When Dad's sister spoke next, I realised I'd
have my work cut out understanding any of them.

As my new uncles and cousins unloaded the car, Dad and
I were led towards an imposing blue-tiled building flanked
by two mighty pillars. Everything about the country so far
had felt alien to me but I still found myself stopping to take
in what I was seeing. The building was quite beautiful and
very, very large. In fact, it was only the absence of any other
buildings that made me realise it wasn't a hotel.

This is their home!

And now for a short while it would be my home, too. By
London standards the sprawling single-storey building
wasn't far short of a mansion – I couldn't believe Dad
owned it. Looking back now and knowing how much less it
cost than our place in Hounslow is scary. The other
distinguishing feature was that it was detached – and had its
own fence and tall metal gate. I'd never seen anything quite
so grand. The only houses I'd been in prior to that were
joined on to other people's, like cards wedged tightly together
in a deck. Where were the terraces and the tower blocks?

I'd certainly never experienced anywhere that required its
own perimeter wall to prevent cattle wandering out. Every
step I took, my senses were struck by novelty. I'd never even
seen a farm before but the closer I got, the more obvious it
was that the smell around the area could only be described
as 'animal'. Cats and dogs I was used to seeing and hearing.
These smells and some of the noises carried by the wind were
something else.

The differences didn't end with the nearby livestock. As
we reached the front door I noticed the house's blue tiles
were peppered with small yellow squares. Looking closely I
saw they contained intricate little paintings of idyllic scenes.
Someone had put a lot of work into this building.

And yet, it seemed, not the inside. After the lavishness of
the exterior, a couple of steps over the threshold proved

something of a disappointment. There was a bathroom and separate toilet just past the door, followed by a sitting room, two other reception rooms, a kitchen, a verandah and stairs leading to the roof. Apart from its size it really had very little to offer.

But I was viewing the building with Western eyes. What I saw as a fairly standard kitchen, for example, I soon learned was state of the art in Patti.

'You won't find a house around here with running water or a gas oven,' Dad said proudly. 'And,' he added, tapping a familiar white object, 'you definitely won't see another one of these.'

'Is that a fridge?'

He nodded, then laughed. 'Welcome to India,' he said.

My tour continued. Despite its size, I noticed the house only had three bedrooms, each fairly basically furnished. A quick tally of the army of people fussing around us told me that I really would be sharing with one of my aunties.

After the initial shock of arriving and meeting everyone, I finally began to relax. I was no stranger to being around large groups of people, so watching Dad catch up with his uncle Tonga and his sister and her family was very nice. I even enjoyed Dad showing me off, although when he presented his nephews to me, I became suddenly tongue-tied. They were only twelve and nine, and in theory we should have had plenty to talk about. But I couldn't remember the last time I'd spoken to a boy. I found myself scanning the grown-ups' faces.

Was it even allowed?

After dinner Dad and I went to bed early. Even though I'd slept so much of the journey, the day's travelling had worn us both out. Any adrenalin from my voyage into the unknown had pretty much disappeared. As I felt my head touch the soft cotton pillow I knew sleep couldn't be far away. But then came the worries. I'd never stayed away from home before.

And I'd certainly never been under a different roof to my mother. Where was she? How were my sisters? What were they doing? Before I knew it the tears were flowing.

Eventually I managed to stop. The last thing I wanted was to let my aunt see how distressed I was by being in her house. That would not be respectful at all.

It will be over soon, I reminded myself. *You'll be home before you know it.*

In the meantime, the house might have been unlike anything I'd seen in the West, but the people inside it lived almost exactly the same way as us – or so it seemed. I would learn the truth soon enough ...

***

Waking up in a strange bed was a new and eerie experience for me. Realising I was in a new country, and not by choice either, sent nervous butterflies into my stomach. There was so much I didn't know about my new home and why I was there. Even though my father was somewhere else in the building and I was surrounded by blood relatives, I had never felt more alone. Fortunately I had been out of bed less than five minutes when my aunt appeared at the door inviting me to join her making breakfast in the kitchen.

My introduction to 'learning the Indian way' had begun.

After breakfast Dad busied himself with overseeing the renovation works on his other property elsewhere in the village. No sooner had he gone than I was being shown how to clear the table, wash up, and put everything away.

If I thought that was the end of lessons for the day, I was mistaken. After breakfast my aunt and grandmother started preparing for lunch – and I was helping. If anyone was impressed by how much I already knew, they certainly didn't show it.

The morning and lunchtime passed quickly. I found myself enjoying the chopping and slicing and being shown the ropes. Tiring as it was using cutlery and bowls that were too big for me, at least it kept my mind focused. I didn't have a chance to wonder what was going on in England. Had anyone even notified my school? Would I be told off when I returned? I hadn't had a chance to tell a soul before I left.

Enjoyable as I found my tuition in food preparation and cooking, Auntie made it very clear that she wasn't giving me lessons for the sake of it. This wasn't an exercise. As my father had said, I was being prepared for womanhood – whatever that meant. And, more pressingly, the family had to eat my food at the end of the day. *My* food. Every time I thought of it, my hand began to shake. That was OK when I was kneading the roti bread, crushing spices or stirring a lentil pot, but nerves when you're chopping ginger with a knife that could cut through bone are best avoided.

The next few days passed in exactly the same way: work, eat, work, eat, work, eat, work, bed. Everybody seemed happy with me – except me. Yet with so little time to myself, not only was I not thinking sad thoughts of home, I was barely thinking anything at all. And even though the blue palace was miles from anywhere, it still felt as claustrophobic as our home. For all its spaciousness, there always seemed to be someone around. The only time I got a moment to myself was in bed, before my aunt took up her space alongside me. That was my only opportunity to reflect on how tired I was after working so hard in a hot kitchen in the Indian summer. And it was the only time I could think of my sisters 4,000 miles away – and cry myself to sleep.

I didn't dare confide in my father how I was feeling and I knew that we could stay there forever and he would never ask. But just as offended by my homesickness would be my gran and her children. Were they not my family, too? Were they so inferior to my British brethren that I would cry to get away? It might not make sense to many people, but that was the Sikh way. They were family. They were community.

I should love them like my own sisters and baby brother. It tore me apart that I just didn't. *But,* I told myself, *I am young. I will learn.*

Cooking-wise, I was convinced there was little my aunt and gran could teach me that Mum or her sisters in England couldn't. That is, until I was asked to fetch the rice.

'Where do you keep it?' I asked my aunt.

She gestured behind me. There were no cupboards or shelves there, just the open window.

'Come with me,' she said laughing, and I followed her outside. 'See that field?' she said.

I was confused. 'The one under water?'

She nodded.

'That is a rice field. Our rice field. And it needs harvesting.'

Coming from London, just the sight of so much open space was mind-blowing. It was odd trying to come to terms with the fact that my family were growing so many of the things I helped my mother buy from supermarkets back home. As well as the paddy fields that stretched as far as I could see, I was also shown crops of wheat, vegetables, fruit, even sugar and cotton. I knew it was a farm and I knew people grew things on farms. But I'd never seen anything like it before.

And then there were the farm animals. Cows, chickens, pigs, buffalo – they all roamed their own fenced enclosures. For a Londoner, each creature seemed very exotic. Like most Sikhs, I was a vegetarian and could not imagine eating any of God's creatures. But that didn't stop me enjoying watching the cows' ponderous movements or the chickens' crazy skittish behaviour. They were either very brave or very stupid, but they only recognised danger at the last minute and then scampered off squawking. In the absence of any toys or hobbies, watching them became my entertainment.

As one week passed into the second, and I prepared my

first curry on my own, I decided it was time to speak to Dad. Waiting for a moment when he was alone was frustrating. Then one night I found him enjoying some solitude on the verandah. Now was my moment. If I dared.

'Dad,' I said in a voice much stronger than I felt, 'when are we going home?'

'Not yet, my darling, but soon.'

'But I've been a good girl. I've worked hard. I have learned the Indian way.'

'Yes, you have worked hard, my dear, I'm very proud. But this is only the beginning. There is much more for your aunt to teach you.'

Not wanting to offend anyone listening, I backed away from the argument. In any case, Dad had said 'soon', and that would have to do. Unfortunately, as week followed week, and I asked the same question again and again, Dad always said the same thing.

'Soon, my darling. Soon.'

I could have believed him more if certain things didn't contradict his words. For example, why was I suddenly told I would be getting a tutor to teach me for two hours every day? If we were leaving soon, why would Dad go to this trouble? He hadn't exactly been interested in my schooling in England. Why the sudden interest now?

Sure enough, a man arrived and I was asked to join him in the sitting room. As usual I wore my headscarf in the presence of a male. He taught me Punjabi and Hindu as well as touching on various general subjects. I enjoyed the attention and couldn't help noticing how much easier I found learning in my own language.

Finally, after four months of trying to fit in with the household and learn as much as I could, my heart nearly burst one day when I noticed Dad beginning to pack. The sabbatical he'd taken from work had run its course.

This is it.

After sixteen long weeks separated from my family, being treated increasingly like little more than a servant in a country where I had nothing and knew almost nobody, I was going home. Back to England. Back to where I belonged.

Or so I thought.

Dad delivered the news as quickly as he could. *He* was going back to England – and I was staying. I couldn't believe it. He was escaping and I was to be stuck there. The one person I loved in this country was abandoning me. I couldn't stop the tears. For once, I didn't even try.

'Don't cry, Sarbjit, don't cry. It won't be for long,' Dad said. 'I just have some things to do at home and then I shall come back for you.'

'When?' I asked.

'Soon. Very soon.'

Those words again. They told me everything I needed to know.

I wouldn't see my father again for two years.

* * *

I'd already woken up once in India feeling alone. This time it was for real. I'd been taken from my family, transported to the other side of the world, and dumped. I knew what my mother had said, I knew what my father had promised. But at eleven years old I'd never felt so scared.

Just as Dad had appeared to take leaving me there in his stride, so my Indian family just got on with things. My auntie and gran didn't treat me any differently after Dad left. But looking back, on top of time with my tutor, I was already working – or 'learning' – fourteen hours a day. How could they possibly have made things worse for me?

But there were changes after Dad's departure.

Spending so much of my time in the kitchen, it was there that I noticed the earliest signs. When I went to the fridge at breakfast I noticed the familiar heavy whirring engine was absent. The contents were still cool, but the light didn't come on. When I traced the lead I discovered the plug pulled from the socket. I assumed it was broken. But when I went to use the gas oven my aunt pulled me aside.

'It's disconnected,' she said, matter-of-factly.

'Why?'

'We don't like to use gas.'

She explained that the fridge and the gas were only employed when Dad came to visit. After all, he was a Westerner now – in their eyes at least – and he would expect such mod cons. Moreover, he had also paid for everything. The least they could do was use it while he was there.

Her explanation made some sort of sense. They, as a family, preferred to live the simple, more natural, Indian life. They lived off nature in the middle of nowhere and that's how they liked it. To a point. But that didn't explain how we were going to cook.

'We use the fire.' She indicated the range in the main room. 'But,' she added, 'we don't burn wood.'

'Then what do we use?'

An amused smile broke over my aunt's face. She called her husband, who led me into the garden and out to the pasture where the cows and buffalo had their noses down in the dry grass. For a while I couldn't understand what he was pointing at. Only when he led me into a field with a bucket and a shovel did I begin to twig. Even then I still thought he was pulling my leg.

But no. He scooped up a giant cowpat and dropped it into the bucket. Then we walked over to the next large black shape and he did it again. Up close, the smell was disgusting and it only got worse when the turds were disturbed. My uncle acted like it was the most natural thing in the world. I knew I was a stranger in these parts and the closest thing to this I'd ever seen was dog's mess on the pavements near our house. But even he had to admit this was odd. Didn't he?

Apparently not.

The bucket was virtually full when my uncle put it down. I assumed – I hoped – he was calling it a day. In fact, he passed me the shovel and invited me to have a go.

Not only was I not dressed for manual labour, I could feel the stench of cow poo seeping into my clothes – and my hair. I planned to spend as long as I could scrubbing down to my roots that night. Within a few minutes, I would need to scrub everywhere else, too. It had looked the most simple, if disgusting, thing in the world to scrape up turds. But the first time I tried, I fell flat on my face – in the mud, fortunately. The second time, I only broke a piece off. The smell, each time, doubled. Not to be daunted, I tried again. This time it worked. My uncle slapped me on the back and for a moment I felt proud. Then I came to my senses. Had it really come to this?

I'm proud to have shovelled a cowpat into a bucket?

If I thought that collecting them was weird, what happened next bordered on the bizarre. We went back to the house and my uncle did the most disgusting thing I've ever seen. He reached into the bucket, pulled out handfuls of poo, and moulded them into a thick oval shape. It looked like a monstrous patti – except nobody would ever want to eat it. He repeated this until the bucket was empty and the low slanted roof had a dozen discs laying on it. Then he led me to another part of the exterior and pulled down a smaller, paler shape.

'We hang them to dry, and they turn into this,' he explained, holding the desiccated patti a little too close to my face. 'And then we burn them for heat and cooking.'

For the first time in my stay I felt genuine respect for my hosts and their culture. Now this really was the 'Indian way'. I could stay at Brentford School for Girls all my life and never learn anything like this.

My uncle also pointed out that the majority of houses in

the village were all built using cowpats smeared on their walls for insulation and strength. You just mix the excrement with water and spread it like cement on walls or floors.

'It's as good as anything you have in the West,' he said.

But distinctly smellier ...

Having been introduced to the business end of the cows and eventually accepting that harvesting their waste for fuel would be another part of my workload, I began to get more interested in the creatures themselves. I chose to watch my uncle milk them early one morning and when he asked if I'd like to try, I said yes. I can't describe anything weirder than pulling on a rubbery teat, manipulating it until the udder began to dispense its white liquid. When it first started to seep out I jumped. Luckily for me, the cow was less surprised. She stayed perfectly still and I tried again, and again, until I got it right. My uncle was so impressed he said I could do it again. Milking a cow was a skilled job, I realised. It wasn't like peeling carrots or chopping spinach. Those were tasks for anyone. This required concentration and ability. Which I appeared to have.

The giant lumbering animals fascinated me, so I also learned how to feed them and accompanied my uncles when they led the cattle to the stream for a bath and a drink. It wasn't long before I was entrusted with that job as well. The cows were huge. Each one weighed ten times more than me. But I practised the right commands and how to use a stick to guide them and they obeyed me like I was their master.

Apart from rearing the farm animals, I also began to explore the more green-fingered aspects of my chores. In time I would be able to tell if chillies were ripe by squeezing them on the vine and checking if they were fat and soft. I'd be shown how to pluck cotton balls from their buds in the field. I would be able to identify, sow and pick potatoes, onions, spinach and all manner of vegetables, as well as bananas, mangos, apples and pears. Everything we cooked was grown or raised on family land or nearby. I would even get the chance to pick sugar cane when it was ripe and be shown how to cut wheat and process it into flour. It was quite a learning curve but, I realised, it was one I wanted to conquer. I was close to being happy.

Close. By day I felt fulfilled by my ability to collect ingredients and prepare quite complicated meals for ten or more people. But it was all distraction. It was all just me making the best of my lot. What other option did I have? To refuse to work and just sob all day?

No. Crying was something I saved for the night-times. For that hour or two when I was alone in my bed before my aunt retired. Whatever image I portrayed in public, this was the true me. I hated being away from my family but I also resented them for sending me there. What was I learning that would be any use at all in London? Even so, my brother and sisters had no part in the decision. They were the ones I wanted to be with more than anything in the world.

But would I ever see them again?

***

I was raised to be a respectful Sikh, to honour and obey my family and my community. I lived the life of a good daughter, even at thirteen. Having been introduced to the ways of the temple before my second birthday, I was not going to turn out any other way.

And yet as tough and orthodox as my parents were, my Indian family were even more strict, especially where I was concerned. If there were two interpretations of a rule, they took the more punishing one. At first I thought it was just their 'way'. Then I realised it wasn't just because it was me. It was because of who I was. Not Dad's daughter.

A girl.

Sikhism is about equality, about all castes of men being the same and about the similarities, not the differences, between men and women. So, looking back, why was I the one not allowed to go out unaccompanied? Why was I forced to cover up if I set foot outside the house? Why did I have to cover my head with a scarf if a male so much as entered the same building, even if it was one of my own uncles? If it had to do with my religion I would not have minded. But this appeared to be only about my gender.

I really should have been a boy ...

My male cousins were excused everything I had to endure. They went to the local school, shortly after I made them breakfast. They were never asked to lift a finger to help with the chores. And they were allowed to roam the property, the village and beyond. It really was one rule for them and another rule for me.

Working in the kitchen or sewing or helping to harvest one of the crops gave me a lot of time to dwell on why I was being treated so differently. I was raised to respect my elders and not question them, so I could hardly ask my grandfather in case it seemed disrespectful. But there had to be a reason. I remember taking a shower one night, the same question still playing in my head. What was it about me that held me back, while other people were allowed freedom? Was it really just that I was a girl? Could that really be the reason that I was expected to work as hard as any male and yet have none of their privileges? There had to be something more, didn't there?

Catching my reflection in the full-length steamed-up mirror, I saw my parents' faces staring back. But, I realised, there was something else, something I hadn't noticed before. After eighteen months of hard labour and harsh temperatures, I'd noticed my clothes all felt looser as the weight had fallen off me. Even looking now, there wasn't an ounce of extraneous fat on my arms and legs. But something had definitely changed. My hips seemed different, wider, softer. My chest was no longer the flat and boyish shape it had once been. I didn't know how it was happening or why. But I had curves. I was changing.

And I was scared.

Of course, I'd noticed before that there were physical differences between me and my mother and grandmother. But I knew nothing of puberty, not then. Whatever change my body was about to undergo was a mystery to me, and a terrifying one at that. Within a second of recognising my new self, any resentment I still harboured for my mother for despatching me to India while she enjoyed my siblings at home disappeared. I was truly conflicted. I needed her like I'd never needed anyone before.

* * *

Alone in India I was becoming a woman. Unfortunately, I wasn't the only one to notice.

One of my chores was to go with my aunt to buy household goods. The best shop was in the next village, an hour's walk or a twenty-minute bus ride away. Sometimes we would walk there, then, laden down with shopping, hop on the bus to return. This was new for me. I had never used public transport in England. My parents would not allow it. I suspect they did not like the idea of us girls being exposed to British males in public, so they would rather a family member drove us everywhere. As I queued to board the former British double-decker in Patti for the first time, I wondered what Dad would say if he ever found out?

I never saw the bus anything less than full, but there always seemed to be room for whoever wanted to push in. If we were lucky, we would get two seats, sometimes together. More usually, we would have to stand wherever we could find space.

I remember one journey feeling relieved that I had standing room by the window. It was a short-lived sensation, as the bus idled at the stop for longer, and more and more passengers somehow boarded into space that wasn't there. In no time I had the elbows and arms and legs and bags of five or six complete strangers pressed against me. I didn't dare look up but I could feel that most of them were men, and all of them smelled of stale sweat. It was horrible, vile.

But it was about to get worse.

As the bus pulled away, everyone lurched forwards before settling back. As I regained my balance without dropping my shopping bags, I became aware of a hand – a male hand – resting on my waist. Instinctively I twisted my body and tried to shrug it off. The hand pressed tighter, then started moving up my body.

I wanted to scream but it was as though all the air had been sucked from the bus. I wanted to kick out but my legs, my whole body, was frozen. I was so shocked I couldn't even cry.

That was the longest twenty minutes of my life. When we reached our stop I pushed so hard through the thinning crowd there were angry shouts from the passengers whose feet I trampled over. But I didn't care. I just had to get away.

The next week I tried desperately to get out of catching the bus again. I even offered to carry all the shopping home by foot. But my aunt insisted. This time we had seats together and nothing happened. But I couldn't relax.

I was never physically groped again, but several times men whispered things in my ear that made me feel ill. Some of them asked me to do things and then laughed at my terrified silence. Others seemed angry and called me names I had never heard before. Yet again, all I could do was wonder why. Why me? What had I done? Why did these men hate me so?

Why wasn't I a boy?

* * *

During my first weeks in India I used to wake up every morning and think, *Is today the day?* Would today be the day I was sent home? I didn't expect any warning; I hadn't received much on the way out. Then as the weeks turned into months, and Dad left and the months became a year and more, I realised I no longer thought it. Once the hope of going home had given me strength. Now it made me sad. Sad that I'd been forgotten, sad that my own family had given me up.

So I had ploughed my energies into being the best student I could, learning as much as I could, praying as much and living in accordance with the Sikh faith as honestly as I could. But it was hard. That very faith promised me that men and women were equal. It promised me that all Sikhs should love one another and enjoy the wider family of community. But I had questions. Why, when I had kept my side of the bargain, was I made to feel inferior to males? Why had I suffered physical and verbal abuse just because I was a young woman?

I didn't know the answer. All I could say for sure was that, after my experiences with strangers in India, and my dealings with my father who, as far as I was concerned, had abandoned me to that fate, I didn't think I could trust any man again.

Life went on. Then, one day, without warning, a man came up the garden path. As I held my hand up against the bright sunlight, squinting to see who it was, I could barely believe my eyes. He had returned. He had come back for me. My father was there.

My heart gave a lurch, and all my anger, all my pain, all my fears vanished, the second I heard him speak.

'Hello, my darling,' my father said. 'It's time to go home.'

CHAPTER THREE

THAT'S THE MAN YOU'RE GOING TO MARRY

I'd spent two years wishing I could go home. Yet when I arrived it wasn't what I was expecting. London had changed. Or maybe it was me.

I had left a girl and returned on the cusp of womanhood, on the cusp of massive physical and psychological change. I needed friendly faces. I needed my mother. But more than anything I wanted to see my sisters.

Our reunion was as magical as I'd dreamed, the hugs and squeals punctuated by tears. But when it came to greeting my brother, I could see in his eyes that I was a stranger. And it was true. I was. I'd missed most of my brother's life. *But, I wanted to tell him, it's not my fault.* I felt a flash of anger at the sound of Mum's and Dad's voices. Yes, I was pleased to see them again – whatever resentment I felt towards Dad, it had eased the second he'd arrived to rescue me. And yes, I understood that they thought it was best for me to learn about my cultural heritage. But could learning how to strip sugar cane outweigh the loss I felt of missing my siblings grow up?

It didn't even come close. But that was in the past. My parents had made their decision and I'd had to live by it.

While I was so happy to be back, my biggest problem now was worrying whether I could ever forgive them. As a Sikh, it was expected of me. As a daughter, I wouldn't survive if I didn't. But how?

Despite my reservations, for the rest of the day there was a carnival atmosphere in the house. Karmjit, Kamaljit and Inder in particular – at three, six and seven years younger than me – couldn't stay away from me. I had so much to tell them and they me. The only difference was, I believed their stories – whereas they called me a liar.

'You never touched cow poo!' Inder squealed.

'I did. And I used it to light fires. We even spread it on the walls instead of paint.'

'Urggh, that's disgusting!'

'I know!'

The laughter continued through the night. It really was great to be back.

***

I'd been away so long and yet in other ways it was as if I'd never left. I'd barely been back in England a day when my mother asked me to help my aunt with dinner. In fact, rather than helping, I was expected to take over my aunt's cooking duties. Feeding a household didn't intimidate me. I could peel onions and radishes and chop veg and cook chapattis like a professional chef. But after two years of enforced distance between me and my family, I resented being stuck so soon in the kitchen on my own. I wanted to be with my sisters. I wanted to be among the people I loved. We still had so much catching up to do.

It wasn't just socially that I needed to reacquaint myself. A week after my return, I found myself dressed in a white blouse, maroon jumper and black blazer ready for my first day at Cranford Community School. Joining a school is nerve-racking at any time, but the idea of trying to fit in halfway through a term gave me butterflies that just would not shift. Feeling so self-conscious about wearing a knee-length skirt didn't help, either. My legs felt naked. What on earth were people going to think when I stepped out of the house dressed like that?

Of course, I hadn't gone far when I noticed dozens of children funnelling down the streets on the same short walk to school – and many of the girls' skirts exposed a lot more than a knee. I couldn't help staring. Why would their parents ask them to wear such revealing clothes? It never occurred to me that the children would have made the decision themselves. Or that some of the older girls had probably pinned their hems an inch or two higher without their mums and dads knowing. The very idea of such independence wouldn't have crossed my mind.

If I felt confused before I stepped inside the school gates, the moment lessons began I thought my brain would explode. What were they talking about? The subject was meant to be mathematics. This was a foreign language – another one. The blackboard was filled with Greek letters and squiggles I'd never seen before in my life. Around me, thirty heads were bowed in application. Everyone understood what they were meant to be doing. Everyone except me.

A long hour later, there was another new language to get my head around. If I had been stunned by how little maths I really knew, then my confidence of walking into an English class and being faced with a play by Shakespeare was shattering. I thought I knew English. I could speak it and I could write it. But this play was in no English I had ever seen. If I was out of my depth in English and maths, how was I going to cope with all the other subjects I knew nothing about?

By the end of my first day everyone in the class knew I was struggling. I'd had no real love of school or any hatred of it before. When I was younger it had just seemed like a place to go and spend time with people my own age while Mum and Dad worked. Even so, the one thing I wanted out of school was to fit in.

What a joke.

I couldn't have been more different if I'd had two heads. Not only was I new, I was 'stupid', I had no friends – and, of course, I was a different colour to most of them. Not everyone by any means. But after two years in the Punjab I spoke with such a strong accent and looked so uncomfortable in Western clothes, I didn't seem English at all. If anyone wanted to insult me, they had no shortage of ammunition.

I quickly got used to people mocking my accent. The sound of exaggerated 'sing-song' conversations followed me along the corridors between lessons. Then as one or two people got bolder, I heard the first shout of 'Paki'. I think once upon a time, Patti had actually been part of Pakistan. But I don't think that was the reasoning behind the name-calling. I knew that other familiar taunt of 'Go back to your own country' wouldn't be far behind, and sure enough I heard it at least once a day.

I'd been the victim of racism before. My whole family had. London in the 1970s and '80s wasn't as forward-thinking as it is today. Even people who weren't trying to hurt you often used language that nowadays we would consider offensive. But just because it was so commonplace didn't make it any easier to accept. When I confided in my father, he shrugged as though to say, *Tell me about it.* He was older than me. He wore a turban. And adults, he said, could be just as cruel as children.

He told me he would speak to my teachers. In the meantime, he said, I should not be afraid of sticking up for myself.

That was easier said than done. Some of the insults left me speechless. Apart from pointing out I wasn't from

Pakistan and England *was* my own country, what could I say? I didn't hate anyone enough to be mean back. But I had to give up when one girl said I stank of curry.

I spend enough of my time cooking it. I probably do smell of it.

Realising that my skin colour and accent were just sticks to beat me with for being slow helped a little bit. But there still seemed to be whole weeks when I cried myself to sleep every night. Upset as I was, however, there was one thing I wouldn't do: ask not to go to school. It was being absent so much that caused my problems in the first place. If I missed any more days it would get worse, not better.

I just wished my family could see it that way. When Mum began work after my brother started nursery, it was made clear to me that as the oldest I was responsible for my siblings. I prepared their breakfast and got them ready for school. That I didn't mind doing. According to Sikh principles, a group's happiness is more important than an individual's. We were all raised to help each other where we could. But if my brother or sisters were ever ill, I was told to take a day off school and look after them. Over the course of a school year I lost weeks playing nurse because it didn't just stop at my siblings. If any of my extended family couldn't go to school for any reason, then neither could I. My aunt rang one day to say my young cousin had a fever – and I should go and look after him. I'd get calls throughout the day saying, 'Have you given him this?', 'Have you cooked him that?'

It got to the stage where I dreaded our phone ringing in the morning in case it was a relative with a sickly child.

* * *

While I was expected to be a woman at home, I was still treated very much like a child outside. Even though

Cranford wasn't very far from our house, I was never allowed to walk to school on my own; one of my aunts or uncles would usually drive me on their way to work. And then, at half past three without fail, my grandfather would be waiting for me, ready to march me home the second I stepped through the gates. And woe betide me if I was late. Usually I couldn't wait to get out the second I heard the bell to escape potential name-callers. But as my first term wore on and the insults gradually died down – one or two people were even nice to me – I was able to take my time.

It was one sunny spring afternoon when I noticed Granddad standing by the entrance. This was unusual. Normally he preferred to wait further away. But today he was pacing agitatedly among the exodus of schoolchildren trying to get home. As I got closer he started gesturing to me to hurry up. By the time I reached the pavement he virtually dragged me towards home.

'Who were you talking to?' he demanded.

The ferocity of his question caught me out. 'Pardon?' I said.

'Who were you talking to?' he repeated, louder this time.

'No one, Granddad.'

'Yes you were. I saw you. A boy.'

I racked my brain. I hadn't spoken to anyone. Or had I?

'Oh, him,' I remembered. 'He's a kid in my class. He was just asking if I'd seen his friend.'

'What did you say?'

'I said no.'

A frown descended on Granddad's face. I quickly looked away. I'd obviously done something wrong but I didn't have a clue what.

'Don't do it again,' he said eventually.

'Don't do what?'

'Don't speak to that boy – any boy – again.'

'What? What if they speak to me?'

'Ignore them. Walk away.'

'But won't that be considered wrong?'

'Not as wrong as being seen talking to them.'

We stomped the rest of the short journey home in silence. Another decision I didn't agree with or understand had been made about my life. Another decision I would follow without argument. I was the good daughter and the good Sikh. That is how I had been raised.

And yet, I couldn't stop thinking about it that evening once I had rattled through my chores. Granddad had said he was protecting me but it felt like I was the one being punished. What had I done wrong? The boy at school was certainly nicer than the ones in India. If my grandfather cared so much about me, why didn't he protect me from them?

* * *

While my schoolwork was never going to win me any prizes – or, I suspected, any qualifications – my time at Cranford grew less painful in other ways. With so many other pupils with Asian or African heritage, the racism that had once rained down on me couldn't be sustained and eventually stopped. Not only were boys in my class willing to say hello and goodbye to me in public – although never in view of Granddad – I also began to make some good friends. A couple of them, Sarita and Suneeta, also had Indian backgrounds, but they were astonished at how strict my life was. While I was escorted straight home each afternoon to clean and cook, they were as free to come and go after school as our other friend, Pam. There was nothing I would have liked more than to visit their houses and play records or talk about fashion, even though I had very little experience of either – but I was forbidden by my father from socialising with anyone. And I still wasn't allowed visitors at home.

Again, however, I held my frustration inside. The happiness of the family depended on me, my parents explained. I fed and entertained my siblings. I should be happy to play my part.

'I am,' I said.

But I wasn't, not all the time. I was raised to obey my parents unquestioningly. I had already proved that I could and would. But that didn't mean I had to be happy.

***

Of all my chores, I seemed to find myself more often than not in the kitchen. Some days Karmjit was asked to help me, as I had helped the grown-ups when I was her age. I don't think she enjoyed it and she moaned a lot more than I had ever dared. But we had fun in our own way, catching up on each other's lives, as uneventful as they were. And from my point of view, at least we were together.

Other times, it would just be me at the stove or Mum would help in between her work or her own chores. I remember the first time she saw me cook a whole meal from scratch.

'You've learned so much,' she said, her eyes beaming with pride. 'You will make an excellent wife.'

Wife? I nearly dropped my ladle into the pan. I was fourteen. I was a child. And, based on my experiences in Patti, I hated men.

How could I ever be a wife?

Mum disappeared out of the room before I could say a word. But that night, after the tattle of my sisters' conversation had died down, I couldn't help replaying her words in my mind over and over again.

Was that all she saw when she watched me cook? Was she really just judging my suitability as a prospective wife?

Suddenly my two-year exile in India made hideous sense. I hadn't been sent away to learn the Indian ways for myself.

I'd been learning them for my *husband*.

I thought I'd been acquiring these new skills for my own benefit, so I could be a good daughter and help my family. I hadn't endured every hard lesson, put up with being separated from my family – even learned how to farm cotton buds – for any man!

Well, I thought, *if my husband has cows that need leading to the stream then I'm ready!*

The idea made me laugh. Calmed by the image of leading cattle through the suburban streets of Hounslow, I decided it wasn't a problem I needed to dwell on. After all, how was I ever going to find a husband when I never spoke to any boys?

***

Apart from the little bit of light relief provided at break times by talking to my friends, most of my days blurred into one. Between cooking, cleaning, school homework and trips to the temple or other relatives' houses, I had very little private time. Once or twice a week we would be allowed to watch half an hour of television, but only once the content had been deemed suitable by an adult. We weren't allowed to watch any programme that might feature a boy and a girl kissing, cuddling or even hinting at a relationship that wasn't brother and sister. That meant that all soap operas were a no-no and sitcoms like *Cheers* and *Diff'rent Strokes* were declared contraband for being too Western.

But I still had Sarita, Pam and Suneeta, albeit briefly during school days, to show me another side of life. Their magazines and gossip seemed so alien and, to be honest, *naughty*, but I was fascinated by the pictures and stories of singers and film stars. After a lifetime in the dark ages, by fifteen and sixteen I felt I had a stronger grasp on the world outside our house. When my friends talked about their favourite pop stars, I no longer had to keep asking 'Who?'

when I heard the names Adam Ant or Boy George. And when they discussed how handsome they found Sylvester Stallone, I was able to agree. Not because I'd seen any of his films, but because he'd been on a pull-out poster dressed as Rambo or Rocky.

The only subject I still didn't contribute on, in fact, was chasing the opposite sex. I just wasn't interested. Not in kissing, dating and certainly not marrying.

There's plenty of time for that.

***

If I'd been better at school then perhaps I would have been more scared of taking exams. But when the end of our fifth year approached and I sat a handful of CSEs – less challenging than the old O-levels – my predicted failure was almost a foregone conclusion. But I knew it was not my fault. I'd done my best but I'd missed so much and had had almost no support at home. Another little sister, Dalvinder Kaur, had arrived in our family when I was fifteen, the year before my exams. Cute as she was, her arrival meant even more responsibilities and even less time to study as I helped out at home. That I passed any of my CSEs was a surprise to me, but it was hardly a ringing endorsement for an academic future. There was no point thinking about A-levels and university was out of the question. The only option left was to get a job.

Unfortunately, finding employment with no skills and low qualifications wasn't easy either, so I signed up for a course in office skills in Feltham. It was only twenty minutes from our home, but rather than lift their embargo on public transport, Dad would drive me. I never thought I'd voluntarily opt to be taught anything ever again, so attending the course was a breath of fresh air for me. For a start, I didn't have to wear a uniform so I could attend in my normal – Indian – clothes. Just that factor gave me more confidence than I'd ever felt being made to dress like everyone else at Cranford. Even if I was still the same shy creature I'd always been, at least I felt more like myself.

More importantly, all the women on the course were starting from the same place as me. We all learned to type, file, answer phones together and for once I wasn't at the bottom of the class. Yet, happy as I was to thrive in my new environment, it only highlighted what I could have achieved at school if my parents hadn't disrupted my attendance. I didn't want to blame them for my poor results, but ...

With everything going so well, it came as a shock when, one evening after my course, Dad pushed an envelope to me across the dining table. Inside was a small photograph of a man I'd never seen before.

'Who's this?' I asked.

Dad smiled.

'That's the man you're going to marry.'

CHAPTER FOUR

HE'S NO ROCKY

It had all started with another one of our family discussions in the lounge. As I sat down, I remembered the horror of what had happened the last time I'd been summoned there.

Surely they're not sending me back to India?

At seventeen years of age, how many more Indian ways could there be for me to learn?

'No,' my father had said. 'Your time in India is done. But I do want to speak to you about your future. Are you sure you do not want to go to college or university?'

I thought about how I'd struggled to keep up at school with all the lessons I'd missed.

'No,' I said, 'that's not for me.'

'Then we will marry you off instead.'

***

It was later, in my room, that I processed what they'd said. 'Marry' someone? Was that how it happened? I could either continue my education or become a wife? Did that just apply to me or all girls? Would my sisters be subjected to the same choice when they reached my age?

Either way, how I wished I'd turned up more for class. But it wasn't my fault that I hadn't learned anything. I didn't choose to go to India or to look after my cousins and siblings at the drop of a hat. In fact, I couldn't go to university now even if I'd wanted to – was it possible that this was my parents' intention all along?

No, of course not. I shook such a disloyal thought from my head. But just the fact that I was thinking such a thing told me how devastated I was at the future laid out in front of me. I didn't want to get married. That was it. End of story, as far as I was concerned.

Unfortunately, I wasn't the one calling the shots. Six months later, when my parents produced a photograph of a small, nervous-looking man, it was a shock to see my fears made true – but not a surprise.

As they pointed to the low-resolution, grainy image, my parents explained that this was how marriages worked. Parents of a boy contacted parents of a girl and arranged a match. That was it, simple. The children had no say. They certainly didn't seek out their own husband or wife. That's how my grandparents in India had married, that's how my grandparents in the UK had married, and that's how my aunts and uncles had found each other as well. Of them all, my own parents' story was probably the most typical. My mother was raised in Singapore while my father came from India. When she had reached marrying age, her parents had let that be known through their contacts in the UK, in Singapore where they had family, and in India, the motherland, where there were still many relatives. A few short weeks later an envelope had arrived at my mother's house – much like the envelope that had been presented to me. Inside there had been a photograph of a young Sewa Singh Bath in his Indian army uniform. The next time Mum saw that face, Dad was standing next to her at their own wedding ceremony. That was the first time they met.

I knew that story well. I knew Mum and Dad considered it normal. And I knew they expected the same of me.

Dad looked at me expectantly as I stared at the slightly blurred image in front of me. I couldn't speak. I didn't know anything about this man in the picture. I didn't know his name, his situation, where he lived. And why was I sent such a tiny picture? Between his turban and his beard, I could barely make out any of his face. And my parents just expected me to say, 'Yes, I will spend the rest of my life with this stranger.'

My father filled in the details. The man was the son of Dad's best friend in India. They were a good family and he wanted to move to England.

'So he doesn't have a job?'

'No. But he'll soon get one,' Dad said. 'He is educated and has many skills. He is a teacher.'

I knew what was needed of me. I knew I had to be the role model for my sisters. It was my responsibility to live the life my parents wanted Karmjit, Kamaljit, Inder and, ultimately, even little Dalvinder Kaur to lead.

But I couldn't do it.

'No,' I said. 'I can't marry him.'

'Why not?' Dad's voice was stern but not angry. I have to believe he had my happiness at heart. But more importantly, he did not want our family to look bad in the eyes of this man's relatives. He did not want to lose face in the community.

'I'm too young,' I explained, meaning every word. I could also have added, 'I'm scared.' My experiences of the wandering hands and vicious tongues of the gropers on the bus in Patti were still so raw. How could I be sure this man from the same country would not be like those? That he would not treat a woman like a second-class citizen as so many had already treated me?

Mum and Dad briefly discussed my response as I sat there, then Dad said, 'OK, Sarbjit. You may say "no" this time.'

The emphasis on 'this time' hung in the air. Dad had honoured my view, and taken into account my young years. He'd listened to my opinion, but we both knew that only went so far. Yes, I could veto this man. What I couldn't do was say I would not get married. My marriage was already a foregone conclusion. That was the Sikh way. That was our family way. And that was the way it would be for me. *Next time* ...

***

As the weeks and months passed, my relief was tempered by the knowledge that at any time I could be shown another photograph. Eventually it arrived.

And I had exactly the same response.

I couldn't say if it was because I was scared of leaving my family or whether it was actually the thought of living with this particular man that disturbed me so much. All I knew was, the second I looked at the photograph, a shiver ran up my spine. It was all I could do to stop my teeth chattering with nerves. The idea of signing away my life to this stranger from a country where I'd been abandoned terrified me.

What's more, I was really put out that this suitor, or his family, had just sent an old passport photo – and not a good one, either. What good was that to me? If he was so desperate to marry me, why hadn't someone gone to the trouble of getting a proper photograph taken, rather than sending off a spare snap from the last photo booth he'd been in? To my mind, it was disrespectful and it just added to my discomfort. There was only one response I could give.

'I can't do it,' I said quietly. 'I can't marry him. I'm sorry, Dad, I just can't.'

I knew I was letting the family down, causing Mum and Dad pain. I also knew I was running out of chances.

***

In early 1989, having just turned nineteen, my parents invited me once again to have a family discussion with them. This time, for the sake of privacy, we spoke in their bedroom. Even though it was so cosy in there, and I could relax sitting on the bed, I knew there was only one topic on the agenda and it wasn't one to put me at ease. I waited to be shown a photograph of another possible suitor. But Mum's and Dad's hands were empty.

'Isn't this about another man for me to marry?' I asked.

'Yes,' Dad said. 'But we don't have a photograph of him.'

'How can I say if I like him then?'

'Because we're all going to meet him. Next week.'

Dad explained his logic. Despite giving me an upbringing that was more Indian than British, he couldn't deny that I was a child of London. I'd been to school here and now I was on a training course that would hopefully lead to a job. Perhaps it was unfair of him to expect me to marry a man from a different culture who might expect more of me than I could give.

'So,' he said, 'your grandmother has found a perfect family. They live in Hayes, they have two sons who have grown up there. One of them is married. The other one would like to marry you.'

Like my mother's family, the Athwals had also lived in Singapore before moving to the UK when the younger son was two. Their connections were still powerful and active. Between the two groups of elders, a match had been arranged.

Having husbands thrown at me from all parts of India was one thing. Having a man lined up for me by people I barely knew existed in a country I'd only heard of was intimidating, to say the least. How could so many strangers be involved in helping me find a husband?

The 'community' influencing my life was bigger than I thought.

* * *

It was a cold January morning when we all squeezed into Dad's car. As usual, practicality outweighed comfort and Mum, Dad, Grandma and Granddad all inched in alongside me and Kamaljit. It seemed ridiculous that we all shared the same car. What was the point of spending all morning getting ready, with Mum and Grandma ensuring I wore my finest *kameez* and *salwar* and matching headscarf, and then it all getting creased and crushed on the way there?

We were heading to my aunt's house in Bedfont, another west London town between Hounslow and Feltham and about five miles south of Hayes. She had agreed to host a meeting of the Athwals and the Baths. Even though my aunt was on our side of the family, the venue was viewed as neutral. We all attended the same temple, we all followed the same God, we were all part of the same community.

But would we become the same family?

My discomfort in the car helped take my mind off what lay ahead. But the second I stepped into my aunt's house, I was gripped by nerves. My stomach felt like it was in a vice. My throat was dry and I could do little more than nod and force a smile at my aunt's and uncle's greetings. They couldn't have been happier if they'd been celebrating their own daughter's wedding.

It was a nice house with a decent-sized lounge. My uncle had arranged chairs on either side of the room, one row for each family. In the middle was a long dining table, like a very visible barrier between the two groups. As the first family to arrive, we chose our side and I sat down. Mum and Dad, Uncle and Auntie, Granddad and Grandma stood around me, laughing and talking, eating chapattis and drinking lassi. It felt like I was looking through a window, watching a party that I hadn't been invited to. The only difference was, I was the guest of honour.

While the others chatted and ate, my sister and I sat quietly. I'm sure she was concerned for me but also, she knew: in a few years' time, this will be me. I was the example for her, my dad had made that clear. I had the family's honour to think of. How I behaved today could shape many lives for a long time to come.

It was a lot of weight on my young shoulders and I thought I might collapse under the pressure. But a noise interrupted my thoughts.

The doorbell.

I listened to the indistinct mingling of new and familiar voices coming from the hallway as my uncle let in the visitors and my grandparents welcomed their fellow Singaporean expats with loud bonhomie. If there were other voices, they were drowned out by the older generation.

After what seemed like an age, the lounge door finally opened and the Athwals filed in.

He's here.

Instinctively they made for the bank of empty chairs opposite ours, but I couldn't look. My eyes were fixed firmly towards the floor and the more people I heard enter the room, the more anxious I became. As spacious as the room had been, it suddenly seemed very small to me. Were the walls closing in?

Breathe, Sarbjit!

The last thing I wanted was to look flustered or hot or unattractive in any way. That would not reflect well on me or my family. Again, it was a noise that snapped me out of my panic. Except this time, it wasn't a doorbell. It was my father's voice – and he was making introductions.

Now I had to look. I saw the frail figure of Gian Singh Athwal, the father of the family. He had a friendly face and twinkling eyes. Next I was introduced to his wife, Bachan Kaur. She was taller than the women in my family; not overweight, but powerful-looking, and dressed resplendently in the finest silks and a severe *dastar* – like a female turban – on her head. Next to her, her three daughters seemed like petite princesses in their traditional dress. Then there was the elder son, Sukhdave, and finally, the reason we were all there: Hardave Singh Athwal.

I knew from my friends' magazines what love at first sight was meant to feel like. But there were no shooting stars, fireworks exploding or swelling chords from a Hollywood orchestra. Hardave didn't turn in slow motion and there was no cartoon sparkle off his white teeth when he smiled a silent hello. I smiled back at him, as he sat flanked by his brother and sisters, then looked away, a second before he did.

From what I saw, Hardave seemed perfectly fine, certainly better presented than the two men whose crumpled images I'd been sent before. *But,* I thought, *he's no Rocky.* He was just a man in the room, one of eight strangers. If anything, he appeared as nervous as I was, but that didn't mean I had to like him.

Introductions over, the families began to mingle around the table. I was struck suddenly by the gladiatorial layout of the room. We weren't two families coming together. We were more like two opposing teams, separated by the field of play. I didn't like it. This wasn't right. This wasn't how you found love. How could a man and a woman meet like this?

More importantly, how can you have a contest if the competitors aren't allowed to step on to the pitch?

While my sister and parents and grandparents stood and chatted to Hardave's siblings and older relatives, I was instructed to stay seated – just as he was. We didn't move, we didn't speak and we weren't allowed to cross to the opposition's half of the room. It was so frustrating. For all the interaction Hardave and I had, he may just as well have sent a photograph.

At least then I wouldn't have felt so much guilt about the decision I was about to make.

* * *

The longer I sat in my uncle's lounge, like a canary in a cage, admired but contained, the more resentful I became. Even when Hardave's sisters came over, I was polite and interested but, at the back of my mind, annoyed. The man they were boasting to me about was barely fifteen feet away. Why couldn't I speak to him myself?

The carnival atmosphere of earlier had been replaced by a more formal air, but there was still the underlying feeling of celebration in the room. All I could think about was, what for? This was meant to be an introduction, wasn't it? Not an actual wedding. The last thing I'd heard was that I would get to choose whether I liked the look of Hardave or not. And yet his family and mine were carrying on as though a decision – a positive one – had already been made.

But it hadn't. No one knew what was in my mind. No one knew how I was feeling about the tall woman who was trying to dominate the gathering, to the extent that her husband struggled to be heard. They didn't know what I thought of the gaggle of brightly dressed women who sang their brother's praises from the rooftops. And they didn't know, either, what I thought about the other woman at the meeting. The one who hadn't said a word all afternoon.

As the Athwals finally left, as noisily as they'd arrived, I caught the woman's eye. She was small and beautiful, if a little rundown-looking, and she'd been introduced as Sukhdave's wife. Her name was Surjit. And, unless I was very much mistaken, she didn't look very happy.

***

I didn't give my answer there. Not at my uncle's house. But then he didn't ask. I think he assumed I had already agreed. It was back in Hounslow, changed out of my Sunday best and relaxing with my family, that my father pushed me for an opinion.

'No,' I said. 'There's something about the family I don't like.'

'What do you mean? They are a good family. Bachan Kaur could not be more respected at temple. She wears the *dastar*, she has been baptised, she is the highest form of Sikh.'

I shrugged. On paper she was perfect. And, in fact, there was nothing I could pinpoint as a fault against the whole family. Hardave wasn't unattractive, he wasn't overweight, he was perfectly fine. But I'd felt uncomfortable in his family's presence. Was I so wrong to mention it?

'You would not like any family,' Dad said dismissively. 'I think you're grasping for excuses.'

I knew I wasn't but I didn't dare argue. Without an actual argument I was aware of sounding silly. Still, I knew what I felt.

'Please don't make me marry him,' I begged. 'Please, Daddy.'

Unlike on the other occasions when I'd rejected potential husbands, this time my father did seem upset. He refused to answer me or engage in an argument. A couple of hours later I realised why. The phone rang and Mum froze. She looked at Dad and he steeled himself before picking it up. A second later and I knew who the caller was.

Please don't say yes, please don't say yes! I was praying into my hands, hoping that my father was not about to consign me to a marriage I did not want. But a few minutes later he came back into the room, his face like thunder, and announced, 'I have asked for more time. We will give our answer in two days.'

'But I have given my answer,' I cried.

Dad shook his head and, without a word, left the room. He was disappointed in me, I could tell.

I've brought shame on him again.

* * *

The next morning I got myself ready for my course as usual. Dad and I passed like silent ships and nine hours later

I returned. The entire journey to and from my course had been hellish. I couldn't get the memory of Dad's sad face out of my mind. But that would pass, wouldn't it? Was his satisfaction right now worth a lifetime of unhappiness for me?

As usual after returning from Feltham I changed into my house clothes and headed straight for the kitchen. My father asked me to cook extra tonight because we were expecting visitors. That wasn't unusual. Socialising at friends' and families' houses was commonplace. We went to them; they came to us. But when the doorbell sounded an hour later I was surprised to see my uncle and aunt from Bedfont.

I would like to say they were happy to see me. But even as I thanked them for the hospitality of the day before, they could not bring themselves to receive my words with a smile. Dad, I realised, had spoken to them.

'Why won't you marry Hardave Singh?' my uncle said. 'He's a good man, with a good job with an electrical company. He's a Londoner, like you. His family are well respected in England, in India and in Singapore. What more do you want?'

'I don't know,' I replied.

'She doesn't know!' Uncle was confused and in a mood to taunt me. Somehow I had hurt his feelings. He fixed me with angry, dark eyes. 'Think about your actions, Sarbjit. Think about your family.' He paused and gestured to the other people scattered around the house. 'Think about the shame you will bring on all our heads.'

Shame? What shame can there be in not getting married? It's just a decision that a boy and a girl need to make.

But there was more to it than that, and I knew it.

My grandparents waded in next. They didn't speak of my happiness or anything to do with me. They merely pointed out that my uncle and aunt had provided a great service by letting us all gather at their house. Was I really going to disrespect them so brutally by making it all for nothing?

I saw their point, I truly did. But were they really saying that I should sign my life away out of gratitude for my relatives hosting a party I didn't want in the first place? Were they really more interested in not looking silly in the Athwals' eyes than in what was best for me? That's how it seemed. If I didn't change my mind, my uncle would have wasted his time. And that, clearly, was annoying him more than anything else.

'How will this look to the Athwals?' My uncle was almost shouting now. 'They are well respected in the temple. This will bring shame on all of us. We will be the laughing stock of the community.'

That word again! I didn't care about the community. They were neighbours, distant relatives, colleagues and strangers. They weren't me. What right did they have to decide my future?

My mother saw how distressed I was getting and tried to calm the situation.

'Remember, Sarbjit, I didn't even get a picture of your father,' she said, smiling, 'and look how happy we are together. At least you got to meet your husband.'

'He's not my husband!'

There, I'd said it. I marched from the room, as respectfully as I could muster, leaving a trail of discontented voices in my wake. I was sad, upset, and sorry for the pain I was causing. But I could not marry a man I didn't love.

It's not what God would want.

* * *

I thought – I hoped – that would be the end of the conversation. But the next day at my course I couldn't hide my feelings. It only took my tutor to put a kind hand on my shoulder and ask what was wrong, and the floodgates opened.

'What's the matter?' she asked.

I managed to say through my tears, 'My parents are making me marry this man I don't even know.'

'Of course, they're not making you. Nobody can make you marry anyone.'

She was white British. She didn't know the Sikh ways. Nothing I said from that point on would make any sense to her.

'Just tell them you don't want to,' she continued. 'It's your body and your life. You're your own woman. Nobody can tell you to do anything.'

Her words were music to my ears but I knew I would get laughed at if I dared repeat them at home.

'You don't understand. My parents want me to marry him. That is our culture. That is what I must do.'

'No, no. This is Britain in the twentieth century. You, not your parents, choose your own husband.'

She was trying so hard to be kind and to help me find a way through the darkness. And she did. I wiped my eyes, threw some water over my face in the toilet and continued on with my work. Then, when I got home that night, I convened a meeting with my mum and dad and grandparents.

'I've got something to tell you,' I said. 'I've decided to do it. I will marry Hardave Singh Athwal.'

CHAPTER FIVE

I'M YOUR MUM NOW

Sometimes you just need to make a decision.

I was no more interested in marrying this stranger from Hayes than I had been the day before. But I'd said I would and, in all honesty, acquiescing was a tremendous weight off my shoulders. There were no more arguments to be had, no more emotional blackmail or plaintive looks, no more pressure from the community. All I had to do now was see it through.

I nearly pulled out again, though, when Dad phoned the Athwal house to relay my reply. He came off the phone and said, 'Hardave has agreed to marry you, too.'

Agreed to marry me? It had never occurred to me he would be in any doubt! In my anxiety I'd forgotten that there was another person being coerced into a position he perhaps hadn't planned for himself. Another half to the whole of my marriage. For the first time I had something like warm feelings for this Hardave Singh. I wasn't the only one suffering. Perhaps our shared experience could yet be the foundation we needed for an actual relationship?

Having met – or at least, seen – each other in January, you would expect fiancés to spend a little time together soon after, to get to know each other, work out each other's likes and dislikes, their ambitions and their desires. But no. That wasn't the Sikh way. There was much to be arranged by the families and the last thing on anyone's mind, it seemed to me, was the two fiancés getting to know each other. In fact, we wouldn't see each other again until August, when the first of the traditional, joint family gatherings to mark our union was due to take place.

For the seven months in between, it was as though nothing had happened. The only obvious sign around our house that things were different was that my parents seemed to have a spring in their step. Personally, I tried my best not to think about my new family. I had my whole lifetime to do that.

***

Perhaps I would have spent more time dwelling on it if I didn't have so much else going on. My office skills course came to a close and, with a successful grounding in admin, reception and secretarial work, I was now a better proposition for a prospective employer. Sure enough, within a week of my last lesson, I got a job at EMI Records in Hayes. I only worked in the production department, miles away from the glamorous parts where the pop stars visited, but it felt great to have some independence for the first time in my life, even if I was still being chauffeured to and from work.

That state of affairs was soon to change too, however, because my course wasn't the only examination I passed. After a dozen or so lessons from my father, I passed my driving test first time and spent my first few weeks' wages on a car, a yellow Datsun Sunny. It was a bit of an old banger, but it was *my* old banger! With money and now transport, I really felt that the future – my future – was taking some shape.

I enjoyed my time driving to and from the EMI plant. Behind the wheel of my Datsun was the only time I could really call my own. What's more, with the company located on the Uxbridge Road between Hayes and Southall – the 'Little India' triangle, as it's known – there was a good mix of English and Asian staff, so I never felt alienated or worthy of comment in any way. Just how I liked it.

With my car bought and paid for and my home still with my family in Hounslow, a lot of my EMI salary was set aside for one important event: my wedding. I may have succeeded in putting it off, but the day was coming. Soon, it would arrive.

* * *

As the late spring of 1989 turned into summer, I finally began to get nervous about my future. Perhaps if I'd had more say in it I could have relaxed. I will never know. Without any consultation with me – or, I imagine, Hardave – a date had been set for 8 October. But the traditional Sikh wedding is a drawn-out affair and by August the ball was already rolling. After seven months of being left to get on with my single life, I now found myself centre stage for eight weeks of celebrations and ceremonies – and, I realised, I was dreading every minute.

The first event was scheduled to take place at our house. The night before I found myself staring in the mirror and panicking. This was it. The first step towards a new life. A life away from this house, away from this family.

Even this mirror.

The more anxious I got, the more vivid my fears and the more I didn't want the next day to come. And not just because of what I was soon to lose. What did I really know about the person I was about to become joined in life with? The answer terrified me.

My husband-to-be is coming to my home – and I can't even remember what he looks like!

I'm sure my family would be horrified now to learn that I didn't dare talk to them about my fears. But I knew how much my marriage meant to them. I knew its significance in our culture and so, after a restless night's sleep, I found myself the following morning joining in with preparations as though it was the most normal day of my life.

***

A few hours later, Hardave and his whole family arrived in Hounslow and were treated to some of my finest cooking. Once again, he and I were not allowed to talk. That pleasure, it seemed, fell to everyone but us. It was only after we'd all eaten that I was called upon to do anything at all.

I tried to busy myself tidying up as the elders prepared for the ceremonial aspect of the afternoon, but any hopes of hiding away in the kitchen were short-lived. I was summoned to stand by my father and, with both families again on opposite sides of the room, I was formally offered to Bachan Kaur and Gian Singh. They each in turn beckoned me and, as I bowed respectfully, Gian Singh pressed eleven pound coins and some sweets into my palm while Bachan Kaur presented a beautiful head covering. As she did so, she said, 'You're taken now.'

You're ours.

It wasn't quite a dowry but it was a token marking my journey, like a down payment on a new car. The first stage in my marriage had taken place – and I had taken my first step away from the family I loved and towards the family that had been chosen for me.

Watching the whole thing from the Athwal side of the room, Hardave's eyes didn't leave me once. I could feel him assessing me, confirming to himself that I was bride material. But he never once came over. We were like animals, dogs, walking around each other, sizing each other up, but not saying a word. When the transaction was complete, I went to my family and his parents regrouped around him. Shortly after, they left. We were getting married in two months and we still hadn't shared a word.

Later that week my father went to Hardave's house and performed the same ceremony with him.

I'm sure I should have wanted to accompany my father but I didn't. I just wasn't interested. I was following a path and taking one step at a time. I was in no hurry and I had no real desire to reach my final destination. All I could think was, *This is the tradition, I'm part of the tradition, don't fight it. Don't question it. Do your duty – and smile.*

But, with October drawing closer, I didn't think I would ever smile again.

* * *

If phase one of my wedding – the exchanging of gifts – seemed protracted, the next phase seemed to go on for ever.

Like other cultures, we hosted an engagement party – but with a few differences. Rather than take place at a disco on a Saturday night, my event was spread out across three days. In place of alcohol we had lassi and juices. And in place of a DJ we had a priest. Three priests, actually. Prayers are an important part of the pre-wedding procedure, and for the three days of celebration at my father's house, a priest was on hand to read out engagement passages from the Holy Book. He would speak for three or four hours then hand over to another. By working in shifts, there was always the word of our gurus being spoken in the house.

The whole event was our family's chance to announce my forthcoming nuptials to their friends and relations. No one was expected to stay for three days but there were no time limits, either. Like at the *gurdwaras* themselves, it was an open house policy and nobody was, or could be, turned away.

Being on show for such a long time was draining. On the positive side, the effort of remaining sociable for so many hours in a row was so exhausting it kept my mind off the reason why everyone was there. But every so often a relative or neighbour would ask how excited I was and I couldn't answer with the truth. So I forced a smile and didn't answer at all.

Dozens, possibly hundreds of people passed through our front door over those three days, but with some exceptions. The Athwals and their close relatives stayed well away. Another example of the Indian way.

The engagement event was for the bride's family only. It was interesting to think that on the other side of Heathrow, in a house I had never seen in Hayes, a similar festival of eating and drinking and socialising was going on at the same time. Only over there it wasn't an awkward girl who was the centre of attention, it was a man. I wondered if Hardave was enjoying himself as little as me.

In a perverse way, part of me couldn't wait to get my wedding over with. At least that way I wouldn't have to endure more days and nights of being in the spotlight for all the wrong reasons. But my culture had more torture in store for me.

With a fortnight to go until the big day, my parents hosted another pre-wedding occasion. Once again it was spread out across half a week. And once again there was no expense spared.

Unlike the prayer festival, this event was designed to be a celebration. The only problem was, I still didn't feel in the mood to join in. One night was set aside for henna painting and all of us women got involved. The cooking night appealed to me because I could hide in the kitchen and help. But the final night's emphasis on dancing was really something I could have done without. Fortunately, my aunties and uncles took care of the dance floor in the way that only aunties and uncles can ...

* * *

I'm sure many readers of this book will not be able to understand why I would go through with something that was so much against my will. The truth is, if you were raised in my family, you would do the same. Yes, perhaps if I had the choice I might have been out enjoying myself like other teenagers. But you have to remember that I had never been out, never socialised, never seen a glimpse of that side of life. I'd never even been on an underground train! You can't miss something you don't know exists.

But that still didn't mean I was comfortable knowing that 8 October was just around the corner. The closer it got, the more nightmares I began to have. They were more stress-related than about Hardave, but when I awoke with a start each night, it was his face I saw – and his face I hoped never to see again.

It wasn't personal. It couldn't be – I didn't know him well enough to bear a personal grudge. And that was the problem with the whole set-up: I just didn't know my fiancé at all. Everyone said he was nice but what did that really mean? After a lifetime being cocooned from male company, and having experienced the worst of it during my time in India, I didn't feel that I needed Hardave or any man.

Was it last-minute nerves or did I really not want to go ahead with things? I couldn't say. And nor would I. It would break my parents' hearts if I shared my doubts with them. They had their place in the community to consider and so did I. So too, I realised, did Hardave.

I thought again of his face and felt the familiar wave of nerves in my stomach. On the positive side, at least I could remember what he looked like now. On the negative, within a week I would be doing more than just looking at him. I'd be talking to him, as well.

***

The day had arrived. Dressed in red, from head covering to footwear, I joined my family in the car. For once we weren't all crammed into one vehicle. When we arrived at Hounslow Civic Centre there was already a crowd of well-wishers. Some I did not know. They must have been from Hardave's family. I was halfway inside the building when a thought occurred to me.

When I leave here, those guests will be my family too.

The magnitude of what I was about to do had finally hit me. I knew I was doing it for my family, for their good name and their honour among their peers. But saying yes to your parents is one thing. Now I was about to say it legally. From this moment on, everything would be different.

There were fifty guests packed into the stark registry office, with the women in particular dressed in every colour of the rainbow. Other couples would marry in the same building throughout the day, but I doubt anyone else's weddings looked quite so beautiful.

My parents took their place in the first row and I was guided by the registrar to a seat at the front. For a few minutes the chair next to me stood empty. Part of me hoped it would stay that way. Another part was desperate for that not to happen. The humiliation would be bad enough for me. I could only imagine what it would do to my family.

But a short while later, and still with plenty of time before the ceremony was scheduled to begin, the doors opened again and the Athwal clan strolled in. The smiles on the parents' faces said it all. I noticed that Hardave was smiling too, especially when he looked at me. I couldn't help smiling back.

I'm going to get married!

For all my misgivings, I had made my bed. I was about to lie in it. Why shouldn't I enjoy it?

When Hardave sat next to me I realised we'd never been so close. If I leaned over, I could actually touch him. But I didn't. That would not be allowed by our families. Not yet.

The registrar ran through the various sections of her script. I listened, half alert, half in a daze. I couldn't really believe what was happening. And then something odd happened: Hardave spoke.

'I do solemnly declare that I know not of any lawful impediment why I, Hardave Singh Athwal, may not be joined in matrimony to Sarbjit Kaur Bath.'

I realised I was staring at his mouth as the words came out. I'd never heard Hardave utter a single word before. How ridiculous was this, that the first time I should hear my groom speak should be at our actual wedding ceremony?

I was so busy concentrating on the sound of Hardave's voice I barely registered his words. The next thing I knew, he had taken my hand in his and was placing a gold band on my ring finger.

He's touching me!

Again, the details of the ceremony washed over me. All I could think about was Hardave's firm, dry skin against mine. Soon enough we would be expected to get even closer – but not now. When it came to the point where the registrar invited us to kiss each other, Hardave and I declined. It was enough that we had touched each other's hands. Any kissing would have to wait.

Until we were married properly.

For the civil ceremony, as fancy and well attended as it was, counted for nothing in our culture. It was merely a legal hurdle we needed to overcome, like sending your children to school. All it meant was that we were married according to British law. But not according to the Indian way.

And not in the eyes of the community.

The moment the ceremony ended, I was shepherded away from my legal husband. We shared a moment of eye contact then he was lost to me.

'All in good time,' Dad said. 'When you are truly married.'

In other words, when we were blessed at the temple in a week's time.

***

Now that I'd got the civil service part out of the way, I found myself willing the Sunday to arrive. In fact, for the rest of the day after the service, I was in a surprisingly upbeat mood. Even more surprising, it was my father who punctured it when he should have been happiest of all.

'I am about to send out the invitation cards for the service at the temple,' he said. 'If you are going to get cold feet, now is the time to tell me.'

Was he pulling my leg?

'Now you ask me if I want to get married?'

I was furious.

'In January I said "no" a hundred times and you all bullied me until I gave in. And now ...' I took a breath. I needed to stop myself before I said something I might regret.

But seriously – he waited until I was legally married in accordance with British law to suggest I didn't have to go through with it. Why couldn't he have offered this choice in August before Bachan Kaur had claimed me for her family? Or in July, June – any time but now?

I know now that Dad only had my happiness at heart. To my teenage self, however, it seemed to be the last thing on his mind. At that moment he appeared to me more worried about wasting the printing costs of the invites than my feelings. But then I realised that that obviously wasn't the driving factor at all. The community was. How would it look for me, for him, for all of us if I did pull out later? He didn't need to tell me the answer.

***

With a week to go until the service at the temple, it was business as usual at home and then at work. But not, it turned out, after work. I came out of my office on the Monday evening and stopped dead in my tracks. I don't think I could have been more shocked if I'd seen a ghost.

'Hello, Sarbjit,' Hardave said. 'Is there somewhere we can go to talk?'

Still in an absolute trance, I led my 'husband' to my little yellow car. I unlocked the passenger door then walked round to my side. I couldn't help taking a few deep breaths before I pulled on the handle. What was going on? Why was he here? And how had he found me?

I soon realised that Hardave was as confused as I was. Like me, he found the limbo between the British service and the Sikh one too much to comprehend. In any other culture we'd be together now. It seemed like torture to keep us apart.

Even though I was in no hurry to leave my family home, I had to agree.

We sat next to each other in silence. All sorts of dark thoughts flashed through my head. One of them stayed. I didn't really know this person and here he was sitting next to me in my car. He could have been anyone. But he wasn't, he was my husband. Then he surprised me by saying, 'Are you happy?'

I thought about it. What did he want to hear? In the end I said the truth.

'Yes.'

Because for all the conflicting – if not downright negative – emotions I'd been going through those past weeks, the mere fact that Hardave had broken protocol and tracked me down just to ask about my feelings filled me with positive thoughts. So, in that car, in that company, at that moment in time, yes, I was happier with my circumstances than I had thought I would ever be.

It was a fleeting feeling of warmth but it was genuine, and even though I was still shaken by Hardave's sudden appearance, we both relaxed at my answer. He thanked me and after a long silence, both of us staring blankly at the misting windscreen, he said he'd like to visit me again.

'I'm here at this time every night.'

'OK,' he said, then left the car as efficiently as he'd arrived.

It was two nights later when he reappeared. Even though I was half expecting it, it was still a shock to see him waiting outside the EMI lobby. Again we walked to my car and again there was an awkward silence. But not for as long this time. The ice had been broken two days earlier. But I still didn't know what to say to him, nor him to me, and attempts at conversation were stilted, almost childlike in their subjects. We fumbled our way around the weather, our jobs, our families. We even touched on the civil ceremony but with neither of us going into any detail. It was enough that we heard each other's voices and grew comfortable in each other's company. In fact, as Hardave made to leave, I realised I might actually like him. When he leaned over and gave me a peck on the cheek, I made no attempt to prevent it.

***

After what felt like two months of continuous family gatherings, ceremonies and rituals, my wedding day had arrived. From being dead against it back in January, I was now almost excited.

Of course, it wouldn't be a Sikh celebration without days of partying. Sure enough, forty-eight hours before the day, my parents had once again declared 'open house'. All those in receipt of Dad's precious invites were invited to come and eat lunch or dinner or both over a couple of days, and take part in dancing and henna painting and generally enjoy the carnival atmosphere in our modest three-bedroom home.

A lot of the guests were strangers to me but that was normal. Our closest relatives had been at the registry service, even more had attended the engagement and prayer drop-ins. But for the actual wedding, it was customary to invite everyone, from neighbours you nodded to but had never spoken to, to friends who had drifted from your lives, to extended family all over the world: this was the opportunity to contact them all and invite them to share in your family's happiness.

Being centre of attention is never going to sit comfortably with me, but now that I had had a chance to actually speak to my fiancé and understand a little about what made him tick, I wasn't so surly. I still didn't dance but I was happier being there. I didn't even mind so much enduring my parents and uncles showing me off with pride.

After two days of constant smiling and celebrating, I didn't think I had the energy for a third. But as I went to bed on the eve of my wedding, I realised I was nervous in a way I hadn't expected. Yes, part of it was fear – fear of leaving my family, of stepping out into the world on my own. But part of it was excitement. I had to be up early to get ready but I knew I wouldn't sleep in. *I'll be lucky if I can sleep at all.*

The next morning, when my aunt arrived to help with my wedding outfit, the size of her make-up bag made my eyes bulge. I'd never worn lipstick in my life. Now she was threatening to paint my nails, style my eyebrows, paint eye shadow on my lids and apply who knew what to my skin. I was slightly nervous but thrilled at the same time. After several false starts, this was the day I was to become a woman.

And I think I'm going to like it.

Mum had helped me choose my clothes. I had a stunning cerise *salwar kameez* that we'd bought in Southall for £300. To a Western eye it might not look too different to the flowing top and trousers I normally wore. But I could feel the quality of the materials and see the effort that had gone into the intricate embroidery. The scarf was also richer and heavier.

It wasn't just my body that was dressed for the day. As is custom, I had been given an ornate gold piercing – or *nath* – that my aunt hung from my ear to my nose. By the time she had helped me on with my bangles, shoes and selected a handbag, I felt like a different person. When she made me look in the mirror I realised I looked different, too. But the longer I stared, the more I began to like what I saw. *And,* I thought, *I hope Hardave likes it too*.

No wedding is complete without every detail captured on film and, with the family dressed in their finery, it was time to welcome the photographer. This one had a video camera as well. I hated the idea of being filmed but I had to admit, I was being spoiled so much I did feel a little like a movie star.

Eventually, the ordeal of posing again and again over, we all drove the familiar route to the temple. Whereas the registry office had all been new to me, this place was a haven. I was comfortable there. I knew the priests and many of the community. It was the house of God, and He would protect me.

For the first hour, we took tea, giving everyone a chance to arrive. Even at nine o'clock in the morning, the air in the main hall was filled with traces of various aromatic spices. I knew if I put my mind to it, I could probably identify each one. Then at ten the formalities began and the members of each family approached each other. My parents went to Hardave's, my uncles met his uncles, and my aunts found his aunts. Everyone met their equivalent from the other family and, even if they already knew each other from outside the temple, made a formal introduction and placed a garland – called a *haar* – over each other's heads. It's our equivalent of the buttonhole corsage but in the minds of many it has the hint of a night in Hawaii.

While Hardave filed into the hall and sat with his family on one side of the room, as close to the Holy Book as possible, I remained outside with my closest male relatives. Despite my father, brother, granddad and uncles being so close, and even after such a relaxed morning, I was stunned to realise how frightened I had suddenly become.

It came out of the blue. One minute I was relishing the theatrics of the day and the next I felt faint, as though my clothes were too tight. I wanted to loosen everything even though I knew that wasn't the problem.

I was really doing it. I was getting married. Dad had been right. The civil ceremony was an irrelevance compared to this. Right here, right now, was all that mattered.

'It's time.'

My father's words snapped me out of my panic. As the door to the main hall opened, suddenly I had all the oxygen in the world.

To the rousing sound of the wedding songs, we walked to the front of the packed hall, past the hundreds of guests sitting cross-legged on the covered floor, and I took my place alongside Hardave before the Guru Granth Sahib. Strangely, I didn't feel any nerves at all. It was as though I were operating on autopilot. I'd rehearsed this moment in my mind a hundred times. It was like putting a jigsaw together. First I needed this piece, then I needed that. Corners, edges, then middle. But there was no emotion. Not yet.

The next piece of the jigsaw was handed to me by my father. As is our custom, he'd brought with him the long red *palla* – or scarf – which he passed first to Hardave and then to me. It was a physical symbol of our union and to drop my end of it would be considered bad luck.

The priest looked around the room, ready to call for silence. There was no need. All eyes were on him. We were ready. Then he began to read the four holy verses – the *laavan* – from the Guru Granth Sahib. As he did so, Hardave

and I walked around him and the Holy Book, stopping only
to bow. We passed four times, once for each verse, sitting in
between. All the time the red scarf seemed to weigh more
heavily in my hand.

Don't drop it!

The more I thought about it the harder it was.

With Hardave and me seated once again, the priest ran
his hand along the top of the Holy Book. Then, shaping
his hand flat like a knife, he dissected the pages and lifted
the giant book open where it fell. It was a random act, a
chance selection, similar to the naming of a child ceremony,
but whichever passage fate had chosen would have great
influence on our lives.

He read the relevant verse as I drank in every word. They
were ours. They were chosen by God specifically for us. And,
more importantly, they were the first words of our marriage.

Forget the ceremony at Hounslow Civic Centre – *now* we
were properly married.

That same tingle of excitement I'd felt at Hounslow came
back. Just the words 'you are husband and wife' sent shivers
through me. I could argue later about whether I wanted to
be there or not, but at that moment, I could not dispute how
good I felt. My training to become a wife had paid off.

The priest continued his duties, extolling the expectations
of marriage and the requirements of the Sikh traditions.
Tellingly, he reminded everyone in the room that Sikh culture
was something to be honoured and respected.

'Listen to your community, listen to your prayers, listen
to your family and listen to your faith.'

Where possible, he preached, we should stay within the
culture.

It seemed to take an age for the temple to empty
afterwards. Then we all drove to a hall near my parents'
house for yet another celebration. I'd arrived at the temple
in my father's car. But that was not what I left in. As I

stepped out of the *gurdwara*, I gasped at the sight of the gleaming cream Rolls-Royce waiting. Hardave's friend was the driver. It was my husband's first act in our marriage and I approved wholeheartedly.

***

If there is a more sociable religion than Sikhism, then I can't imagine it. More food, more laughter and more dancing filled the next few hours. Then at six o'clock, after a full day, we began to say our goodbyes to the extended family and our neighbours and more distant friends. The next – and, thankfully, final – part of the tradition had arrived. It was time for those closest to the happy couple to travel to the bride's family home for one last ritual.

A ritual I wasn't looking forward to at all.

After about forty or fifty minutes of yet more sweet snacks and tea, I watched as the two families – now united as one – began to assemble in a guard of honour leading towards our front door. As I stood in the centre of the room, my legs felt like they were made of lead. I knew what was coming.

As my parents hugged and kissed me, I knew my time in their family was coming to an end. We were nearing the final act in a performance that had started back in August. Through each stage I'd been guided by my father or mother or aunt's steadying hand – like I had been, I realised too late, for every single step of my life. The ritual that was coming now would put an end to that relationship once and for all. When the day was over, a link in the family chain would be broken.

I'll be on my own.

But in reality, I wouldn't be on my own at all. I just wouldn't be with *my* family.

The next few moments were meant to be a celebration of my growth as a woman. But as my parents each said that they were passing their love on for my new life, it felt more like a wake. When, with symbolic seriousness, they pressed a clutch of rice into my hands, it felt like burning coals in my palm.

I don't want it.

To the dozens of watching eyes, the rice signified my parents passing on their blessing that I was ready to leave the nest and take my place in the world. But that's not how it felt. I wasn't being given my freedom; I was being divorced. From them, from the Bath family. From my brother and sisters. When I should have felt overjoyed at starting a new life, all I could think was that I was being cast out.

Conscious of each grain prickling my palms, I scanned the room and picked out my family. Grandparents, aunts, uncles all beamed proudly back at me, oblivious to my pain. Then my eyes landed on Karmjit, Kamaljit, Inder, my brother and five-year-old Dalvinder. The girls were all crying, with happiness or sadness I couldn't tell. I forced a smile and watched them respond. In that instant I remembered my power as the eldest child. They counted on me to show them the way. However I felt inside, I needed to appear strong.

My gaze fell on the Athwals, poised by the door. Bachan Kaur, Gian Singh, Hardave's brother Sukhdave and his beautiful shy wife stared back. At my side, Hardave turned, touched my elbow, guiding me, encouraging me to turn as well.

We walked towards the open front door. A second before I reached it, I stopped, folded my hands more tightly over their contents, then, as was the custom, flung the rice dramatically over my shoulders. With it I symbolically returned to my parents all their claim on my future life. It was done.

I didn't look back. I didn't acknowledge the cheers and whistles. I just cried as I stepped out of the front door and walked forwards, towards the smiling group of Athwals huddled by their cars. As I reached the Rolls-Royce, two figures stepped in front of me. Gian Singh placed his hand on my head and blessed me, welcoming me to his family. I smiled, recognising the sincerity in his words, but still unable to speak through my tears.

Then my mother-in-law, Bachan Kaur, pulled me to her.

'Welcome to the Athwal family, Sarbjit,' she said. Then, embracing me closer, she added softly, 'I'm your mum now.'

CHAPTER SIX

DON'T BELIEVE IT

You shouldn't judge a book by its cover. That's what I'd been told. And yet, as the Rolls-Royce purred to a stop outside an unremarkable semi-detached house in Hayes, I felt my heart sink.

I'd been assured that I'd married well. I'd been promised that my husband came from a successful family and that he had prospects. But this place, 90 Willow Tree Lane, looked less impressive than the home I'd left behind – and I knew there were at least six adults who needed to squeeze in. After the highs of the last three days, I felt a genuine thump as my hopes took a blow. *Still,* I told myself, *I'm sure it will be fine inside ...*

In fact, although the house was smaller than the one I'd left behind, at least the space had been divided sensibly. A long lounge to the left of the front door stretched from the front of the house to the back. It was a combination of subtle beige and grey shades, with only a large fish tank in the corner adding any colour.

Upstairs there were three bedrooms and, in honour of my arrival, there had recently been a change-round. Sukhdave, as the elder son, shared the main bedroom with his wife, Surjit.

The box room, previously Hardave's, was now taken by my father-in-law – or 'father' as I now had to call him. Gian Singh was suffering very badly from asthma, I was told, and needed space to himself. 'Mum' moved into a room downstairs which had once been a kitchen before a new extension.

Which left the mid-sized bedroom, once Bachan Kaur and Gian Singh's, for the newlyweds. It was an OK room, a decent size, with white furnishings and enough space for my clothes and a good spot on the wall where I could have my favourite portrait of Guru Nanak Dev Ji and a photograph of the spectacular Golden Temple in Amritsar. It was a fresh start for everyone.

Everyone had their place – including a large Alsatian called Ricky who had a kennel in the garden – but it was undoubtedly a tight fit. I knew, however, that space wasn't everything. My family's house in Patti had been five times the size, but that place could still feel claustrophobic. A house is made by its inhabitants.

I hoped the inhabitants of 90 Willow Tree Lane would surprise me. Right then, I wasn't confident at all. After all, what did I really know about any of them?

But the Athwal family could wait for a few hours because first, we had yet another social engagement to get through. No sooner had we pulled up at the house than the doors of a dozen other cars opened. Many of the people who had not gone to my parents' house had come straight here instead. In their honour there would be further celebration.

The majority of these guests I did not know because they were from my husband's side. But as they eventually disappeared into the night after another round of chapattis and snacks, I was glad that two faces I recognised remained: my grandma and my little brother. I hadn't been abandoned, thrown to the wolves, not quite yet. They were here to guide me through my first night away from the family home.

People from other religions, and especially those who do not follow any faith, might find this practice extremely odd. But it is a Sikh tradition for a bride to share her bed on her wedding night not with her husband, but with a male from her own family. That way the transition from one family to another is supposedly smooth. A bride will have enough change to contend with. Why not let her start one step at a time?

My brother was the obvious candidate, but at ten years old he was too young to have the sole responsibility, so my grandma had volunteered to accompany him – and me. I couldn't have had anyone better. For so much of my childhood she'd been the one who was around while Mum was at work. It seemed only natural that she would be with me now. More natural, in fact, than sharing a bed with my husband.

As positive as my thoughts towards Hardave were after such a thrilling day, he was still mostly a stranger to me. The idea of him touching me was not one I was relishing.

Fortunately, our culture also had a timetable for that as well. Like other faiths, we would be going on a honeymoon – but not yet. So, in accordance with custom, I had two weeks before we entered the next phase of our relationship. As the following days passed by, I realised I was willing time to slow. As much as I wanted to go on holiday, I really did not want to give myself to this man. To any man.

I wouldn't even know how ...

* * *

My passage from Bath to Athwal still wasn't over. The day after our wedding, my husband and I, my in-laws and relations from that side of the family, all drove over to Hounslow. My parents had prepared a beautiful feast with tea and my sisters couldn't wait to talk to me about my first night away. It was good to see them. But if I'd hoped the occasion would be the first of many between my extended family, Bachan Kaur had made it clear en route what the day was actually about.

'You're visiting this house as a guest,' she explained. 'It's no longer your home. You're only going to show your parents how happy you are.' She took my hand, pressed it and smiled. 'And then you come back with us, to your real home. As my daughter.'

Later that night, after I'd driven my dad's wedding present to us – another Datsun, this time a bright red Cherry – to its new home outside the house on Willow Tree Lane, Bachan Kaur reiterated her point.

'This is your home now,' she told me. 'Everything you need is here.'

She didn't actually say, 'You are forbidden to go to your old house', but it was implied. I nodded in agreement and smiled. It was my wedding weekend, after all. I didn't want to cause a fuss. But inside I was so confused – and worried. *Everything I need isn't here. I have four sisters and a brother. I've already been separated from them once – we can't be cut off again.*

The embargo on me leaving only covered my family, it seemed. Going to work was still expected of me, although, in truth, my new home was so much closer to EMI I probably could have walked.

After my first day at work as a married woman I drove home, wondering how to spend my time. The idea of a world where my father or mother didn't control my every move was strange. I was looking forward to actually making some decisions of my own. Perhaps I would take a walk or maybe watch some television.

Or perhaps I would cook a meal for twenty people.

It seemed that my marriage still had more celebrations to run. It was, Bachan Kaur explained, part of Sikh culture that the bride cooks a meal for her new family. And tonight, she said, was the night. I was happy to do it, naturally, although considering that all the guests – Bachan Kaur's daughters and son-in-laws – had been at every other stage of the proceedings to date, I couldn't see why we needed to celebrate again with them. But, if that's what 'Mum' – as I had been told to call Bachan Kaur – wanted …

Just as I moved from chopping spinach to peeling carrots, another figure appeared in the doorway. The sad girl I'd seen before. Surjit. We nodded at each other and said, 'Hello.' Over the course of my never-ending wedding we'd barely shared a dozen words. But she, it seemed, had also been sent to prepare food. I was pleased for the help, and for the company. If anyone knew what I was going through entering a new family, it was her.

Over the next few years, Surjit would tell me so many things. Many I was glad to know, some I wished I'd never heard. But that night she only let slip a few stories. I suppose she was as nervous around me as I around her. But why? She was the wife of the older son. Her status in the family was higher than mine. When the parents eventually died, Sukhdave and she would control the family and its name together. That was how it worked in the community.

Actually, I learned, death might be coming to the family sooner than I realised. My father-in-law's asthma complaint was more severe than I knew.

'That is why it was so important for Hardave to find a wife,' Surjit said. 'Father wants all his children married before he dies.'

'That's sweet,' I said.

She shook her head. 'Don't believe it.'

The next few minutes followed in silence. I surmised that Surjit was upset about her father-in-law. After all, he seemed a particularly decent man. Despite knowing him for such a short time, I too was sad for him. But no. Surjit also, I learned, had married because her grandmother was said to be on her deathbed. The old woman's wish, possibly her final one, was to see her granddaughter wed and so Surjit and Sukhdave had found each other – or been found for each other – in haste.

'I had to,' Surjit said. 'My grandmother was at death's door.'

'I'm sorry to hear that.'

'Don't be. She was the first one on the dance floor at my wedding. I'm sure she'll outlive us all.'

Surjit also hinted that I should get used to working in the kitchen. She had been just sixteen when she married Sukhdave. Two years on, she said, after a full day's work at a local tool-selling firm called Buck & Hickman, she was still expected to prepare and serve a meal for the family. It was not the dream life she'd been expecting. But maybe that was always going to be the reality, whatever family she married into. She was young and she was female, so of course her place was in front of the oven. That was the Indian way ...

* * *

I couldn't easily begrudge my new in-laws for expecting me to help around the house – not without criticising my own mum and dad, who had expected me to do the same. They'd even trained me to do it for my husband. In that respect there were no surprises. Not yet. Surjit, on the other hand, had not arrived with the same attitude as me. Her Coventry family wasn't exactly Westernised – far from it – but she had never been shipped to India for intensive training. Nor had her parents restricted her from socialising with Western girl friends at school. Entering a world that was far stricter and being expected to toe the line was like a splash of water on the face.

And then there was her age. At sixteen, Surjit was not even considered an 'adult' in some quarters when she married

Sukhdave. Added to that the fact that her family were so far away and she must have felt very isolated indeed. No wonder, I supposed, she seemed so pleased to see me.

The feeling was mutual. I enjoyed Surjit's company and her wisdom. Even though she was younger than me, her life as a grown-up had started so much earlier than mine that she had a word to say on most subjects. But there was one area that we did not talk about. It was a journey I had to take alone, and I was not looking forward to it.

My honeymoon.

A week's holiday in Majorca should have been something to look forward to. But, excited as I was about leaving the country for the first time – apart from my exile to Patti – there was a cloud hanging over me. As the day of our departure drew closer, my nerves grew steadily worse.

What was there to be worried about? I asked myself. What could be better than having time alone with the man I had pledged my future to? It was only right that we got to know each other properly. We had to find a way to make things work between us.

For the past two weeks Hardave and I had lived almost as brother and sister, sharing polite conversation around the family table at mealtimes or when he came and stood in the kitchen doorway and chatted while I prepared food. It was a pleasant enough relationship, although not exactly natural. But despite our amicable interaction, there was one looming duty that was worrying me.

For as welcome as time away with my husband was, at the back of my mind, I knew there would be other expectations as well. Ones for which I really was not ready.

Everything I knew about the human body had come from one biology class at Cranford Community School. That had been perfunctory to say the least, although perhaps there were more lessons and I just didn't attend for family reasons. Certainly I had never had any sort of conversation along those lines with my mother or father or any of my aunts. What I knew – or, at best, half-remembered – had come from a lecture and pictures in a textbook. And the idea of doing anything like the action discussed seemed the most unnatural thing in the world.

I could only hope that Hardave shared the same apprehension.

***

The flight out was exciting and we had a beautiful first day in the sunshine. As I'd never been on holiday before, I only had my traditional *salwar kameez* to wear. By contrast, Hardave had packed shorts and T-shirts. While I would never have worn those, and certainly nothing like the scantily clad women on the beach around us, I still wished I'd been allowed to pack something like jeans or other tops more suited to the environment. It was the first time I'd ever longed for something from the 'West'.

I remember enjoying myself over dinner until I realised that it was getting late and we would soon be turning in for the night. Everything I was dreading would be taking place soon. Perhaps I put too much pressure on myself, and filled my head with too many fears. But as we took the lift up to our floor and made our way to the room, I just wanted to flee back down.

The only way I made it to the bed was to remind myself that Hardave was my husband, that I had enjoyed my time with him so far that day, and that what we were about to do was perfectly natural and expected of a married couple. But, I have to admit, it didn't go smoothly for me. I wanted so much to be the good wife but, as much as I was confused by what he wanted me to do, he was confused by my reluctance.

He seemed genuinely puzzled by my reaction, and, to his credit, we soon stopped, the atmosphere between us ruined for quite a while.

The rest of our honeymoon passed without a repeat of that first-time awkwardness and, as the physical side of our relationship naturally developed, we grew closer. But even at its very best, at the back of my mind I could not help remembering that I was giving myself to a man I barely knew. How could this be right?

And what would be expected of me in the future?

CHAPTER SEVEN

A BAD DAUGHTER

I'd arrived at Willow Tree Lane with every intention of devoting my life to becoming an Athwal. I wanted to be the good wife, the good sister and the good daughter. I'd been raised to become that, even if I wasn't aware of it at the time. But it was hard.

And I wasn't the only one struggling.

Shortly after returning from my honeymoon, I asked Bachan Kaur – or 'Mum', as I had to remind myself to address her – if I could go to visit my mother.

'It's her birthday,' I explained. 'It would mean a lot to her – and me.'

My mother-in-law thought about it. Then she shook her head and said, 'Out of the question. My daughters are coming today. You will make tea.'

'But what about my mother?'

'You may visit her tomorrow.'

But that's not her birthday!

I'm surprised I even dared think it. But the matter was closed. Mum had gone to her room and, once I calmed down, I knew where I had to go. When I reached the kitchen, Surjit was already there.

I really wanted to confide in her but I didn't dare. Bachan Kaur was my mother now. To disrespect her in her own house was a low blow I couldn't stoop to. That would not be right. Fortunately, I was able to vent my frustration slightly by listening to Surjit – who was not impressed at having to give up her time to host a tea for her – *our* – sisters-in-law.

'All of them are so lazy,' she fumed. 'They expect to be waited on hand and foot.'

I didn't say a word.

'They never help, they don't even offer to clean up. Would it kill them to pick up a few plates? Obviously I would never let them, but they should offer, shouldn't they? I do in their houses. You would, too, wouldn't you?'

Surjit was ranting, clearly angry, but all I could do was smile. I'd never heard anyone talk like her. Even the more rebellious girls at school didn't have a tongue to match hers. It was as though she didn't have a care in the world. Whereas all I could think was, *What if Mum hears? What if Hardave or Sukhdave walk in?*

We prepared the tea and, to the sound of our sisters – Bhajan, Ajmar, Kalwant and Baldave – and their husbands gathering in the lounge, began to take everything through. Bachan Kaur made a grand show of praising us, me especially, as we served the snacks and drinks. But when Surjit and I went to join our guests at the table, I realised there were no spare chairs. I looked for Surjit, desperate for guidance. This was my first family function of this kind. I did not want to cause offence.

Surjit was sitting on the floor.

I was used to sitting like that at the temple. I enjoyed it, in fact. But I'd never done it while my family sat at a table. How could we communicate if we were all on different levels? The answer soon became apparent. We didn't.

Afterwards, as I washed up in the kitchen, I mentioned the seating to Surjit. She shrugged, as though she hadn't noticed anything was wrong. Or perhaps, as though she were so used to sitting on the floor when her sisters-in-law visited that it didn't even register to her as wrong any more. Given everything I already knew about her, Surjit's blasé reaction told me all I needed to know.

I don't think this is a one-off.

* * *

When I finally visited my mother after her birthday she looked at me with sadness in her eyes.

'I thought you would visit yesterday.'

'I could not, Mum.'

'I thought you would phone.'

What was I meant to say now? That Bachan Kaur had forbidden me from even calling? No, that wasn't right. It would portray my new family in a bad light and I would not be responsible for that. I knew the ways of the community. I knew how quickly judgements were passed. I was an Athwal now. I needed to be loyal to them. To us. To our family name.

'I'm sorry, Mum,' I mumbled. 'I'm a bad daughter. I will remember next year.'

* * *

While it was taking a little while longer than I'd hoped to get used to my mother-in-law's ways, I was glad of my relationship with Surjit. I just wished she could be happier. While I got on with my chores, she couldn't chop a tomato without resenting the fact it was only ever us two in the kitchen. It was bad enough that the men weren't expected to help but Bachan Kaur was one of us. And yet she wouldn't lift a finger around the house unless it was so I could dust underneath it.

I was still very shy around the whole family, so I rarely asked Surjit anything. My role was more of a listener. So when she confided in me one day that she and Sukhdave rowed so much they were sleeping in separate beds, as much as I wanted to probe, I couldn't say a word. I stood there with my mouth open, while Surjit rattled on to her next revelation.

After my experience in Majorca I didn't find the news about single beds that shocking. In fact, I liked the idea and secretly wondered whether Hardave and I might copy it eventually. But at that moment I was actually quite comfortable with how my relationship with my husband was developing. The physical side of our marriage had reached a rhythm and he tried to be friendly and funny when we were alone. We were both in this union together; neither had chosen the other, but he was as determined as I to make it work. And yet, for all his attentiveness when we were alone, when we were downstairs, as part of the family, only one woman ruled his life.

And it was not me.

When his mother was around I may as well have been invisible.

As hurtful as it was to be ignored by my husband during every family meal or discussion, the fact that Surjit appeared to be going through the same treatment from Sukhdave gave me hope. Hope that I wasn't doing anything wrong. Hope that my marriage was strong and on the right track. Both men wouldn't treat their wives badly for no reason, would they?

Often the only man to pay heed to me at mealtimes or family gatherings was Gian Singh. He was a generous soul and quick with warm comments. It was fun seeing Bachan Kaur bite her tongue in his presence and I'm sure he played up to that. Both sons loved him, too.

Father's ill health was the reason Hardave and his youngest sister, Baldave, had married within months of each other. There was also another wish of his that the family was desperate to see.

A grandson.

But this is where Baldave and her sisters could not help. The grandson had to take the Athwal name, which meant it had to come from Gian Singh's sons. Yet, despite two years of marriage, Surjit and Sukhdave seemed as unlikely as ever to have a child. Perhaps, I wondered, Hardave and I would provide an heir first.

Unfortunately Gian Singh died within six months of my wedding, aged only fifty-nine. As feared, it was a giant asthma attack which proved too much for him to fight. I'd only known my father-in-law briefly but I was very sad. He was a lovely person and well respected by everyone. More importantly to me – if not the community – he was clearly loved as well. Distraught as I was at Gian Singh's passing, watching my husband almost crumble with grief was somehow worse, and consoling him was a painful process. For once I was grateful to have the distraction of chores.

Sikhs do not believe that death is the end of a soul's life, and so – in theory at least – we are meant to be less despondent when a physical form passes away. Having said that, the traditional cremation and service afterwards at the temple were sombre and heartbreaking. I cried and cried and, for the first time, I truly believed I belonged in the family.

The next few days at home were very hard. I lost myself in household chores and hosting a memorial supper. My parents came over to pay their respects and join in the prayer sessions. I was so pleased to see them, but sorry it had taken such a terrible event to bring them to my house.

Hardave took his father's death very badly. And, I'm sure, Sukhdave did as well. But he needed to maintain a strong public face. After all, with Father gone, he was now preparing to take on the mantle of 'head of the family'.

But that is not how things worked out.

A couple of days after Gian Singh's death, we all gathered to eat in the dining room. Before we began, my mother-in-law raised a toast to her dear departed husband. She spoke thoughtfully, then concluded with words that I remember to this day: 'I am the head of the family now.'

I sensed Hardave flinch and I'm sure I saw Surjit jump. But all eyes were suddenly on Sukhdave. His rightful place now was at the head of our family. That was what everyone inside and outside of No. 90 expected. That was the normal way of things. And yet, right before his eyes, someone else was claiming the position for their own. And that someone was the person Sukhdave loved most in the world. Someone who was grieving at the loss of her dear husband. And someone who was already more respected in the community than he would ever be. What could he say?

Bachan Kaur smiled. 'We shall be very happy.'

*　*　*

The effects of my mother-in-law's accession passed like shockwaves through the family, touching every aspect of our lives. Whereas Gian Singh had been laid-back, Bachan Kaur suddenly had an opinion on everything. She'd always been bossy and nosy but now she had the authority to back it up. Whatever she said became law in Willow Tree Lane. It quickly became tiring having to explain myself to her time after time. I couldn't believe how Hardave and Sukhdave let her get away with it. If Bachan Kaur said, 'Jump,' her sons would say, 'How high?' – and then make their wives do it for them. At least, that's how it felt some days.

With my first wedding anniversary coming up, Hardave surprised me by saying he'd like to take me out to dinner to celebrate.

'That would be lovely,' I said.

The day came and I couldn't help being excited as I got ready. Going out with my husband was a rarity. We usually socialised as a family. Having any time alone with him at all in such a packed household was hard. As I got downstairs I saw Bachan Kaur pulling on her coat.

'Are you going out as well?' I asked her.

'Of course,' she said. 'You can't celebrate without me.'

She's not coming on my date with my husband!

But she was. And Hardave refused to stop her.

My job at EMI was an enjoyable balance to my austere home life. Soon, Bachan Kaur managed to affect that, too.

'OK,' she announced one day, 'you will have to pay your salary to me.'

'Why?' I asked. She was not my husband. My salary went into a joint account I shared with Hardave. I had to ask his permission if I wanted to buy something.

'Because I have to pay the mortgage on this house on my own.'

That was rich. I already helped out for food and, as far as I knew, the mortgage was only around £200 a month. She certainly didn't need my salary to pay for that.

'Hardave will not agree to this,' I said.

'Speak to him.'

I promised I would. But I had no intention of trying to persuade him. Bachan Kaur was out of order and she had to know it. Unfortunately, she also knew her son. A few weeks later, my next cheque from EMI was paid directly into Bachan Kaur's account. Hardave hadn't even tried to fight it.

She already controls my movements. Now she's pulling the purse strings as well. What on earth is she going to bully me about next?

I soon found out.

* * *

I had never considered having a baby as anything other than a natural progression after marriage. While Sikhs are not opposed to contraception, Hardave and I did not use any.

We discussed it and assumed nature – and God – would take their course. What we didn't account for was influence from anywhere else.

'You must not have a baby,' my sister-in-law, Ajmar, instructed me one morning.

I was completely taken aback. Yet I was almost certain Ajmar hadn't come up with this edict herself. Only one woman would have the power – and arrogance – in this family to do that. I felt the message must have come from Bachan Kaur at source.

Ajmar went on to say that as the elder son, Sukhdave should have the right to bring the first child into the house.

Then he'll have to start sleeping in the same bed as his wife! I thought. I could only imagine what the family's response would have been if I'd dared say that!

She continued. 'Are you listening to me? Do you understand? You will not shame him.'

Shame him? He and Surjit had been married for nearly three years by now. Was Bachan Kaur – through Ajmar's edict – really going to risk never having grandchildren for the sake of not embarrassing the son whose status she had so brutally stolen?

Obviously, I kept those thoughts to myself as well.

'I will speak to Hardave' was all I said.

Later that night that was exactly what I did. With my husband I had no reason to hold back.

'She has no right to tell us not to have a baby!'

'Calm down. It will not look good on the family if we shame Sukhdave.'

'How can we shame him by having a child? He might never have a child. There might be a problem with one of them – it happens. Then where will we be?'

I could see in Hardave's eyes that he agreed with me. But what he said was, 'You will obey. We'll have to wait. Mum knows what is best for the family.'

I held his gaze defiantly until he was forced to look away. That told me everything. He didn't agree with his mother but he would rather please her than me. At that moment, I could not have respected him less.

Despite my desire not to criticise my in-laws in public, I needed to speak to someone outside the house: my real parents. If they told me I was being selfish then I would back down and apologise. But Mum was furious.

'No one can tell you not to have a baby.'

'But they have.'

'Well, that's not right. You ignore them.'

'What about bringing shame on them?'

'They are bringing enough shame on themselves.'

Despite my mother's emphatic support, feeling betrayed by my own husband was hard to bear. He and I had to share a room and a house and a future. Why couldn't he put me and our future baby ahead of his mother's wishes?

Sadly, it wasn't just the Athwals putting pressure on me. When I passed Surjit in the house one morning, she acted as though she hadn't heard me say hello. That evening, she didn't show up in the kitchen when I was cooking.

Then it occurred to me. Was she in on this ridiculous plan as well? Had Bachan Kaur reported my response back to her? Was I going to lose my only ally in the house if I didn't make a public guarantee that I wouldn't get pregnant too soon?

Apparently so. In Surjit's defence, I could only imagine the amount of pressure she was under to provide a son. Bachan Kaur, the sisters-in-law, her husband – they were all telling her what her body should do. It was no wonder that she snapped. It was just a pity she took it out on me.

Still, it helped me make up my mind.

You can worry about your own baby. No one is telling me not to try.

* * *

Despite our religion, Christmas was a fun time in the Athwal household. We celebrated it as much as anyone else on our street and, even if we didn't believe in the stories behind Santa Claus himself, it was still a national period of family and togetherness, which we embraced. Finding the perfect gift, however, is a pressure in any culture. Fortunately, I had the ideal one for Hardave. I was pregnant.

'Are you sure?' he asked, happiness written all over his face.

I nodded. I didn't want to tell my husband how I'd bought the home-testing kit and sat nervously watching the little stick, praying that it would change colour. When it did, right before my eyes, I'd been sad to be on my own. When Hardave had come home I'd barely been able to wait until we were alone before blurting out the news.

As delighted as Hardave was, I saw a flash of concern pass momentarily over his face. For a second he'd worried what his mother would say. Then, by the look on his face, he remembered that Surjit had declared herself pregnant a week earlier. We wouldn't be stealing his brother's thunder. If things went to plan, they would still have their baby first.

We could shout our forthcoming new addition from the rooftops and not worry about repercussions.

* * *

I loved being pregnant – although I could have done without the swollen feet. Everything was new to me, so each new phase brought fresh experiences. It was a pleasure to share and compare my pregnancy with Surjit. Having someone in the same house undergoing the same physical and chemical transformation was pretty weird. But we both enjoyed it. Whatever she was going through privately was put to one side and whenever we passed in the house we shared the secret smile of mothers-to-be.

As the months passed, our mutual bond only grew stronger. Each time I saw Surjit, I hoped that I looked as happy as she did. Then one day, while we were alone in the house, she confided in me why she was so happy. In September 1988, a year before my wedding, she'd fallen pregnant but had lost the baby shortly afterwards.

'I'm so sorry, Surjit. I had no idea.'

I didn't know what else to say. But that wasn't the worst of her story. Or her suffering. Bachan Kaur hadn't taken the miscarriage well and had accused Surjit of having an abortion.

'Why would she say that?' I asked my sister-in-law.

'Because she's evil.'

Evil? She's domineering and selfish. But evil?

'What did Sukhdave say?' I asked.

'What do you think? He agreed with her.'

Now that I could believe. I'd seen with my own eyes the sway Bachan Kaur held over her sons.

Surjit broke down at the recollection. 'They called me a murderer,' she sobbed.

I tried to comfort her but what could I say? I couldn't imagine anything worse for a woman than suffering a miscarriage. However upset Sukhdave had been, there was no justification for him to accuse her of wanting it to happen. And as for Bachan Kaur – what woman accuses another of such a thing?

No wonder Surjit was so desperate to get pregnant again.

***

At Surjit's request, we never spoke of her story again and I tried to put the thought of my mother-in-law's behaviour out of my mind. Usually I could find solace in the tedium of housework. Unfortunately, juggling EMI with chores at home while I was feeling more and more exhausted was far from comfortable. By the summer of 1991 I was struggling to keep up.

If Bachan Kaur saw how hard things were becoming for me, she made no acknowledgement. I was still expected to clean and tidy and cook as often as ever. It didn't matter to her that my feet ached so much after a day at work. It didn't matter that it was becoming hard for me to even stand close to the oven or worktops. It was almost as though she didn't care about my baby at all.

Outside of No. 90, however, it was a different story. To her friends in the community, Bachan Kaur could not have been prouder of her forthcoming grandchildren. When we were at the temple, she loved to drag me around to all her friends. I didn't mind that. What did stick in my throat, a little, was keeping quiet while my mother-in-law described how caring and supportive she was to me during my pregnancy.

Does she know she's lying or does she really believe this?

I couldn't tell. But what I did know was that public opinion was incredibly important to her – especially when that opinion came from fellow temple-goers.

Maybe that explained the increased frequency with which we began attending friends' prayer sessions or the temple after her husband's death. Once again, Surjit and I bore the brunt of her great shows of faith. If we weren't out visiting fellow temple-goers in their homes, Mum often demanded to be taken to the *gurdwara* at all hours of the day and night – and usually I was the one charged with driving her. No one who knew me would have said that I was not a devout Sikh. I prayed every day, I attended temple and, most importantly, I lived my life in accordance with the teachings and beliefs of the ten gurus. I was raised following strict principles and I even served an apprenticeship in India. What more could I have done? And yet, even I had never been to an all-night prayer session before I joined the Athwal family. Now it was a regular occurrence, with me alongside my mother-in-law. Turnout was never that great, but I noticed we only left as the *gurdwara* filled in the morning. It seemed important to Bachan Kaur that as many people as possible saw her leave, and noted that she had been there all night. Just as I suspected she had chosen to be baptised in order to earn the right to wear a turban – the sign of a higher level of Sikhdom.

Being religious wasn't enough to her. She needed to be *seen* to be religious.

Which misses the point of Sikhism altogether.

***

Towards the end of August 1991, our already packed house greeted a new arrival as Surjit and Sukhdave brought home their first child. I was so excited for them, especially knowing that I would be experiencing the same joy myself within a week or so if the due date were to be believed. Sadly, not everyone was as thrilled as me. Bachan Kaur could barely manage a smile when she looked at the little bundle. It took a few seconds to work out the problem. To me, baby Pawanpreet was perfect. But, I realised, she wasn't the grandson the head of the house had demanded.

Suddenly there was pressure back on me again. What on earth would Bachan Kaur say if her younger son dared to have a boy?

On 17 September 1991, we would find out. My baby had been due a fortnight earlier and was showing no signs of arriving. As a result, my GP announced I would have to be induced. That was scary. Any medical intervention worried me. Would my baby be all right? This was my first child. I wanted it to be special – for all of us – but most of all I wanted it to be so safe.

I was admitted to Hillingdon Hospital the evening before and told the procedure would begin at nine o'clock in the morning. Hardave was told to arrive no later than ten.

'Please come before that,' I begged. 'I don't want to go through this alone.'

'I'll be there,' he said. 'I promise.'

The midwife was punctual with her pessary and gel and by 9.30 my contractions had started. Twenty minutes later they were much more frequent – and more painful. It felt like a combination of sudden cramp and an electric shock every time.

Where is Hardave?

The nurse could see my distress and asked if anyone would be coming. I told her my husband was due at ten.

'It's already ten past. Do you want me to call him?'

'Please!'

She reported back that he was still at home. 'But he's just leaving. He'll be here soon.'

That might not be soon enough?

With the pain now becoming unbearable, I was wheeled into the labour ward and given gas and air. When I next looked at the clock it was 10.50. My husband was going to miss the birth of our child.

Or was he? One of the side effects of gas and air is it can make you drowsy and slightly confused. When I realised someone was holding my hand a few minutes later, it took me a few seconds to recognise Hardave.

He was just in time. Less than fifteen minutes later, I was staring into the wide brown eyes of my beautiful daughter, Taran Kaur.

I've done it!

But even as the gas-and-air-induced happiness swilled around my brain, I could still picture Bachan Kaur being disappointed. Before, I'd been worried that I might give her a grandson; now I was worried that I hadn't. What was she going to say?

CHAPTER EIGHT

YOU'RE OUT OF CONTROL

If I thought that being a new mum would mean getting some help around the house, then I was mistaken. I don't think I'd been out of hospital for one day when Bachan Kaur knocked on my bedroom door.

'My daughters will be coming later. Have tea ready.'

I've just sat down …

'What about Taran?' I asked.

'I'm sure they will like to see her.'

Discussion over. I had my orders. No option but to get on.

There was no let-up in my cooking, cleaning and chauffeuring duties. Nor, as far as I could make out, in Surjit's either. As both of us had taken maternity leave, at least we could help each other out. But if the other was out on a rare visit to her family or shopping, we'd have to have Taran or 'Pav' – as everyone called Pawanpreet – in a basket on the floor while we chopped and sliced and stirred and boiled.

Over the two years I'd been living in Willow Tree Lane, I'd snatched every opportunity to visit my old family home. It wasn't easy to persuade my mother-in-law to give permission, even when the reason was for a birthday or Christmas or some other important date. But I'd gone when I could. And now, with Taran on my hip, I wanted to visit more than ever.

My parents did everything I'd hoped Bachan Kaur would have done. They took the baby from me, made a fuss of her, prepared food – and told me to put my feet up! It was a treat to be cooked for at any time. But in truth, I didn't care if I ate anything. I just wanted to close my eyes ...

How much I would love to have stayed with them. But sadly my life was in Hayes now. I didn't even dare complain in case it reflected poorly on my parents' choice of family for me. And I also did not want them to worry. I was a mother now. I had responsibilities to my little girl. Whatever my problems with Hardave and his family, I would make it work.

I have to.

***

Having a daughter brought Hardave and me closer. I liked watching him play with her. And, while I was expected to do all the childcare when he was at work, he even occasionally looked after Taran while I popped out on errands. Like all mums, being able to hand her over so I could switch off for just half an hour was incredibly valuable.

Hardave surprised me in other ways, too. Watching me get dressed one morning, he said, 'You can buy some jeans if you like.'

Pardon?

'Did you say I could buy some jeans?'

He was smiling. 'Only if you want to. I've seen the way you look at other women. I don't mind if you wear trousers if you find them more comfortable.'

'What about Mum?'

'She doesn't mind.'

So he's checked with her then.

I shouldn't have been surprised that he'd felt he needed her permission. But I was pleased, touched even, that he'd thought of suggesting it. It had never occurred to me to dare ask. I hadn't been allowed to dress like that at home. In a house that made an even greater show of its traditional values, I'm sure I would never have mentioned it if Hardave hadn't.

Stepping outside of the house for the first time not wrapped in layers of cotton and polyester felt alien to me. I was nervous, too. Were people staring? Was I being accused of not being a good Sikh? Did they think I was disrespecting my family? I contemplated carrying a sign that read: 'Bachan Kaur gave her permission.' That was the only way I was ever going to relax.

Or so I thought. It didn't take long to realise that nobody was staring accusingly. I was just another woman in a headscarf, top and trousers.

With my paranoia subsided, I realised there was a reason so many millions of people, men and women, wore jeans. They were just so practical and comfortable.

I never want to wear anything else!

In hindsight, I'm amazed at myself for never having questioned why I was expected to wear traditional clothes around the house when Surjit often appeared in jeans and even my sisters-in-law occasionally turned up in Western clothes. Like me, they kept their scarves on and always reverted to traditional garb for religious events at home, a friend's house and especially at the temple. But it had honestly never occurred to me to dream I could act like them. It just wasn't how I was brought up.

***

From what I knew of Surjit's upbringing, she too had come from a reasonably traditional family, albeit far less extreme than the Athwals under Bachan Kaur's leadership. But somewhere along the line she had started to think for herself – another lesson I seemed to have been absent for. I was a woman, I was put on this earth to be a daughter, a wife and a mother. That was my lot, that was what I'd been trained for. I didn't question my role in life, I just got on with it.

So why didn't she?

Looking at my sister-in-law, sometimes I had to remind myself that she was so young. She'd been part of the Athwal clan two years longer than me so it was easy to forget she was actually two years younger. But it was more than a difference in age between us. She wasn't happy living how we did. She loved her daughter and she didn't mind working around the house. But she did object to her domestic duties being thought of as the be-all and end-all of her life.

'This is meant to be Britain in the 1990s,' she complained to me once. 'You'd think it was the 1950s.'

'What do you mean?' My knowledge of the era wasn't good.

'You know: the man goes to work, the wife cooks and fetches his slippers when he comes home.' She shook her head. 'We're barely more than servants.'

I nodded. She spoke sense. The only difference was, I couldn't see the problem.

That's how things are.

* * *

There was only a two-year gap between our ages but sometimes it felt like we were from different generations. I wanted nothing more than to fit in and be a respectful wife and bring my daughter up to do the same. Like my mother and her mother before her. But Surjit wanted a life outside No. 90.

I began to wonder if Surjit would have been more content if she'd liked Sukhdave more. I worked hard to make a success of my relationship with Hardave. Yes, he'd let me down not being around enough during my labour, and I hated the way he was happy to be in his mother's pocket, but it had been his initiative to allow me to wear trousers. He cared about me. That's how I saw it.

By contrast, I never heard Surjit say anything nice about her husband. I wasn't comfortable talking about her relationship in the house, even if we knew we were the only ones in. But some days she wouldn't hold back. Sukhdave was so stingy with money, she said. He wouldn't let her go shopping even though she earned more than he did. He wouldn't let her wear skirts.

'He won't even let me see my friends.'

Friends? I didn't even know what a friend was. I'd enjoyed hanging out with Sarita, Suneeta and Pam at Cranford Community School, but when my father and grandfather had explained they weren't to come to our house and I wasn't to go to theirs, that was the end of the discussion for me. So we never saw each other after school and we lost touch the day of our last exam. They certainly hadn't been invited to my wedding – but then I hadn't invited anyone. I didn't have anyone I *could* invite.

I'm twenty-two and I don't have a friend in the world.

I wasn't the only sounding-board for Surjit's rants. Sometimes I would hear her have the same hushed conversations with our eldest sister-in-law, Bhajan Kaur Bhinder. For whatever reason, Surjit felt she could trust Bhajan, and would often visit the Bhinder household.

I don't know what Bhajan's advice to Surjit was, but I had to admit – on the subject of clothes and a wife's place in the family – I probably agreed with Sukhdave!

I would never have said this to Surjit, but rightly or wrongly I'd been raised to believe we had our roles in life.

Whatever my instincts, it had been hammered into me long before my finishing school in India that we needed to concentrate on being good daughters, mothers and wives. But then, Surjit was so young when she joined the Athwal family.

Looking back, I can't believe I was so prim and so pious. But that's how I'd been raised. That's how deep the indoctrination of my culture ran inside me. I suppose we were two sides of the same coin. Except, where Surjit questioned everything, I just plodded along the path that had been chosen for me. I regret it now and I would certainly never wish my old docility on my daughters today. But my entire life had been an education – and my young sister-in-law looked like the naughtiest girl in the school.

While I was secretly horrified by Surjit's acts of independence, others were more vocal. Our mother-in-law, of course, was the loudest dissenting voice.

What would the community say if they saw Surjit out with friends and not her husband? How would she, Bachan Kaur, be able to face her peers at *gurdwara* knowing her daughter-in-law was shopping for skirts and dresses and other Western paraphernalia? It was ridiculous but that's how Bachan Kaur felt. So she came up with a plan.

'You're going to get baptised.'

* * *

Baptism in the Sikh religion is not something to be taken lightly. It is a ceremony that any male or female can undertake when they feel ready to take the next step in their faith. Inwardly, the subject commits to pure vegetarianism, a greater presence at temple and a more God-loving lifestyle with prayers in the morning and evening. Outwardly, they pledge at all times to carry the 'five Ks' (*kes*, *khanga*, *kara*, *kirpan* and *kacchera* – uncut hair, a wooden comb, a steel bracelet, a small dagger and certain underwear), in keeping with the guidance of the Tenth Guru. They will only eat specially prepared food – cooked by themselves or someone of the same spiritual level (something Bachan Kaur conveniently ignored when it came to being waited on) – served on metal plates. Everything about baptism, from the turban she would be expected to wear downwards, seemed a pronounced and very public show of faith – and one I wasn't sure Surjit was ready to accept.

Bachan Kaur must have known this. But she obviously saw baptism as a way of controlling her daughter-in-law.

In fact, she saw it as a way of controlling *both* daughters-in-law – I was ordered to take part as well!

I didn't dare speak out against Bachan Kaur but Hardave felt the full extent of my anger.

'Why does she want me to do this?' I demanded as soon as we were alone. 'I'm religious, I pray every day, I dress the right way, I attend temple. Does she think I'm not a true believer?'

Hardave seemed stunned by my fury. It wasn't something he was used to seeing, but then nobody had ever questioned my faith like this before.

'I don't think it's you she's worried about ...'

I knew he was right but it was typical of his mother to rope me in as well. She knew better than anyone that baptism should be a personal matter, a contract between a Sikh and God. When I was ready, I'm sure I would have considered it. But that wasn't enough for Bachan Kaur. She was going to force me to go through with it because it would reflect well on her at the temple. My own feelings, my own faith and my own connection with God were of no importance to her. However hard I worked, Surjit and I were both still pawns for her to move around whenever she saw fit.

***

The ceremony took place in Birmingham. Five high-ranking baptised Sikhs performed the ceremony and dozens of us repeated their words and sang hymns with the large gathering. Then we were offered a sip of '*amrit*' – holy water – to signify our purification and the taking on of God's essence. It was a beautiful and reflective occasion but that wasn't what I objected to. Having more restrictions placed on how I lived, and especially being ordered to wear a turban at all times, was hard to take.

Even though it was a major family event, my own parents and siblings were not invited to the ceremony. Obviously this wasn't my choice. As soon as I could get away from home I went to visit them. The first thing they commented on, of course, was what I was wearing on my head.

My sisters were shocked.

'Why are you wearing that thing?' the youngest, Dalvinder, squealed. 'Turbans are for dads.'

My own father was just as confused. What did I think I was doing?

'I have to wear it, Dad,' I explained. 'I've been baptised.'

'Were you ready to be baptised? It's a commitment one must obey for life.'

My silence told him everything.

'If I had been there, I would not have let you go through with it.'

Which is obviously why Bachan Kaur had not invited them ...

Mum was upset. 'I agree with your father. You should take it off unless you want to wear it.'

'But I can't.'

'Of course you can. Nobody can make you wear it if you don't want to.'

'You don't understand!'

'What don't we understand?' Dad asked. But I knew I couldn't tell him, so once again I bit my tongue and left their house knowing I'd upset the people I most cared about.

***

I think I wore my turban for a year. Surprisingly, Surjit managed the same. Then one day we both decided to remove them. Giggling conspiratorially, like mischievous schoolgirls, we both walked down the stairs at the same time and waited for the fallout. It was incredible how invigorating it felt. Even more incredible was our mother-in-law's reaction. She didn't howl or rant as I'd feared. She just looked disappointed and carried on her day, almost as if she didn't care at all.

Did she put us through all that for nothing?

I wouldn't have put anything past her.

Whereas I'd removed my turban because I felt I was living fraudulently by not really believing in what it stood for, I think Surjit threw hers away in protest. But she didn't stop there. When she came in the next day, she hadn't just removed her turban.

She'd cut her hair.

Losing the turban had been one thing. But this was actually breaking one of the five Ks. Mother-in-law was not going to be happy.

She wasn't, but her reaction to Surjit was strangely restrained. Or so we thought. But when Sukhdave flew into a rage later that night, there was only one reason for it. Bachan Kaur had told him what to say.

'How dare you cut your hair!' Sukhdave yelled at his wife.

'Your sisters have cut theirs,' Surjit responded coolly.

'That's different.'

'How is that different?'

'Their husbands gave their permission.'

'So?'

'So – you didn't even ask me.'

'It's got nothing to do with you how I wear my hair.'

'Yes, it has. I'm your husband.'

The argument went on and on. Living on top of each other, in a house with paper-thin walls, it was impossible not to hear every word. After a while, Sukhdave and Surjit didn't even bother hiding their fights. But I didn't need my ears to know how bad things were between them. Surjit didn't respect Sukhdave – not as her boss or her partner – and she wasn't afraid to let him know. In her defence, she had married the man she thought would be head of the family. She'd ended up with a puppet controlled by his domineering mother, which left her even lower.

'You need to learn some respect.' Sukhdave shook his head as he marched angrily from their room. 'You're out of control.'

***

Over the next few months, the argument about hair proved just one of many. Ironically, considering how much they seemed to provoke each other, Surjit's biggest complaint about her husband was that he was never around. As well as his part-time job as a mechanic, Sukhdave spent a lot of his spare time fixing or tinkering with cars on the driveway – time he should, in Surjit's opinion, be spending with her and their daughter.

The atmosphere in the house turned unpleasant for everyone. Even me. Surjit took less care about what she said, and the last thing I wanted was for Mum or her daughters to accuse me of colluding. It seems cowardly in retrospect, but it wasn't my fight. It was something Surjit needed to sort out with her husband – ideally without his mother interfering.

I realised how lucky I was to have Hardave as my spouse. Given how much say I'd had in events, I knew it could just as easily have been me married to his brother. Alone in our room, when Taran was asleep, I felt comfortable enough to discuss what was going on. Without criticising his mother in any way, Hardave agreed that things would be better if Sukhdave and Surjit had their own space. It turned out we weren't the only ones who thought so.

On 1 January 1994 Surjit moved out.

CHAPTER NINE

IT'S A BOY

The *shame*.

Bachan Kaur was beside herself.

'She can't have gone. That's not allowed. Why didn't you stop her?'

Poor Sukhdave heard the same question again and again. It was bad enough his wife walking out on him. The tirade from his mother accusing him of it being all his fault was so unfair he must have felt like leaving as well.

But, as Surjit told me later, it wasn't the first time she had left. But it was the first time she'd gone of her own accord.

* * *

It had happened back in 1988, before I'd even heard the name 'Athwal'. As if the horrific accusations of murdering her own unborn baby weren't bad enough, Sukhdave and Bachan Kaur had then ordered Surjit to move out.

Still distraught at losing her baby, Surjit had gone to the only place she could think of: her parents' house in Coventry. Where else could she go? Who else would take her?

She'd thought that would be the last time she saw

Sukhdave. But she was wrong. He appeared one day in her father's house and begged forgiveness.

'I'm sorry, you have to believe me. Please come back.'

He said he would change. He said he knew it wasn't her fault that she'd lost the baby. He pleaded with her to come back with him. As much as she wanted to say 'no', a Sikh woman who'd left a marriage was not looked on too well in the community. Whether it was pressure from her parents or brainwashing from her in-laws or simple faith, what the community might think played on Surjit's mind.

'I can't come back to that house,' she said finally.

Sukhdave considered it. 'That's fine. We'll get our own place. Just please come back with me.'

'OK.'

They set off that night. By the time they'd reached the M6 the atmosphere in the car had already taken a turn for the worse. Within half an hour Sukhdave was shouting, repeating all the insults and accusations that had driven Surjit away in the first place. Obviously she told him she'd made a mistake and didn't want to go back.

He pulled over at the side of the motorway and screamed, 'Get out!'

She looked out into the midnight darkness. It was cold, there was no path and they were miles from anywhere.

'I'm sorry,' she said. 'Let's go home.'

* * *

Fast forward to 1994 and this time Surjit had definitely left of her own volition – which Bachan Kaur did not like at all.

Once again Sukhdave was despatched to woo her back. He found his wife in a bedsit in Lothian Avenue, Hayes. This time, she later told me, Surjit refused to be swayed by his words. There was too much bad blood, she said. At first, Sukhdave kept his cool. I think he assumed his wife would cave in. When she didn't, he didn't just revert to name-calling. He let his fists do the talking, too.

Surjit called the police but he left before they arrived. She changed address soon after but Sukhdave tracked her down again. When Surjit refused to open the door, he began shouting through the letterbox. It started with begging, and a declaration of love. When that didn't work the messages turned darker.

'Come back to me, Surjit, or I'll kill you!'

His words were confused and threatening. But at least they weren't his fists.

The second she realised who was at the door, Surjit dialled 999. Once again Sukhdave was gone before a response unit had turned up. But he returned several times more, shouting his weird mix of apologies and threats through the front door in the short time before the police were called.

Another month passed and by now Surjit had moved to a different Hayes address. Money was incredibly tight for her and the only way she was going to make a separation work was if she increased her own income. Maybe then she could afford to collect Pawanpreet and look after her.

In early 1994 Surjit was hired by the tax department of Customs & Excise at Heathrow Airport. I only heard about this from gossip in the house. Hardave had got it from Sukhdave and he in turn had learned it *by following Surjit!*

I don't know how long he was doing it but he was spotted.

'Sukhdave? What are you doing here?'

'I just want to talk to you.'

Hearing about it reminded me of Hardave appearing at my workplace all those years ago. Coincidentally, where my surprise visit ended in a wedding, this one eventually had a positive result as well. Perhaps it was with the added confidence her job gave her or perhaps she was lonely, but when Sukhdave asked her again to take him back, Surjit decided to put all the threats and bullying behind her and say yes. But with one proviso this time.

'I will not go back to that house.'

Like he had six years earlier, Sukhdave agreed. But Surjit was older and wiser this time. She would not be tricked into going back temporarily while Sukhdave claimed to look for a place. And, because she was also better off financially this time around, she was prepared to wait.

Sukhdave had a choice to make. In the end it was decided that he and Pav should move into a flat in Hillingdon with Surjit. Whether he made the choice or his mother, Surjit never knew. But she was glad to have her family together again.

And glad to be out of Bachan Kaur's clutches.

***

Surjit's gain was my loss. Without my sister-in-law, my childcare and chores seemed to take longer. Worst of all, I was the only one left for my mother-in-law to torment. Whether she did it on purpose or because she was naturally unpleasant, she was quick to criticise almost everything I did. My cooking wasn't good enough and my cleaning always needed redoing. Of course, she could have helped out herself if she were that worried about falling standards. But that wasn't the point. It never was with her.

Hardave also seemed unsettled by his brother being absent. He never admitted to me that he too was getting too much attention from his mother, but it was definitely true that she asked him to spend more time with her. She liked to have a cup of herbal tea with a family member. Sometimes she called for me, like she used to call for Surjit. Sometimes Hardave was dragged in to have a conversation with her about nothing in particular. I think we were all relieved when she went to work, also at Heathrow, like Surjit. Fortunately for my sister-in-law, it's a big airport. If she was worried about bumping into Bachan Kaur she never showed it.

After two months away, Sukhdave suddenly returned home. But rather than it being an admission that his marriage was over, he claimed it was just part of their plan. The old man who lived next door to us had agreed to sell the house. The only problem was, Sukhdave's salary in his new job as a coach driver – again, part-time – wasn't enough to secure the mortgage. Even with Surjit's new income the building society still said no. In the end, Bachan Kaur told Hardave and me that our names would be going on the deeds. We didn't mind. We weren't actually being asked to pay anything. We were just included as security. I couldn't pretend to understand the small print. All I knew is that on 23 September Surjit moved into 88 Willow Tree Lane.

***

From the amount of fuss my mother-in-law made about the purchase it was as though she were the one buying it. Which was bad news for Surjit. When she'd said she didn't want to return to No. 90 it was for one reason: to escape Bachan Kaur. The moment No. 88 was finalised, however, Mum announced she'd be moving next door, too. Did she do it to spite Surjit? Or to keep an eye on her? All I know is, her favourite son didn't object – and I couldn't have been happier.

Unfortunately, I wouldn't be shot of her completely. After moving out, Bachan Kaur then converted the box room in our house into her prayer room. The Holy Book was given a corner under its traditional canopy, and every morning and night she would appear to pay her respects upstairs. I saw her as much as if she still lived here. Worst of all, she never knocked. Hardave and I would be in the lounge or upstairs and we'd hear the snap of the garden gate. A few moments later the back door would rattle as Mum let herself in. And despite never warning us when she was coming, if she weren't met with a welcoming committee there were complaints.

Still, having Surjit nearby again was nice for me. We weren't the closest of friends – I suppose our different outlooks would always give us a certain distance – but apart from my sisters she was the nearest thing I had. I was never going to pry about why she'd run away; she would tell me in her own time. But when she came round to visit one day it was with news I hadn't been expecting.

With Surjit now working at Heathrow as well, I had wondered if she and Mum would bump into each other. It hadn't happened so far, although Surjit had discovered something through a colleague. Yes, Mum worked at Heathrow, but not in the storage area as she claimed: she was a toilet cleaner.

As far as I'm concerned a job's a job. You do what you need to do to make a living. But obviously Bachan Kaur was worried about her place in the community. The irony, of course, is that no one at the temple should have judged a person on their job, not if they were good Sikhs. But they would have had rules on lying. That was not allowed. Especially lying to your family and friends. But Bachan Kaur would never see it that way. Despite her outward piety, it was as if her ego were more important than her faith.

There was one other question that I was glad Surjit cleared up. I had to ask why she didn't take her daughter when she left.

'They wouldn't let me.'

'But you're her mum. You should have insisted.'

'I know. I should have done. But the truth is, I thought Pav loved our mother-in-law more than me.'

That was ridiculous and I told her so. 'What on earth makes you think that?'

'Because she calls Bachan Kaur "Mummy".'

'Bachan Kaur makes her do that! You know she does.'

I realised then how sad and confused my sister-in-law must have been. To add to all the other reasons to distrust her, bullying Surjit out of being with her daughter was one of Bachan Kaur's lowest moves.

But it would not be her last.

* * *

Whatever reasons Surjit had for returning to Sukhdave, they obviously hadn't talked much about them. By the time she arrived back on Willow Tree Lane, she was a very different woman to the one who'd left. And, what's more, she was still changing. How would Sukhdave cope with that?

I think he tried. They both did. But as usual someone else got in the way. When Sukhdave gave permission for Surjit to see friends after work, Bachan Kaur told him he was wrong.

'She is your wife. Her place is at home with you, not in the homes of strangers.'

I'm sure he resisted. He knew the only reason Surjit had been persuaded to return to him was on the condition they lived away from his mother. It was bad enough that Bachan Kaur had ruined that plan. If Surjit saw that her mother-in-law was still calling the shots he would never hear the end of it.

Eventually Sukhdave did what he was always going to do and caved in. His mother's gossip still bubbling in his ears, he put his foot down with Surjit as instructed. It didn't go well.

'I know who's put you up to this.'

'I don't know what you mean.' However many times he said it, Surjit wasn't convinced. And she certainly wasn't about to go back to the old life she'd run away from once.

* * *

As the months rolled on, the wedge between Surjit and Sukhdave became greater than ever. The longer she worked, the more friends she made. And the more friends she made, the more invites she received. Whatever Surjit seemed at home, to the outside world she was still a radiant, young twenty-three-year-old – and a Western-looking one at that.

Sukhdave and Surjit had always argued about what she wanted to wear, and who was going to pay for it. When she moved back in, one of Surjit's concessions was to drop that argument. However, as Sukhdave quickly broke his pledge not to fuss about her seeing friends, Surjit couldn't see any point in keeping her side of the bargain. At first she at least made a show of respecting the family's wishes by leaving the house dressed in a traditional outfit. But that is all it was: a show. Between arriving at Heathrow and making her way to her desk, a transformation would take place. Ten minutes in the toilets gave Surjit all the time she required to change into her preferred Western skirt and blouse. And as for a headscarf, even that joined her *kameez* in the holdall till home time.

The reports I got from Hardave suggested Surjit didn't stop at a change of clothes. According to his brother, she occasionally appeared to be wearing make-up when she returned home. Sometimes, he reckoned she even seemed to leave in one outfit and return in another. While they were still traditional he couldn't really complain. But that didn't stop him ...

Eventually Surjit stopped even pretending. Bachan Kaur was the first to tell me what a disgrace her daughter was, but I wasn't in the mood to listen to her. I knew she didn't care much for my sister-in-law in the first place. Then a few days later I caught a glimpse of a woman dressed in a skirt making her way out of Sukhdave's house one morning. It took me a second to put two and two together.

Is that Surjit?

The black skirt finishing above the knee told me it wasn't. But as the woman turned on to the pavement, I recognised her familiar bold features.

I can't believe it ...

Sukhdave was losing her. Even I could see that. When Surjit began to come home drunk and, he claimed, would put on the stereo to dance in her bedroom, it was the final slap in her husband's face. She had been baptised. She had sworn never to touch alcohol. But there she was, giggling and unstable on her feet as she picked her way into their home and up to bed. There are many ways that Sukhdave could have responded, but he chose hitting and abuse. Yet again, if it was designed to bring her into check, it had the opposite effect.

I admit I was part in awe, part horrified by Surjit's behaviour. Mainly I couldn't imagine doing the same things myself. But whatever my conflicting feelings, there was no excuse for violence.

As a result of her husband's aggression, Surjit made less and less effort to please him. She would agree to be home by seven, then arrive after midnight. And she wouldn't apologise. She didn't care what Sukhdave thought, that was clear. What was he going to do to her? Smack her again? It was only a matter of time before someone snapped.

In the end, it turned out, I snapped first. I became weary of being caught in the crossfire between Mum, Sukhdave and Surjit. No one had a kind word to say about the other and, as much as I was worried about Surjit's behaviour, I knew the root of all her problems. It was the same root causing mine. And I knew the way to solve it – I just needed to persuade Hardave.

'Your mother owns this house,' I explained, 'and Sukhdave has next door. It's time we had a place of our own.'

He took some convincing. While he would never admit that his mother was the poison ruining our entire family, he did see that a little distance could be a positive thing. In January 1996 we picked up the keys for a three-bedroom house in Bishop's Road, still in Hayes.

I had my daughter, my husband and my freedom. It was everything I could have asked for.

So of course somebody tried to spoil it.

I heard the phone ring one evening and Hardave pick it up. When he found me in the kitchen I could tell something was wrong.

'I have to go to Mum.'

'What for?'

'She's on her own. She's scared.'

'Don't be so gullible – she's got Sukhdave next door.'

Hardave sighed. 'I know. But she says she doesn't want to keep disturbing them.'

'Pah!' It was all I could think of. 'She's using you, Hardave. She'd disturb Sukhdave and Surjit all day every day if she felt like it. No,' I said, 'she just wants to show you she's still in control. Don't go.'

'What if she's really scared?'

'Fine, go then.'

I was furious with him for not putting his foot down as usual. Not because I begrudged him comforting his mother – but because I knew it was just a power game on her part. And one that she had won already. We'd only been away a month and the writing was on the wall.

Two months later we moved back into Willow Tree Lane.

* * *

If anything, the relationship between Surjit and Sukhdave and Bachan Kaur was worse than ever. Surjit was making no effort to hide her contempt at their efforts to control her and Sukhdave was at his wit's end. He was a part-time coach driver who wanted a stay-at-home wife to do his bidding, although he also enjoyed her salary. He was married to a young, beautiful woman who'd had no adult life before being pushed into marriage.

Everything about my upbringing told me that what Sukhdave wanted wasn't so outrageous. And yet, the more I thought about their relationship, the more I saw myself reflected back.

Where was *my* life before marriage? Where were *my* nights out with friends? More to the point, where *were* my friends? For the first time in my life I began to doubt my own decisions.

It was so easy to see Bachan Kaur as a monster, but did she really expect much more than my own family? Or other families out there in the community? In her world, men worked and women looked after them – even though she'd adopted the 'male' role in the family now. Surjit and I had both been raised in that fashion. The only difference now was that my sister-in-law realised there was another way. The question was, what was she prepared to do to follow it?

***

While my sister-in-law's pursuit of her own path was planting one or two seeds in my mind, it would take a lot more than watching her fight with Sukhdave to unpick twenty-seven years of learning. For every doubt I was beginning to have, I was still the good wife at heart. So I could not have been happier, in the spring of 1997, to discover I was carrying Hardave's second child.

The whole family was delighted. Even Surjit. There had been no whispers that this time I should hold back to let someone else try to get pregnant first. It was a wonderfully happy and, more importantly, a straightforward time.

And then, three months later, it all became incredibly complicated again when Surjit announced that she too was expecting a baby.

'I didn't think they were sleeping together.'

If Hardave was as confused as me, he put a brave face on it. 'They obviously are,' he said. 'The evidence is there.'

He was right. But I had heard the raised voices through the wall partitioning our houses on so many nights that I was amazed they were even sleeping in the same house, let alone the same bed.

If Bachan Kaur was surprised she didn't show it. Only one question mattered to her and, at the earliest opportunity, Surjit was marched down to the doctor's for a scan. Mum didn't want to have to wait six months to be disappointed again. If she was going to have another girl in the family, she wanted to know now.

To be honest, I was too wrapped up in my own world to notice what was going on next door. But when the result of the scan came in, Bachan Kaur made sure everyone knew.

'It's a boy! We're having a boy!'

Anyone would have thought it was her baby. But then, considering she made us all call her 'Mum', maybe that's what she genuinely felt.

The only person happier than Bachan Kaur was Surjit – and not for the obvious reason. The moment we found out that a male heir was joining the family, Surjit had power over her mother-in-law. The next time Bachan Kaur criticised her behaviour, Surjit replied, matter-of-factly, 'I thought you'd be happier that you're having a grandson.'

Whatever she was accused of, that became Surjit's reply. It was the one response that Bachan Kaur could never argue with. If the old lady genuinely did believe that her daughter-in-law had once terminated a child on purpose, there was no guarantee she wouldn't do it again. So Bachan Kaur bit her tongue. Again and again and again.

Even though I was pregnant first, I was largely invisible in Surjit's shadow. I didn't know if I would be having a boy or girl – which suited me fine. We already had plenty of girls' clothes, and if we had a boy we'd just buy some for him. The main priority – the only priority – was that he or she was healthy. Everything else was a bonus.

On 11 November 1997 I returned to Hillingdon Hospital. This time Hardave was more reliable. And this time I had another girl, gorgeous little Balveen Kaur Athwal. It was a magical time – and one that I hoped Surjit would enjoy as much when her time came. Then, on 7 March 1998, when her little boy finally came into the world, she had her chance.

If my mother-in-law had been excited before, now she was uncontrollable. I tried not to be envious of how much attention she paid Surjit's baby over Balveen, and in fact I was glad not to have her taking over. But when she declared, 'We'll have to have a party for the baby!' I was upset.

But not as upset, it turned out, as Sukhdave.

'I don't think that's a good idea, Mum,' he said.

'Why ever not? The world should know I've got my first grandson and you have your first son.'

'Yes,' Sukhdave said. 'The only problem is he's not mine.'

CHAPTER TEN

A GOOD SISTER

He discovered it by chance.

Four years earlier Sukhdave had taken to stalking Surjit to and from her job at Heathrow. On that occasion it had been in order to grab the chance to talk to her while she was living on her own. Later, with his wife's behaviour becoming even more of a problem for him, he wanted to learn who else she was talking to.

In hindsight, I think Sukhdave would have been happier never to find out.

Usually when Surjit worked, he looked after their daughter. But when his mother happened to be around, Sukhdave phoned his boss and if possible changed his shift. That sorted, he was free to drive to Heathrow and wait. Wait until he saw Surjit come out. Wait until he saw where she went. Wait until he saw who she was with.

And then follow.

Sometimes Surjit told him she was going to a friend's flat after work for an innocent pizza and TV wind-down evening. She would maintain the story even after Sukhdave had seen her enter a pub and stagger out several hours later.

But it was when she did go to a friend's house that he became concerned. First, because this time she'd told him she was going to a party.

And second, because she'd entered with a man.

There could have been any number of explanations. But Sukhdave couldn't think of any. The next week, he followed Surjit to the same address. She was with the same man. And this time they were kissing.

He challenged her that night.

'Where were you tonight?'

'I told you. I went out with my friends.'

'Where?'

'A bar. You don't know it.'

'You're lying. You were with a man.'

'What are you saying?'

Confused and hurt, Sukhdave was desperately trying to keep his temper. 'I saw you. I saw you with him.'

Surjit denied it, as she denied it every time. But Sukhdave knew. And later, when his wife became pregnant, he knew the baby couldn't be his.

Because they hadn't touched each other in months.

Once upon a time, I would have been horrified at Surjit's infidelity. Even then, I struggled to believe what Sukhdave was telling his brother about her. *Surjit's young but she's a good Sikh. She would not do this.*

Even when I could no longer deny her actions, I couldn't blame my sister-in-law. How unhappy she must have been. Sukhdave had bullied her, belittled her, driven her from her house, abused her and hit her. Much of that had been at his mother's behest. Of course Surjit had wanted to escape from that. And by finding a new man to love, she figured that was the best way. It made sense, even to me.

What she didn't bank on was falling in love with another married man.

The man – whom I can't name for legal reasons – was older than Surjit. He also, like Surjit, had a family and children waiting for him at home.

But Surjit fell in love. And yet, when she announced she was pregnant, she found herself on her own. She was pregnant, desperately lonely and feeling betrayed. Of course she let Sukhdave believe the baby was his. But he knew. He always knew.

Even I suspected. But certain other people refused to believe the truth when it was standing in front of them. Bachan Kaur, predictably, seemed on a course of her own. She resolutely refused to believe that Sukhdave wasn't the new baby's father, even when it was her own son confessing to her.

'Don't say that,' she snapped. 'You don't know that. He's your son and don't forget it.'

Would she have been so blinkered if it were a girl they were talking about?

I didn't have to ask.

***

On the face of it, Bachan Kaur was in utter denial. But I soon learned she had her own agenda and once again, I found it out the hard way. We all did.

Shortly after my daughter Balveen was born, Surjit called round to ask a question.

'Remember how you and Hardave helped us get a mortgage for next door?'

'Of course I remember,' I said. 'We were happy to help.'

'Now I'm earning enough to get a mortgage without you, would you mind taking your names off it?'

'I don't see why not,' I said. 'I'll ask Hardave tonight.'

'Thanks – but why do you have to ask him?'

I shrugged. 'I ask him everything. He's my husband.'

I could see Surjit thought I was mad. Maybe I was. But that's the way I'd been raised. The problem was, Hardave had been raised to ask permission for everything, too. No sooner had I mentioned Surjit's request to my husband than he disappeared to ask Mum. If I'd wanted her opinion I'd have asked her myself.

'Where are you going?' I said. 'You're the man. You're in charge of our decisions. You tell me what to do for once.'

He stared at me for a second then left the room. I wondered how much more of his spinelessness I could take before I lost all respect for him.

Ten minutes later, I wasn't surprised to see him return with Bachan Kaur. At least she wasn't shy of making a decision.

'You can't do it,' she said. 'I forbid it.'

'Why ever not? We don't live there, we don't pay for it. It's Surjit's and Sukhdave's house, not ours.'

'Yes,' Bachan Kaur snapped. 'But if Surjit decides to divorce Sukhdave then she'll take the house from him. My son will be out on the streets.'

'That's ridiculous. They won't divorce.' I don't know why I was so confident. I think because I'd been raised to believe that ending a marriage was never an option.

'You don't know that woman,' Bachan Kaur said. She lowered her voice, conspiratorially. 'She's evil. She hates my son. She's trying to trick you into hurting him.'

Now she was just being paranoid. Surjit would never think like that.

'Mum's right,' Hardave said. 'Our names are staying on.'

'I'll let Surjit know,' Bachan Kaur said.

I thought that would be the end of it, but the next time Surjit came for a gathering she totally snubbed me. I wasn't prepared to put up with that in my own home.

'Is there a problem, Surjit?'

'What are you playing at?' she asked angrily. 'Why won't you give me back my house?'

'Mum told me not to,' I explained.

'Liar. I know it's you. You want my house for yourself.'

'Surjit, that's not true.'

'Save it. I don't believe you.'

The rest of the evening was most unpleasant. For the next few weeks Surjit refused to speak to me. Hardave reported the same treatment.

Then, out of the blue, I got a phone call from my father. This was unusual. Normally he waited for me to ring him. After the pleasantries he came out with it.

'Who owns No. 88?'

'No. 88? Do you mean the house next door to me?'

Even when he said 'yes' I couldn't work out why on earth he would be asking.

'Is your name on the mortgage?' he asked.

Now I was really confused. 'Yes, Dad, it is. Mine and Hardave's.'

'Why?'

'Sukhdave and Surjit couldn't get a mortgage without it.' I explained the situation.

'I see,' my father said. 'Do you have a share in the house? Have you put money into it?'

'No, I haven't. It was literally just our signatures they needed.' I didn't let him ask another thing. 'Look, Dad, what's this all about?'

He told me that Surjit's mother had rung the house. She was demanding to know why I was refusing to give her daughter the rights to her own house. So Dad had rung me to get to the bottom of it.

'It's clear,' he said, 'you have to take your name off the deeds.'

'I can't do that.'

Now it was his turn to be confused. 'Why ever not?'

'I'm not allowed. Mum – I mean, my mother-in-law – has told me not to.' I explained her fear that Surjit was planning to divorce and evict Sukhdave.

'Well, that's not what Surjit says Bachan Kaur has been saying. According to her, you are refusing to take your name off the mortgage because you want to make a profit from it.'

'Dad! That's a lie.'

'You know the problem?' he said finally. 'Your mother-in-law is telling you and Surjit different stories. She is playing you off against each other. It gives me no pleasure to say that she's not being honest with either of you. I'm sorry.'

It wasn't his fault. But he was the reason I knew Mrs Athwal in the first place and he knew it. I had always restrained from telling my parents anything negative about my new family. Finally Dad was beginning to work it out for himself.

He rang me back later to say he'd spoken again with Surjit's mother. The next time I saw Surjit she was much friendlier. We both knew now what the problem in the whole matter was.

'I'm sorry. I should have known – you're a good sister,' Surjit said. 'But she's done it again. She's played us all like puppets.'

I had to agree. It was embarrassing that we hadn't seen through her meddling sooner. But at least the harm was mended between Surjit and me.

***

My mother-in-law did not take kindly to our parents' intervention. She was furious that my parents and Surjit's had got involved. This was family business. What right did we have to go outside Willow Tree Lane? She forgot how often her daughters from all over London interfered.

I couldn't help cowering as she shouted at me. I wished I could have brushed the criticism aside like Surjit managed.

But Bachan Kaur was powerful, she was angry, she was tall. And she was the head of my household. Whatever I thought of her, she was the boss.

Not only was Surjit not intimidated by Bachan Kaur, she didn't think twice about disobeying her. Once again Surjit planned to move out of No. 88.

But this time she would take the children.

To this day I feel guilty that I stopped her going. I happened to spy the activity by Surjit's little red car one morning and mentioned it, by way of conversation, to Hardave. He'd obviously had instructions from his brother. Where I saw my sister-in-law and her children popping out, Hardave saw a conspiracy. He leapt on the phone and dialled his sister's house in Ilford, where Sukhdave and Bachan Kaur were visiting.

'Sukhdave, Surjit's packing the kids and a case into the car. What do you want me to do?'

'Stop her! Do anything you have to. Do not let her leave with my kids.'

A second later my husband was racing out the front door to grab Surjit's keys. When Sukhdave's car came hurtling up Willow Tree Lane an hour later, his wife's car was still there. Hardave had done his job.

Surjit admitted defeat and unpacked the car. But it was a temporary truce. A few weeks later I cried when I heard her screaming next door. Our hallway joined on to No. 88's and I could make out every smack that Sukhdave landed on his wife as she tried to leave. I felt sick as I heard my sister-in-law hit the floor. Then I gasped as I made out a different voice. It was Bachan Kaur. And she was attacking Surjit as well.

I looked at the phone. I knew I should call the police. But I was numb with fear.

If they do that to Surjit, they'll do it to me.

* * *

It was only a matter of time before Surjit left again. This time there was no nosy neighbour to alert her husband. Even if I had seen, I wouldn't have told Hardave. I'd learned my lesson there. His allegiance was to his brother and mother. Not to me.

Having fled, where else could Surjit go but to her parents? While she was there, she began looking into schools for Pawanpreet. She was serious. Enough to move into new accommodation and pay to furnish it. Enough to apply for a job transfer to East Midlands Airport. So serious, in fact, that she contacted a solicitor and began divorce proceedings. And, in a move designed to strike at the core of the family, she also initiated another legal process.

She wanted Sukhdave's name removed from her son's birth certificate.

Despite being 99 per cent sure that the baby wasn't his, Sukhdave was mortified. He refused to admit defeat and continued to beg for his wife's return. After three months he got his way. I don't know what was said or what promises were made, but Surjit finally agreed to come back. Sukhdave couldn't have been happier. Typical of him, rather than collect his wife and children in the car, he arrived at their home in a white van. Yes, he wanted his family back, but he also knew there was a brand-new fridge in the house that his wife had paid for. That would be coming back to Willow Tree Lane, too, along with all the other white goods Surjit had bought. He was his mother's son ...

So Surjit returned from Coventry after a couple of months. But it wasn't, I discovered later, for the reasons Bachan Kaur and Sukhdave and even I thought. Surjit had rekindled her relationship with her ex-lover, the man she believed was the father of her son. Surjit wanted to be as close to him as possible. She also had her job and her children to consider. So back she came.

How I wish she'd stayed away.

***

It was a Friday afternoon in late November. I was upstairs putting laundry away. Hardave was pottering around, wandering in and out of our bedroom. Surjit was working a night shift, so both her children were asleep in our spare room – as they often were when Mum was meant to be looking after them.

I heard the back door slam and a few seconds later Mum's voice called up.

'Sarbjit, come and make tea!'

No hello, no please, no manners – no surprise.

I went to the kitchen and realised Sukhdave had also come in with Mum and they'd both gone into the lounge. It didn't matter, except I'd need more water. I thought nothing of it and leaned against the side unit, watching the pot. True to reputation, it didn't seem in any hurry to boil.

Suddenly my mother-in-law appeared in the doorway.

'Sarbjit, come into the lounge.'

What now?

'I'm doing the tea,' I said.

'Turn it down low. It can wait.'

I followed her into the lounge. Was I imagining it or was there an odd atmosphere in the room? Mum took her place on the large grey sofa, flanked by her sons.

As I took a seat at the table, I could sense something was wrong. Was it me? Had I offended someone? Even the way the others were sitting apart from me made me feel nervous. Then I realised both brothers' eyes were on Bachan Kaur.

'I've spoken to a contact in India,' she began. 'It's all going to be taken care of.'

Sukhdave nodded. I didn't have a clue what she was talking about, and from the mood in the room I didn't dare interrupt.

'It's her own fault. She's out of control,' Bachan Kaur continued. 'She's bringing shame on the family.' She looked sad. 'We're the laughing-stock of the community.'

So now I knew who she was talking about – but what did it have to do with India?

I didn't get the chance to ask.

'So, it's decided then,' Bachan Kaur concluded, without any discussion having taken place. 'We have to get rid of her.'

***

It all happened so quickly. I couldn't believe what I was hearing. 'Shame', 'India', 'get rid of'? All I understood for certain is that it couldn't mean what I thought it meant. Not even Bachan Kaur would think of something like this.

Could she?

She could.

'I have spoken to someone in India,' she explained. 'He says to bring Surjit to India and he will take care of her. We won't be troubled by her again.'

For the first time since I'd been in the lounge I found myself relaxing. This crazy plan would never work. Surjit was barely talking to any of us. How would Mum get her anywhere near India?

But when Bachan Kaur then revealed that there were family weddings the following month, and that she was going to invite Surjit to accompany her, my heart froze.

She's serious. She's really thought this through.

Or had she? At that moment in time, Surjit wouldn't have travelled to the end of the garden with Bachan Kaur. What made anyone think she'd go to India and the weddings of two people she'd never met with a woman she hated? Then another thought struck me.

But what if she did?

I felt sick. But my mouth was dry. Even if I'd dared to try to speak up, I couldn't have said a word. Luckily, Hardave could.

'This is stupid, Mum,' he said. 'You can't do this.'

'It's decided,' she said. 'I won't have her shaming our family.'

'Mum, it's Sukhdave's wife you're talking about.'

All eyes flew to Hardave's brother. But he just sat there, silent, emotionless.

'Enough,' Bachan Kaur said. 'We have discussed it.'

'But, Mum!'

'I said, enough! The decision is made.'

I'd never been so proud of my husband. In fact, I'd never been proud of him before at all. But at that moment he was the only one in the room brave enough to question his mother. Even I didn't do that. But then, as I was always reminded: I wasn't blood. Why would Bachan Kaur listen to me?

More importantly, I couldn't help thinking: *Look what she's planning to do with another person who isn't blood either ...*

* * *

We were all dismissed eventually and I almost ran up to the bedroom. My head was spinning. I couldn't believe what I'd just heard. But what had I heard? In the Punjabi language, 'get rid' can mean several things. Was I misinterpreting Bachan Kaur's intention? The second Hardave walked into the room, I asked him.

The look on his face proved I hadn't got it wrong.

'What's she playing at?' I said, shocked.

He looked devastated. 'I don't know, Sarb. She won't listen.'

'But they're not really going to go through with it, are they?'

'It sounds like it.'

'Well, we've got to stop them.' I was getting hysterical now. If I wasn't careful, Bachan Kaur would hear me.

'I tried,' Hardave said.

'Well, speak to Sukhdave. He can't want to do this. Not to his wife.'

Hardave fell silent. He had argued long and hard with his brother, but there was no convincing him.

'Then we have to tell Surjit,' I said.

'No!' Hardave's face changed. I'd gone too far. It was one thing to get him to talk to his mother and brother, but to suggest going behind their backs? That was unacceptable. He was still an Athwal.

'Mum won't like it if you say anything.'

All the respect he'd built up in me disappeared in a second. My true husband was back, passing on his mother's threats.

'Well, then,' I said, 'the only hope we've got is if Surjit refuses to go.'

* * *

My head felt like it was going to burst. I'd been raised never to question my elders. I'd been trained for marriage, almost programmed to be the perfect wife from as early as I could remember. Obedience and honour were ingrained in my soul, in everything I thought and did. But surely my parents had never intended me to stay quiet in the face of something like this?

For a couple of days I barely left our room unless it was to feed my children. Then I'd dart into the kitchen, grab the quickest snack and run back upstairs. Taking Taran to school or picking her up was a welcome respite. I turned a fifteen-minute trip into an hour-long exercise. Any longer and my mother-in-law would get suspicious. And the last thing I wanted was to have to speak to her.

Coincidentally, Bachan Kaur chose those days to eat next door. Maybe she was having second thoughts, giving Surjit the chance to change her ways. Or maybe she just wanted to keep an eye on her daughter-in-law in case she decided to run away again. Either way, I was relieved to stay out of her way.

I was just as scared of running into Surjit. Eventually my luck ran out one morning as she appeared in my kitchen. I didn't know where to look. I wanted to tell her to run, to get out, to go to the police. But I couldn't get a word in. She was so excited, she had news she was desperate for me to hear.

I looked at Surjit's happy face. She was almost unrecognisable from the sullen woman I was used to seeing. Over the last couple of years I'd barely seen her smile. Whatever was making her so bubbly had to be pretty amazing. Maybe it was a divorce? Maybe she had come to tell me she was escaping.

'Guess what, Sarb?' she said, her dark eyes sparkling with energy like they once used to all the time.

'What is it?' I asked. 'What are you so happy about?'

'You'll never believe it – I'm going to India!'

I hadn't eaten for days – but at that moment I felt like being sick.

CHAPTER ELEVEN

0800 555 111

Friday 4 December 1998: the day I hoped would never come and the day I will never forget.

I was going mad during the run-up to Bachan Kaur's and Surjit's departure. I couldn't concentrate on anything other than what was going to happen in India. I still couldn't believe it. It was too far-fetched. The more I worried, the less I ate and the less I ate, the more light-headed I felt. If it weren't for the need to focus on my children I would have collapsed.

I still couldn't get over how easily Surjit had been talked into going. By the sound of it, it had been typical mother-in-law tactics. She'd first asked Surjit to accompany her so she didn't look bad in the eyes of her Indian relatives.

'It will bring shame on my name if I turn up alone.'

Surjit's days of caring about Mum's good name had long gone. Even when Bachan Kaur turned on the waterworks and cried how terrible it would be, Surjit held fast. Only when Bachan Kaur said that obviously she would treat her daughter-in-law to any number of outfits while they were over there – and not just clothes for the wedding – did Surjit's steadfastness start to waver.

'There's been too much bad blood between us, Surjit,' the old lady said. 'I want to make it up to you. I want to spoil you.'

The year before, Bachan Kaur's eldest daughter Bhajan had gone on a shopping spree while visiting India and raved about it to Surjit when she returned. I think Surjit imagined herself buying the same amount of wonderful finery and couldn't wait to get going. Vain as it might make her sound, any time she could spend away from Sukhdave was time well spent. And if she got to play Supermarket Sweep in Delhi's finest clothes stores, that was a bonus.

Bachan Kaur must have known that. But she also knew that there was something else that Surjit could be tempted by. To this day, I suspect that Bachan Kaur may have offered her a prize that money couldn't buy, a priceless, glittering jewel that Surjit had longed for for so many years: her freedom. I imagined the conversation: 'Do this for me, Surjit, in front of my family, and if you still want a divorce when you return, you will get it with my blessing.'

Deal.

It could have been that easy.

As the day of departure drew closer, I realised Bachan Kaur was spending more time back in our house. If anything was going to ruin her plan, I imagine she thought it would be me. I got on the best with Surjit, I was the only other non-blood relative, and I was married to Hardave. Even though he'd been the only one to speak out against the plan, I had no doubts that he would have passed on every doubt, every angry comment I'd made about it. Bachan Kaur was going to keep a very close eye on me, it seemed.

She was also going to stop me speaking to Surjit. Several times I was on my way next door to borrow something or pick up the kids when my mother-in-law appeared with an urgent errand or task that could not be delayed or done by anybody else. Even indoors I felt her watchful gaze burning into me wherever I went.

Hardave was useless. Following his outspoken performance at the meeting, Bachan Kaur had slapped him down hard and he'd stopped trying to change her mind. Sukhdave wouldn't be swayed either.

'I've done everything I can,' my husband reported. 'Now just drop the subject. This is family business.'

He's as scared of his mum as me.

On the Thursday night there was a gathering at No. 88 to see the travellers off. Mum, Hardave, the children and various others went round. But I was held back. There was no way Bachan Kaur wanted to risk me puncturing the atmosphere. She was so close to success.

Alone in No. 90 I didn't know what to do. So I did what I always did whenever I needed guidance.

As I looked up at the kind eyes of Guru Nanak Dev Ji, my own filled with tears. He had never let me down before, so I prayed he wouldn't this time.

'Dear Guru Nanak, please save Surjit. Please stop her going to India. I fear the worst for her if she steps on that plane. Please, please, I'm begging you, please!'

I don't know how long I sat there, distraught and heavy of heart. I knew I had to do something but I didn't know what. I'd been forbidden to speak of it to anyone outside the house. My husband and the head of the family had agreed. However despicably I thought they were behaving, I wasn't to meddle in family business. I had to protect the family's honour.

Like them.

* * *

Confessing all my fears to my Guru was cathartic. But as much as I had every faith in him, I knew in my heart I had to tell someone else. I owed Surjit that. I owed Guru Nanak that. And I owed it to myself. I'd been silent long enough. But who?

The thought of going to the police sent a chill through me. I'd been raised to believe that everything could be sorted out within the family. My father thought this, my grandparents thought this, and my mother-in-law did as well. Even if she was taking it to extremes, I still couldn't face the idea of walking into my local station in Hayes and confessing all I knew. What if someone saw me? What if Bachan Kaur or Sukhdave discovered what I'd done?

Then I remembered a series of adverts I'd seen recently for a helpline that encouraged people to call in with information about illegal activity. What made it so appealing to a lot of people was that informants could phone in anonymously. But what was it called? I racked my brain for ages until it eventually came to me. 'Crimestoppers'. The only problem now was how to contact them without anyone finding out.

As I went downstairs to make breakfast on that fateful Friday morning, I stopped by the telephone in the hall. I just wanted to pick it up and get everything off my chest. But it was too dangerous. I could hear Hardave upstairs in the shower. Taran was crashing around in her room, Balveen was calling out to be fed and who knew where Bachan Kaur was.

I can't do it here.

I realised the only chance I would have was when I drove Taran to school. But knowing what I was going to do turned me into a bundle of nerves. I was dropping cutlery and shaking as I cleared up the breakfast things.

'Are you all right?' Hardave asked.

'I'm fine.'

But I wasn't. I was about to go against my family and that made me nervous as hell. But it had to be done. A woman's life depended on it. She depended on me.

I was shaking like jelly even as Taran and I walked to the car. I felt Bachan Kaur's eyes on me as I put the key in the lock and prayed she couldn't see how much my hand was shaking. Even as my car pulled away, I couldn't relax. Why did I feel guilty, like I was the one doing something wrong? When I pulled up alongside a public phone box a few minutes after dropping Taran at school, my anxiety got worse. I nearly drove off without getting out, but I knew I had to try. I owed it to Surjit to at least do that.

This is the call that could save her life ...

***

My first call was to directory enquiries. Even asking them for the number of Crimestoppers made me feel sick.

Was I really going to do this? Was I really going to betray my husband's family?

Everything that I'd been raised to believe about relationships was on the line. I was going against my whole culture. I was going to bring shame on us all.

I still remember my shaking fingers hovering over the keypad of the public phone. Eventually I realised that the only way to stop the quivering was to do it, to press the buttons.

0-8-0-0-
I'm doing it ...
5-5-5-
Nearly there ...
1-1-
I can't! I can't risk everything.

Suddenly the whole weight of everything I was doing – breaking the promise I'd made to my husband to keep quiet, going against the family name – hit me. Twenty-nine years of upbringing hadn't led me to this. But then I thought of Surjit's happy face when she'd told me about her trip. She had no idea what was in store for her. I pressed the final button.

1

'Hello, Crimestoppers ...'

The voice echoed in my ear for a few seconds before I could muster the strength to reply.

'Hello,' I said, my voice small and quiet. 'I want to report a murder that's going to happen.'

Once I'd started, the floodgates opened. I told them everything. About the meeting, about the plan, about the trip. About Bachan Kaur and Sukhdave. I told them it was happening today. I told them the flight time, the flight number, where they were going. And what they were going to do.

Then I stood there, frozen, while the operator thanked me for my bravery.

Bravery? I was just doing what was right. Then I remembered the time. I'd been out too long. My mother-in-law would be getting suspicious.

I hung up, ran to the car and drove home as fast as I dared. What had I done? What can of worms had I opened? Suddenly I was very afraid.

That wasn't brave – it was stupid!

* * *

By the time I got home there was a flurry of activity outside No. 88. Suitcases were lined up on the path. In my house, things were happening too. Hardave didn't raise an eyebrow when I came home later than usual. But I did more than that when he said, 'I'm driving Mum and Surjit to the airport.'

'Are you serious?' I asked. 'After everything you've said? You know what's going to happen to her.'

'You don't know anything,' he snapped. 'Mind your own business.'

I ignored that. I already knew too much.

'Why can't Sukhdave take them? It's his wife. It's his plan!'

Hardave looked at me with pity in his eyes, as though he couldn't believe my naivety.

'Sukhdave can't do it, can he? Surjit's told her friends at Heathrow all sorts of lies about him. He can't be seen there with her, can he?'

I couldn't follow his logic. But then I couldn't follow any of the logic that had led to this point in time where my husband was going to collaborate, as I saw it, in the potential murder of his sister-in-law.

But I knew he was as opposed to it as I was. So I had to try again. With tears streaming down my face, I begged and begged him not to go.

'Think of what you're doing. Think of us. Think of Taran and Balveen – and me!'

Then we got down to it. The real reason why he wouldn't listen to a word I said.

'Look, I have to, all right?' he shouted. 'Mum says!'

I knew then that this was a fight I would never win. Because when Mum said Hardave had to do something, he did it, whether he agreed with it or not. It was pathetic, but it was in keeping with his character.

I was ashamed to be his wife.

* * *

It was time. Bachan Kaur finished her packing in our house then went down to the front door. Hardave and I followed. The door to No. 88 was already open so she just shouted at Surjit to hurry up while her son loaded the car. Through the wall I could hear clomping on the stairs next door and the unmistakeable whoops of a young woman excited to be going on the holiday of a lifetime.

This is my last chance, I thought. *I have to stop her.*

It was as though my mother-in-law read my mind. She suddenly spun round and glared at me standing in the doorway behind her.

'Go inside, Sarbjit,' she commanded, her voice as cold as Surjit's was happy.

I didn't move. I was transfixed by the sight of my sister-in-law almost skipping towards Hardave's car.

'Sarbjit! Go – in – side!' Then the front door was slammed in my face.

I ran to the front room, lifted the curtain and stared out. Bachan Kaur was taking her place in the front passenger seat. Hardave had finished loading the car and was starting the engine. I watched as Surjit climbed into the back seat and waved at Sukhdave and the children standing on the lawn.

And I knew I would never see her again.

***

When you give up hope, you give up everything.

Even as Hardave returned that afternoon, I had to believe that I'd got it all wrong. That when Bachan Kaur had said she was going to get rid of Surjit, it had just meant that she was going to take her on holiday for a while, get her out of the country and show her the culture that she should be honouring. The phrase in Punjabi, after all, was open to interpretation.

I'm sure Hardave could see I'd been crying, but he didn't mention it. There was nothing else to say. All I could do was hope that I'd been mistaken – and that if I hadn't, then Crimestoppers would be able to do something.

***

The hours ticked by. I don't know what I was expecting to happen next. Each minute that passed felt like it would never end. But what was I hoping for? A phone call from Surjit to tell me she was OK? A comforting hug from Hardave to say it had all been a misunderstanding? All I knew for sure was that my stomach was churning all day every day.

Maybe I imagined the police in India were right then swooping in to arrest Bachan Kaur and save Surjit's life.

That was their job, wasn't it?

That first night I couldn't sleep for worry. Every time I closed my eyes I just saw Bachan Kaur's smug face as she announced Surjit's fate at the family meeting. It had been bad enough being there in person without it polluting my dreams. But I couldn't shake the chilling memory.

The next day, I demanded that Hardave call India.

'What for?' he said.

'Just to check they landed OK.'

'I'm sure we would have heard if they hadn't.' But he called anyway, to shut me up, probably.

The next few days passed in a blur. They'd left on 4 December. The first wedding, of Charan Singh's daughter Harjinder Kaur, was due to take place the following day, followed by his son Bhupinder Singh's nuptials on the sixth. I pictured Surjit dancing and letting her – shorter – hair down at these festivals. And I counted down the days until she returned on the eighteenth.

Over the weekend Hardave refused to discuss anything. He told me to stop imagining things and to get on with my chores. How I wanted to believe him when he said that nothing was going on. But then, the following Monday, I became aware of noises coming from No. 88 when I knew Sukhdave should have been at work. He'd taken the baby to stay with Surjit's parents while she was away, so he wasn't at home looking after him. When my brother-in-law came to visit Hardave later that day I had a bad feeling.

'Why aren't you at work?' I asked.

'I've taken sick leave.'

'What's wrong with you?'

He didn't answer, just glared and stomped off to find his brother.

***

Living so close to that man, and with traces of his mother all around me, was hell. My mind was in turmoil, wondering what more I could do. I spent a lot of time in our box room, praying to the Guru Granth Sahib, asking for advice. On Sunday I went to the temple. I needed to be there, among my peers, I felt, to ask for forgiveness for any wrongdoing on my part but also to pray to God to give me the courage to carry on.

On the face of it, nothing changed. Nothing helped. I woke up one morning in tears. I was breathless, panicking. I must have had a terrible nightmare but I couldn't recall it. I just remember lying in bed, deep in thought, feeling sad, desolate, isolated. Outside of my gurus, I had no one to talk to. I couldn't breathe a word to my parents. I couldn't wish the torture I was enduring on them, not even for a minute. No parent wants to imagine their child suffering in any way. Especially as they might feel responsible for me being there in the first place ...

In their absence, I drew on the one being who would listen. I felt tears running down my cheeks as I listened to myself have a conversation with God. I really felt like I was watching, eavesdropping on myself. It was bizarre. I was asking Him for the courage to find a way to help. Then, as my emotions grew even stronger, my questioning grew darker.

Why is all this happening, Lord? Why have You let my sister-in-law disappear? Why can't You make it all stop?

Why?

I was tired, numb. I wanted to stay in bed all day with the covers over my head. Only the sound of my husband stirring beside me spurred me on.

I'd rather spend the day in front of the oven than share another minute with him.

Yes, he'd tried to object to his mother's plan at the meeting. But he could have done more. Of the two of us, he was the only one Bachan Kaur would ever listen to. So why hadn't he made her?

Surely he wasn't scared as well?

* * *

Over the next few days there were plenty of calls to and from India. Each time I asked Hardave if Surjit was all right and each time he said, 'Of course she is.'

Then, after about a week or eight days, the calls to Bachan Kaur became less frequent. When I realised it had been forty-eight hours without an update I begged Hardave to phone. He did, but begrudgingly. When he hung up, he said, 'Mum told me to stop pestering her. She's meant to be on holiday.'

My stomach churned hearing that. There was only one reason I could think of that my mother-in-law wouldn't want to be contacted.

'Did she say how Surjit was?' I asked, my voice weak and shaking.

'What do you mean?' Hardave's eyes flashed with anger.

'You know what I mean! You were at the meeting. You were the one who stood up against her. Tell me she hasn't done what she threatened to do.'

'Look, Sarb,' he said, but the words wouldn't come. Eventually, head in his hands in a pose of pure exasperation, he cried out, 'Just shut up about it, will you?'

I didn't care how upset he was. I was already in floods of tears.

'Just tell me, Hardave, is she all right? Is Surjit all right?'

'For God's sake,' he shouted and threw down his mug of tea. 'I forbid you to mention this again, OK. Surjit will be home when she's ready.'

With Hardave struggling to keep his patience, I turned to Sukhdave. As he wasn't at work he was able to call India every day. What had he learned?

'Mum says they enjoyed the weddings. She wished we all could have been there.'

Why? Because she wanted to kill us as well? I tried to put the idea out of my head but the conversation lingered with me. It had just been innocuous chat but a chill passed over me every time I thought of it. How could anyone in Sukhdave's position be so cold, so matter of fact? Was it possible I was wrong? Or, as Hardave said, that I was imagining things?

No. It was too much of a coincidence that Sukhdave had taken time off work. There was nothing wrong with him – apart from in his head. It was happening, I knew it. On the other side of the world Bachan Kaur's despicable plan was being enacted.

I have to do something else.

With my mother-in-law out of the country I had more freedom. But there was still no way I could go to Hayes police station. Members of the community were everywhere. It only took one pair of eyes to recognise me, and one loose tongue to pass on to Bachan Kaur that they'd seen me, and I would be in trouble. But that shouldn't stop me writing. I found the address and wrote a long, detailed letter imploring them to act. Once again, I questioned myself on every detail, but I knew it had to be done. The shame I was bringing on my family was nothing to the shame it was bringing on my faith. Sikhism had not been founded to be used as a motive for murder. I would not let my gurus' names be tarnished by the evil in my family.

My letter contained all but one detail: my name. I could not risk being found out. But it was only as I sealed the envelope that I fully appreciated why I was so determined to maintain my anonymity. It was obvious in many ways. Readers of this book have probably worked it out already. But I had been in denial for so long that when the penny dropped it came as such a surprise. A hideous, terrifying surprise.

If my mother-in-law was prepared to kill Surjit to protect her honour in the community, then she would happily do the same to me.

* * *

I must have been blind. Why didn't I see that was a possibility? But even as I'd called Crimestoppers in secret, I hadn't put two and two together. I knew if Bachan Kaur had discovered what I was up to that she would be angry – but I put that down to her proud defence of her family and the perceived shame Surjit was bringing to it. And not the fact that she was prepared to kill anyone who got in her way.

Some ideas are too big to think about. And, I soon realised, I wasn't the only one having trouble in the logic department.

Friday 18 December finally arrived and Hardave and Sukhdave decided to do the Heathrow pick-up together. After the longest fortnight of my life, they weren't the only ones who wanted to go. The local schools had broken up for the Christmas holidays the day before and both Pav and Taran begged their dads to tag along. They'd both missed their 'Mummy' – Bachan Kaur – terribly, and of course Pav looked forward to seeing her real mother.

Sukhdave was a sucker for his daughter's imploring eyes. 'OK,' he said, 'jump in.'

The girls were delighted and, watching from the house, so was I. If the men were taking Pav with them, then Surjit had to be coming back. There was no way that Sukhdave would risk disappointing his own daughter by taking her to Heathrow, knowing her mother wouldn't be stepping off that plane. However much he hated his wife, he loved his little girl. I was sure of that.

With that realisation, the next couple of hours passed more quickly than any time over the last fourteen days. I was so happy, I even found myself telling Surjit's little boy, who'd been collected from Coventry the day before and left in my care, 'Mummy will be home soon.'

When I finally heard the unmistakeable sounds of an engine stopping and car doors slamming, I picked up the baby and rushed to the window. I saw the boot open, the luggage stacked on the pavement and Sukhdave and Hardave talking to their mother.

But Surjit was nowhere to be seen.

PART TWO
SHAME

CHAPTER TWELVE

I'M NOT COMING BACK

'Where's Surjit?'

I was alone with Hardave and I wanted answers. If he wouldn't give them to me, then I would go to his mother.

'She decided to stay a few more days,' he said. 'She'll be home soon.'

'OK.' I wasn't convinced. 'Where are our daughters?'

He looked momentarily confused. Almost as if he'd forgotten what he'd done with them.

'We dropped them at your parents' house.'

'My parents'? Why on earth did you go there?'

'We drove past their house on the way to Heathrow and Taran wanted to see them,' he offered eventually.

'More than she wanted to see your mother? More than Pav wanted to see Surjit?'

It made no sense. Was it really possible that he and Sukhdave had only realised en route to Terminal 3 how bad it would look if Surjit's daughter turned up and Surjit wasn't there? *Tell me they weren't so stupid.* But from the way Hardave was getting flustered, I had my answer.

'I don't want to talk about it,' he snapped as he stormed out. 'I said she'll be home soon, so leave it at that.'

* * *

Although Hardave was acting weirdly, I still refused to believe they'd gone through with it. But if that was the case, where *was* Surjit? I was dreading seeing my mother-in-law but I needed to know.

'She loved India so much she decided to stay on,' Bachan Kaur said. She was staring directly into my eyes as she spoke. Even though I desperately wanted to believe her, if she was lying it was very convincing. Especially as she knew *I* knew her original plan.

I didn't dare push the subject because part of me didn't want to know the truth. But there was someone who would not take no for an answer.

On the day of the flight to India, Surjit's brother Jagdeesh Singh Dhillon had called No. 88 to speak to her. Jagdeesh Singh was surprised when Sukhdave had answered. He was even more surprised to discover his sister had left the country.

'But my wife and I were meant to be staying with you tonight,' Jagdeesh Singh said. 'Surjit wanted to talk to me.'

'What about?' Sukhdave asked.

There was an uneasy hesitation.

'I was coming over to discuss things with her,' said Jagdeesh, and he didn't need to explain exactly what. Sukhdave was fully aware of the ongoing tension in his own relationship with Surjit, and Jagdeesh's attempts to mediate between them. Jagdeesh had spoken one-to-one with each of them about these problems over recent months.

Now, Jagdeesh said, 'I understood she was going to Bombay as part of work training – at some point. Is that where she is?'

'Bombay? That's bullshit,' Sukhdave laughed. 'She's gone to India for two family weddings.'

If Jagdeesh Singh was shocked at why she had gone, he was left open-mouthed at whom she'd travelled with.

'Mum asked Surj to go with her. It's got nothing to do with work,' Sukhdave said.

It didn't make sense to Jagdeesh Singh. Why would his sister not tell him the truth? Unless she knew that he would try to talk her out of going with her mother-in-law. After all the things Bachan Kaur had done to her – and he was sure he'd only heard a fraction of it – how could she be thinking of going on holiday with the woman she detested?

I thought I knew the answer. There wasn't much light in my sister-in-law's life, or mine. Whatever promises Bachan Kaur had made, they had been enough to tempt Surjit – and make her lie to her brother. And then, of course, there was the deal she might have struck with Bachan Kaur about her divorce.

On the phone to Sukhdave on 4 December, Jagdeesh Singh had heard enough. Told that Surjit would be back on the eighteenth, he said, 'OK, tell her to call me then.' He also asked if Sukhdave had a contact number for his family in India.

That number was never forthcoming; Sukhdave said his family's house did not have a phone connection. So who was he phoning and receiving calls from every other day?

But Sukhdave did keep one part of his bargain. On 18 December 1998, Surjit's family received a call. Bachan Kaur herself, fresh off the plane from India, called Surjit's mother in Coventry.

'Surjit's not here,' Bachan Kaur told her. 'Have you heard from her?'

'What do you mean she's not there? Isn't she at your house?' responded Surjit's mother.

'No, she decided to come home early. We spoke the other day and she said she missed the kids, so she was jumping on an earlier flight. But I haven't seen her. I thought she must be with you.'

Surjit's mother – and her whole family, when told of the call – immediately feared the worst. Something horrible had happened to Surjit.

Something that demanded more action than a simple phone call.

* * *

Day 2.

The following morning Jagdeesh Singh and his wife arrived at Willow Tree Lane. I don't know what was going through his mind, but Jagdeesh Singh was adamant that Surjit had to be in trouble. Perhaps he could understand her not wanting to travel back with Bachan Kaur – he knew his sister didn't like her mother-in-law – but if the ticket was already bought and paid for, that was madness. Especially if she'd said she was going home early to see the children and she hadn't set eyes on them yet.

'I think we should go to the police,' Jagdeesh Singh said.

Sukhdave wouldn't hear of it. 'No, no,' he said. 'She'll be here soon enough. Give it a couple of days.'

'What's that going to achieve? She should have been on the same flight as your mum.'

'She changed her plans,' Sukhdave said. 'You know what she's like.'

'No, I don't like it,' Jagdeesh Singh insisted. 'She should have been back. I'm calling the police.'

But that was the last thing Sukhdave wanted.

'Don't get them involved.'

Jagdeesh Singh shrugged him off and went to leave. He knew where Hayes police station was. He was already planning what he was going to say when Sukhdave played his trump card.

'Think of the shame in the community, Jagdeesh Singh, if you make a fuss with the police and she comes back in two days' time.'

Jagdeesh Singh did not respond.

But, inside, he remained unsure. He had his suspicions, but he needed to be certain before voicing them – to anyone.

***

If Sukhdave was dismissive with Surjit's brother, he wasn't much better with her children. When Pav discovered her mum hadn't come back when she should have done, she was very upset. Even the baby realised something wasn't right. At first Sukhdave tried to cheer them up, telling them not to worry. Then he began to lose patience, ordering them to stop moaning. It wasn't what they needed.

I saw how those little kids suffered. Again it raised such doubts in my mind. Would a father really be so callous if he knew the mother of his children was never coming home? Surely not.

Selfishly, I thought of something else. *If Sukhdave really has got rid of Surjit and he's so cold with the children he loves – then what will he do to me?*

***

It was only hearing Bachan Kaur on the phone to someone that I realised her story had changed overnight. She'd told me that Surjit had stayed on. Now she'd left two days earlier. Did that mean my sister-in-law was more or less likely to be OK?

Speaking to Bachan Kaur and Sukhdave was out of the question and Hardave would only parrot back to me what they'd told him to say. That didn't matter. I was used to avoiding them. But when it came to speaking to my own family, what could I say? I wanted so much to tell them about my suspicions. But who would that help? How would my father react when he heard me spreading unfounded rumours about my family? It would bring shame on all of us; I was sure he would see it like that.

Even so, it was agony speaking to him shortly after Bachan Kaur returned.

'Did your sister-in-law have a good time?' Dad asked.

'I don't know.'

'Haven't you spoken to her?'

'She hasn't come back yet.'

There was a pause on the other end of the line. 'I thought you said Bachan Kaur had returned?'

'Yes.'

'So where is Surjit?'

'I don't know.'

'You must know. You're neighbours. You're family.'

'I don't know. She's not back, that's all I can tell you.'

I'd started out not wanting to worry him, but I think I achieved the opposite.

***

My mother-in-law had been back two days and despite what she and Sukhdave were saying, there had still been no word from Surjit. The atmosphere in both houses was terrible. The children seemed to get on everyone's nerves. Ricky the Alsatian's barking seemed louder and more invasive than ever. And I couldn't look a single member of my family in the eye. I was too scared of what I would see there.

I thought again about my letter to the police at Hayes, my phone call to Crimestoppers. They must have had some effect, surely. Maybe that was the reason we hadn't heard from Surjit – because the police had acted on my information and rescued her? I'd heard about safe houses and witness protection schemes. Was it possible the police had spirited my sister-in-law away to safety in the nick of time? Maybe that's why Bachan Kaur seemed so confused? Perhaps she genuinely didn't know where Surjit was.

The very idea put something like a spring in my step. But it was short-lived. Under pressure from Jagdeesh Singh,

Sukhdave had decided to inform the authorities about his wife's unexplained absence. Hayes police station was the obvious place to go, but when he'd explained his story he wasn't slapped in handcuffs. No one said, 'Yes, we've heard about your plot to kill your wife.' They just wrote down his statement, confirmed that Surjit had not left Delhi on 14 December or later, and passed on their hope that she would turn up soon.

It had all been a waste of time.

I'd risked my life and my sanity for nothing.

***

Day 3.

Hope.

If I was confused already about Surjit's whereabouts, when Sukhdave decided to return to work on Sunday 20 December I couldn't help feeling relieved. He wouldn't be able to do that if he'd just murdered his wife, would he? And according to the story he later told the police, there was even better news: he'd bumped into a friend of his wife's.

And she'd told him Surjit was alive.

According to Sukhdave, he was unloading luggage from his coach at Terminal 3 Arrivals when he became aware of a woman standing a short distance away from the passenger group. She was about five foot five, with shortish ginger hair – and she was clearly waiting for something, but it wasn't a suitcase.

'Are you Dave?' she asked when the crowd had dispersed.

'Yes, I am.'

'And your wife's name is Surjit?'

Warily, he replied, 'There are plenty of Surjits.'

'Has yours gone to India with her mother-in-law?'

'That's her,' he said. 'What do you want?'

'She called me with a message. She wants you to know

that she's OK, she's happy and she'll be away for about two months.'

'Have you got a number for her?'

The woman shook her head.

'Then can you tell her to phone me or her family in Coventry? Just call one of us to let us know she's all right.'

The stranger agreed. As she turned to disappear inside the terminal building, Sukhdave said he called out after her, 'What's your name?'

'It's Kate.'

It was 11.20 a.m. According to my brother-in-law, the whole exchange had lasted barely five minutes. But the time didn't matter. As Sukhdave told officers at Hayes police station the following morning, Surjit was alive and well so there was no point in them searching for her any more. At worst, she was just having a break. Who from, however, Sukhdave wouldn't conjecture.

Either way, it was really positive.

I'm so glad I didn't say anything to Dad!

* * *

Day 5.

By now, the impact of Surjit's disappearance was starting to be felt beyond the circles of family and community. Surjit's boss, Mike Beglin, was called upon to say when he was expecting Surjit back.

'She'll be here tomorrow morning for the early shift,' he said, '6 a.m. start.'

Beglin wasn't the only Customs employee expecting her that day. Apart from her date with her brother, one of the other appointments that Surjit had missed by her sudden holiday was pre-Christmas drinks with her colleagues Kellie and Theresa. She'd rung Kellie at home the night before leaving for India and promised to be back in time for the Christmas party. But of course she hadn't made it, and her friends were now concerned.

And when she failed to show up for work for that December morning shift, the questions just kept coming. Where was Surjit?

***

Day 6.

It was 23 December. Bachan Kaur had been back – alone – for six days. The house was full of excitement for Christmas and New Year. But it was all a front. We were only doing it for the children. When Pawanpreet showed Sukhdave her list of what she wanted from Santa it broke my heart. There was only one thing on her list that she really craved.

And we didn't know where she was.

But at least Sukhdave got to speak to her. Once again, according to the report he gave to the police, he was at work that day, this time dropping off at Terminal 1, when he saw a familiar figure.

'Kate?'

'Surjit wants to speak to you,' the woman said.

'Thank God. Give me the number.'

'No, I'll call her for you.'

She pulled out her mobile phone and dialled a number. Nothing.

Sukhdave said he began to think it was a wind-up. But Kate told him to have patience as she tried again. And again. And again.

On the fifth attempt she smiled. It was ringing. Even standing two feet away, Sukhdave heard the unmistakable sound of his wife's voice crackling down a bad international line.

'Let me speak to her!' he said. As he took the phone Sukhdave tried to read the number on the screen. He

couldn't. Kate had wrapped black tape around the little
Nokia to prevent just that.

Right then, it didn't matter. He just wanted to hear Surjit's
voice. Five minutes later, he wished he hadn't.

'You need to know I'm not coming back,' Surjit told him.

'What do you mean you're not coming back?'

'What do you think I mean? I'm not fucking coming
back!'

'Surjit, please mind your language.'

If that was intended to calm her, it didn't. She went on to
reveal that she had had enough of England and she was
happy with her boyfriend, Raj.

'Please tell my family I won't be coming back. Not in two
months, not ever.'

'How can you say that? What about Pav? And have you
forgotten you've got a nine-month-old son?'

'Look, if you don't want the boy, take him to Coventry.
My parents will be happy to have him.'

Then she hung up. Sukhdave was silent, numb, as he
handed back the phone. Once again he asked for Surjit's
number. Once again, Sukhdave reported, Kate refused him.

'It's for the best.'

And then she was gone again.

***

Christmas came and went. It was a sombre affair despite our
best efforts. Sukhdave's report that Surjit was out there was
great. But what sort of a mother just abandons her children
like that? I didn't want to ask Sukhdave anything. For all he
was going through, I still wasn't sure about him.

But Sukhdave seemed to have a new sense of purpose. He
spent all his spare time at Heathrow trying to press Surjit's
colleagues into talking about her. None of them could help
with her whereabouts. However, he seemed to be more
interested in asking them about her social life. Reporting

back to Hardave, he said she had a reputation as a troublemaker who would go out with any man who took her fancy. And, although no one could confirm it, he was convinced she was also on drugs.

When the police launched an official missing person's enquiry for Surjit and came to No. 88 on 29 December, he told them the same things. When the police returned on New Year's Eve, Sukhdave had even more to share from his Customs network, none of it very flattering.

The picture Sukhdave was painting of his wife was getting worse and worse. Despite my misgivings about him and Bachan Kaur, I had to admit that the idea of my sister-in-law just escaping the family was so much better than what I'd feared had happened. Perhaps Bachan Kaur had paid her to go away? I wouldn't have put that past her. Considering how important it had seemed to Surjit to be spoiled by treats on her trip, maybe that made sense. And it explained why Hayes police station and the Crimestoppers people hadn't appeared to do anything – because there was nothing for them to do.

I felt a weight lift off my shoulders. I'd obviously misjudged Surjit. It hadn't been the first time she'd behaved in a way I wouldn't have done. Yes, I found it inconceivable that a mother would abandon her children – and I would tell her that the next time I saw her – but the main thing was that she was alive. My worst nightmares were just that: nightmares. I could relax and get on with my own life. Enjoy my own family and try to help out with Surjit's children whenever I could.

Then I got a visitor who changed everything.

It was January 1999 and everyone, apart from the children, was acting like it was just another start to the year. I was in the kitchen, as usual. The children were playing upstairs and Hardave had gone to work. I heard the back door swing open and immediately tensed. I nodded at my mother-in-law as she passed through and into the lounge. On her way she called quietly, 'Sit with me.'

It was the last thing I wanted to do but I followed anyway, as she knew I would. I'm glad I did.

By the time I arrived Bachan Kaur was unrecognisable from the woman who had seemed so strong and imposing a few minutes earlier. She had her chin to her chest and she was shaking, tears streaming down her face. Not the fake waterworks that she seemed able to summon on command. These were genuine, as far as I could tell. And the shivering was authentic, too. This was a woman in distress.

Despite all the pain Bachan Kaur had put me through over the years, I couldn't help rushing over to her side.

'What's happened? What's wrong?'

She was sobbing uncontrollably. I'd never seen her like it. This woman, this powerhouse of a personality, was rocking in her seat, sniffing and incoherent. I'd never known her to be lost for words but it took her several attempts to speak.

'Take your time,' I said.

What on earth had got her so worked up? She hadn't even been like this when Gian Singh had died.

She took a deep breath. 'It's really bad ...'

'What is? What's happened?'

'Surjit's not back.'

'I know. You said she was leaving after you. Then you said she'd left two days earlier. Tell me the truth. Where is Surjit?'

I was breathless when I'd finished speaking. I'd never spoken so directly to my mother-in-law before. I don't know where I got the strength from this time, but whatever she wanted to say to me, it seemed important. And with her so distressed, I felt confident enough to take chances.

Bachan Kaur still didn't look up. 'It's really bad,' she repeated, 'really bad. Maybe I shouldn't have done it but she was bringing too much shame on the family.'

Oh no …

'Done what?'

I think I already knew, of course. It had been my living nightmare ever since that family meeting. Even so, I needed to hear it from the horse's mouth.

'I couldn't continue like that. People were starting to talk and my son would be left out on the street if she took the house away.'

'Tell me, where is Surjit?' I said again. But it was as if I weren't there. Bachan Kaur had something to get off her chest and I was going to hear it, whether I wanted to or not. And all in her own good time.

'We went to the weddings,' she continued. 'She met the relatives, we had dancing and everything. We were happy. Then she wanted to go shopping like I'd promised so I said to her, "Here's some money, enjoy."'

'Did you go with her?'

The weeping woman shook her head. 'No, she wanted me to but I didn't.'

The memory of that moment brought another bout of howling. I just wished she'd get on with it. I was so desperate to hear what was on Bachan Kaur's mind I had to remember to breathe. What *was* she going to say?

'So, Surjit was taken out in a jeep as arranged. But they didn't reach the shops. She was given some water to drink and as soon as she'd swallowed, Surjit knew she had been drugged.'

As she relayed the details, Bachan Kaur's confidence returned. The more she spoke, the more normal she sounded. From seeming so distraught a few minutes before to now sounding holier-than-thou – as she did when making small talk outside the temple – it was a remarkable transformation.

'When she was unconscious, the two men who had driven her there strangled her, removed her jewellery and threw her body in the Ravi River.'

'So she's dead?'

I had to be clear.

'Yes, she's dead.'

That was it. So matter-of-fact, so cold. She'd just told me about the murder of her own daughter-in-law and the way she was sitting there she might have been telling me about a conversation in the supermarket. Her tears had dried on her face. She sat with her back straight and her head up. Her usual proud, confident self, like on any other ordinary day.

As for me, even sitting down my legs were trembling. I had goose bumps running all up me and I was flushing between boiling hot and freezing cold. I couldn't have felt worse if I'd given the order for her death.

And why was she trusting me with this information? I didn't want to know. I didn't want to share her dirty secret. Or was that not the point? Had it all been an act? Was this my mother-in-law's way of telling me that I too could be despatched in the same way? At that moment I honestly didn't know what to think.

Then, as suddenly as she'd arrived, Bachan Kaur rose, ready to leave. Scheming or overcome with remorse, she was done.

'Surjit won't be able to bring shame on us any more,' she announced, back to her usual confident self. 'We can start living like a proper family now.'

I couldn't believe it. Surjit had just wanted to get away from her husband and his family – and they'd killed her.

The answer was divorce.

Not death.

I'd never felt so scared.

CHAPTER THIRTEEN

HE'S THE ONLY GRANDSON I'VE GOT

Idiot.

They must have been laughing at me the whole time. Hardave, Bachan Kaur, Sukhdave. They'd all stood in the same room as me and lied. Lied to my face, lied to my children. Lied to Jagdeesh Singh, his family. Lied to the police. I'd never felt so stupid.

Or so afraid.

Mum and Sukhdave hadn't physically put their hands around Surjit's neck, but they'd asked someone to. I suspected they'd paid for the service as well. Surjit had been encouraged to wear her gold and jewellery for a reason. Was that a down payment from the family?

I thought back to the previous spring. Sukhdave had flown to Singapore for a week to visit his mum's family. I hadn't questioned it at the time. I was glad not to have him around. When I quizzed Hardave after I had been told of Surjit's murder, he revealed Singapore hadn't been the destination at all. Sukhdave had gone to India, to the Punjab.

'Why do you want to know?' Hardave asked.

I couldn't tell him. Not yet. He was my husband but I needed to work a few things out in my own mind before

I confided in him what his mother had said. But could there be any doubt?

It was all falling into place. Sukhdave had been to India to arrange the deal face to face. Whatever the price for slaughtering his wife, he must have shaken hands on it then.

And I was living with them.

How had it come to this? A few weeks ago I had the pain of not knowing what was going on and fearing the worst. Then I'd let myself believe that Surjit was fulfilling her own destiny, albeit not in the way I would choose. And now I knew the truth. There were no more doubts, no room for wondering. No room for *hope*. Surjit was dead.

***

After Bachan Kaur confessed to me, the atmosphere in the family changed instantly. Sukhdave had largely kept out of my way before. Now he sought me out with a message. He wasn't angry, just cold and unsmiling. As I stared at his serious-looking face I could only think of one thing.

I'm looking at a murderer.

'I hear you had a chat with Mum today?' he said.

I nodded.

'So you know?'

Another nod.

'And you also know the same thing will happen to you if you dare breathe a word of this to anyone.'

He stared at me a few seconds longer then left the house. I wouldn't have been surprised if he'd whistled on his way. He couldn't have seemed calmer.

And that just made him all the more terrifying.

***

I couldn't believe Sukhdave hadn't even tried to deny his mother's claims, to pass them off as hysteria. But there was no mistaking the menace in his words. I thought of Taran and Balveen. I was a mother of two daughters in a family that had already killed one woman. Of course I would take his threat seriously. If I were gone, who would be around to protect them?

Not Hardave.

I'd been told not to speak to anybody – but Sukhdave had said nothing about God, so I immersed myself in the prayer room to talk over the mess I'd found myself in. When that didn't work, I ran to the *gurdwara* in Havelock Road, as though being around other religious people would give my prayers more power. Only childcare stopped me being there all day. But there was only so much solace I could get from confessing my problems to my gurus and the Almighty. Despite Sukhdave's threat, I was bursting to tell someone else. But I knew I couldn't. The silence that I'd have to demand was too much of a burden to put on anyone. And I knew what would happen if my brother-in-law discovered I'd opened my mouth.

Then, a few days later, my sister Inder asked me to go shopping with her. She wanted to take advantage of the January sales. I had no money but it was an excuse to get out of the house, so I said yes.

Knowing I was seeing my sister, Bachan Kaur warned me to watch my tongue. She needn't have bothered. I was too scared to tell anyone. And I certainly wouldn't burden my little sister.

But I'd followed her around all morning, trying to smile when she looked at me, but lost in my own thoughts the whole time. Then we were in Argos, Uxbridge of all places, waiting for an order and I just broke. While Inder stood open-mouthed next to me, I poured out everything. She knew Surjit. She couldn't believe what she was hearing.

But one look at my face, the relief mixed with tears, and she knew it was the truth.

'You have to tell the police,' she said.

'I can't. They made me promise.'

'You have to. They killed Surjit.'

'And they'll kill me too if I say anything. Promise me you won't tell anyone.'

'I don't know ...'

'Promise me! You have to!'

I shouldn't have told her. It was unfair, selfish of me. I'd been unable to keep it secret, why should I expect it of her? But she promised. And, as Inder and I parted company later that day, I knew I could trust her. I also knew I was glad I'd told her.

If anything happens to me, at least someone will know the truth ...

***

But nothing would happen to me. I had to believe that. Desperately, I tried to convince myself again and again that I wasn't Surjit. That I'd done my best to fit into the family. That, simply because of the way I'd been raised by my own parents, I'd lived the way the Athwals would want a daughter-in-law to live. Surely they had no reason to be mean to me. But, I realised, they'd never had a reason to be mean to me.

And that had never stopped them.

But, like Surjit, my sisters had a more independent streak running through them. I don't know if it was a personality thing or to do with being allowed to mix with others of her generation. All I do know is that I later discovered that Inder had ignored my pleas and taken the information about Surjit to the police.

She didn't do it immediately. Out of deference to me and my precarious position, she fought off her instincts to report it the second we'd parted company. But working in the Strand in central London, and having to walk past Charing Cross police station on her way to work and then again on her journey home, the temptation to call in grew. Yes, she would be betraying my confidence. But, as she saw it, she might just be saving my life.

A desk sergeant took her details and the rough outline of my story. He passed it on. Then she was called back several more times for a fuller run-down with more senior officers. She didn't tell me what she'd done and I didn't find out for years.

There was a reason for that. Because the police did nothing about it.

It was the third time they'd been told, and the third time they'd failed to respond.

Why? Did they think it was just a family matter? Or maybe the disappearance of one more Sikh girl wasn't enough to trouble them? Perhaps they just misfiled the information. Whichever way I look at it now, there's no good answer.

* * *

Oblivious to what my sister was planning, I returned home from our shopping trip more content than when I'd left. Sharing the terrible burden of the past few weeks had lifted a weight from my shoulders. It was short-sighted, I know that now. And it wouldn't bring Surjit back. But I was too terrified to think so far into the future. All I knew right then, in January 1999, was that I had to find a way to live in that horrible household for the sake of my children. And by talking to Inder, I felt I'd found renewed strength to carry on.

But for how long?

My new resolve was tested almost immediately. When I saw Sukhdave later, he had just returned from telling Hayes police about his last meeting with the woman called 'Kate'.

The imaginary woman.

He'd told them everything. About how Surjit had run away with this man called Raj, how it had all been part of an elaborate plan. And how she'd told him to give the children to her parents if he didn't want them. He played the crushed, cuckolded husband to a tee. But it was all a performance. How could he do it? What sort of a person can lie like that?

If I didn't know it already, I realised this was a man to be feared. But he was also a man to be hated – and not just for what he'd done to his wife.

It was one thing telling the police that Surjit had run off with Raj, but repeating it to his own children was unforgivable.

'Your mother doesn't love you,' he told a distraught Pav. She was only seven years old but she knew exactly what those words meant. Her brother was too young to appreciate the details but he would get the chance many times over the next few years. 'She's run off with another man. She doesn't want to live with you any more.'

Who would tell their own children such lies? The kids were already hurting so much that their mother was missing. But to blame them for her running away was despicable – and cowardly. He must have known how it would destroy them inside. But Sukhdave didn't care. The more they hated Surjit, the more they would love him. And Bachan Kaur.

Luckily I didn't see much of Sukhdave over the next few days. Discussions with his family tended to take place next door. Even visits from his sisters happened there. I was glad. He was such an outwardly friendly person, jolly, really approachable. Of him and Hardave, most people would warm to the older brother more naturally. But knowing he was living a lie made me think how fake his bonhomie had to be. I did my best to get on with my life normally for the sake of my children, and the less I saw of him the better.

The same went for my mother-in-law. From the moment she emotionally confessed all to me, and then switched so effortlessly into her usual in-control self, I realised what an actor she had to be. I dreaded seeing her. But unlike Sukhdave, she had round-the-clock access to my house to visit the prayer room. Whenever I knew it was time for a visit, I'd hide in my bedroom. If I timed it wrong or she came round unexpectedly, I had palpitations. It felt like the air was sucked out of the room the second she stepped into it. I'd struggle to breathe, struggle to look her in the eye, struggle to speak. If she picked up on it, she didn't say. Not then. Not at first.

* * *

Sukhdave's statement to the police about Raj was designed to stop them asking questions. Perhaps normally that would have worked. Unfortunately for my brother-in-law, he wasn't the only one pushing to find Surjit. Jagdeesh Singh became a constant presence at Hayes or Uxbridge – where the CID team were operating from – either in person or on the phone. His father, Mohinderpal Singh Dhillon, also pushed police in Coventry and even contacted his local MP. As a result, the missing person's enquiry continued long after Sukhdave had tried to shut it down.

The CID officers in charge of the case spoke to Jagdeesh Singh and Sukhdave many times. They also made regular visits to No. 88. And then on 7 January 1999 they decided to combine the two, and asked Jagdeesh and Sukhdave to meet at Willow Tree Lane.

I didn't enjoy calling next door, but I imagine it was far worse for Jagdeesh Singh to be in the house where his sister had been so unhappy. Arriving early and feeling suddenly stifled, he offered to take Ricky the Alsatian for a walk. When Jagdeesh returned twenty-five minutes later, the police were waiting. The detective updated them on the case –

much of his news inevitably based on Sukhdave's revelations about 'Raj' and 'Kate' – and in reply to one request was told that the Athwals' Indian family was not contactable by phone, despite many calls made from Willow Tree Lane to Bachan Kaur while she was on holiday staying with the family. The detective also asked for a sample of Surjit's hair. He left with one of her hairbrushes.

The following week a similar event took place. Once again Jagdeesh Singh walked Ricky rather than endure the company of his sister's family for longer than necessary. Even if he didn't suspect them of foul play, he knew too much about how they'd treated Surjit during the marriage to be comfortable in their presence. This time, the police announced that the next stage in a missing person's case was publicity. Did Sukhdave have a photograph he could give them for a poster? They also said they would pay for adverts to be run on the hour on London's Indian radio channel, Sunrise AM.

It was only when Jagdeesh Singh had left that Sukhdave contacted the police about their plan.

'Because my brother-in-law was here I didn't want to speak, but when you run the advertising campaign could you not use the name "Athwal"? It will bring shame on the family.'

Shame? That word again.

The police agreed.

On 20 January Sunrise radio broadcast a lengthy 'Have you seen …?' message every hour. They described Surjit's last reported sighting and the fact that she could have taken an internal flight from Delhi and might even be back in the UK now. Her description was given as five foot three, short hair, possibly tied in a bun. The only problem was, the name of the woman police were searching for was Surjit Kaur Dhillon.

This was a London-only radio transmission. And no one in London knew Surjit by that name.

What were the police thinking?
1–0 to Sukhdave.

* * *

The official investigation took another turn for the peculiar on 1 February when Surjit had been missing for six long weeks. In an attempt to push events forward, it was decided to interview both the Dhillon family and the Athwals again. Everyone was invited to Uxbridge police station – which was where the police dropped their bombshell.

They would all be spoken to together.

I wasn't aware of what the police knew or what Mohinderpal Singh and his family suspected, but I did know that from the moment Sukhdave opened his mouth, there was going to be no information that his in-laws would want to hear. And, I feared, certainly nothing that would help with Surjit's discovery. I couldn't understand why the police had chosen to proceed in this way, but perhaps they had their reasons, the best of motives behind the decision. Maybe it was felt that getting everyone together would lead to a breakthrough. But it wasn't to be.

According to Jagdeesh Singh, who attended with his father, it was a very bizarre meeting. The police sat the Dhillons on one side of the table and the Athwals on the other. The police sat in the middle. Then the two sides squabbled and argued over the details of what had happened – or could have happened – to Surjit.

When I heard about the meeting, I felt so sorry for Jagdeesh Singh and his family. For that day at least, they weren't just up against the Athwals. As far as they were concerned, they must have felt they were up against the police as well.

2–0 to Sukhdave.

* * *

The torment of living with the truth but being too intimidated to act on it was dragging me further down every day. I had to keep myself busy or rot. Any idle moment and my brain would suddenly be filled with Bachan Kaur's description of Surjit's last moments. I couldn't stop myself from picturing what she must have gone through: alone, frightened, fighting for her life. I knew, too, that I should *do* something – but the horror of what had happened to Surjit and the fear that it could happen to me left me paralysed. I couldn't see any future. I was too scared even to look. Instead, I buried myself in cooking, cleaning, taking care of the children; literally existing minute to minute to minute.

By contrast, Sukhdave and his mother always seemed to have one eye on the future. Everything they did, and had done to date, had been with all their tomorrows in mind. Misleading the missing person's investigation was just the latest example. As I would discover later, one of the reasons for Surjit's murder had been the fear of what would happen if she'd been allowed to live. Namely, if she'd succeeded in divorcing Sukhdave.

And taken the children away.

In the end, the fear of that longed-for baby boy disappearing from Bachan Kaur's life had been the final straw.

'He's the only grandson I've got. I'm not going to lose him.'

Even though she knew the boy probably wasn't Sukhdave's, she was prepared to kill to keep him in her family.

Suddenly I was very glad I'd only given her granddaughters.

She wouldn't kill to keep them ...

CHAPTER FOURTEEN

I'LL FIX THIS

Surjit had been missing less than two months. But already, I felt like I'd aged several years. Between jumping out of Bachan Kaur's way whenever she popped by and maintaining as much normality around my children as possible, I felt as run-down as I did scared. My relationship with Hardave was hardest of all. He was the man whom I'd seen stand up to the others in the meeting. But he was now the man who ensured that I toed the family line. Other than that one time, Sukhdave never spoke to me himself about Surjit. He got his message across via his brother.

Sometimes I wondered why Hardave went along with it. I knew that, like me, he was scared of his mother – but surely there were limits? Gradually I realised that Sukhdave was feeding my husband all kinds of lies about things Surjit had allegedly said about Hardave. I couldn't believe he would try to manipulate his own brother like that. But it worked. And that, I believe, is why my husband maintained his silence about what had gone on.

3–0 to Sukhdave.

* * *

I don't know how much of what happened after Surjit's murder was planned by Sukhdave and Bachan Kaur, or how much they improvised. When my brother-in-law rang the Dhillon family on 24 January, it was a little bit of both.

According to Sukhdave, Surjit's mother answered the phone. He asked if she'd heard from her daughter.

'No. I think she is dead.'

'Don't say that!'

Then Mohinderpal Singh took the receiver. He too was convinced that Surjit had not run away and that she'd been murdered during her trip. What's more, he was sure who was responsible – and he wasn't afraid to track them down on Indian soil.

'I have friends over there,' he said. 'I will send them to the village and get to the bottom of this.'

Sukhdave knew just how deep Mohinderpal Singh's connections in the Punjab extended. He was genuinely shaken by what he saw as a threat. What if the Athwals' contact decided to reveal everything they might know?

But to the police, Sukhdave bleated that he was scared for his children's safety. That he genuinely believed Mohinderpal Singh's friends could attack him in London while he was out with his kids.

As if he cared about them ...

In truth, I think Sukhdave was genuinely scared by the ferocity of his father-in-law's commitment to finding Surjit. But an Athwal is an Athwal – and Sukhdave soon turned that conversation to his advantage.

If the Dhillons thought that their daughter was dead, then surely Sukhdave should be able to claim on the £100,000 life assurance that he had taken out in his wife's name? He started calling Scottish Amicable and tried to push through the claim. Confident of it going through, he left his job as a coach driver. In the end, he was told 'no'.

As usual, I found out about this only after it had happened. When I did, I was surprised that Surjit even had a policy. My instincts proved correct. When I saw the date of the policy I was chilled to the bone. The policy had been taken out on 4 December 1998.

The very same day Surjit had left the UK.

Another clue, another admission that Sukhdave knew what was going to happen. Another sign of how calculating he was and how arrogant.

And yet more proof of how wary of him I needed to be.

***

If he couldn't profit from Surjit being dead, Sukhdave went for the next best thing. He filed for divorce.

I couldn't understand why he would be so bold. If you were genuinely upset that your wife was missing, would you act so swiftly to cut her out of your life? No. But if you'd already invented the lie of her telling him to move on with his life and forget her, then maybe you would. That was clearly the version of reality Sukhdave was clinging to.

And it explains why he had the audacity to cite as reason for divorce: 'Surjit is an unfit mother'!

He'd only been alone at No. 88 a month or so when I noticed a woman coming and going. She was a familiar face at my daughter's school, although I'd never spoken to her. I asked Hardave about her. After consultation with his brother, Hardave said, 'She's just a friend. Sukhdave is paying her to look after the house.'

That would have made sense coming from anyone else. But Sukhdave would never part with money if he could get something for free. This woman had three children and no longer any husband. I knew what she was hoping to get out of her relationship with Sukhdave. But he would not admit that she was anything more than a cleaner. Unfortunately for him, as soon as we'd exchanged nods and hellos outside

No. 88 once or twice, it made sense that his 'cleaner' and I would get into conversation at the school while we waited for our children to come out.

The problem for both of us was that Sukhdave knew this, too.

I don't know if he had actually followed one of us – although given how he'd tracked his wife, I wouldn't be surprised – whether he was spying on the school or just happened to be passing. But one day Sukhdave saw us talking in the playground and he was waiting for me when I returned home.

This time there was no going through his brother. No issuing orders or dictums that I had to follow via Hardave.

'I saw you talking to her.'

'Who?' I said.

'You know who. What were you saying?'

'We were just talking about the kids. General chit-chat.'

'So you do know who I'm talking about?'

I stared at the floor. Sukhdave wasn't a big man but he was intimidating. Anyone with blood on their hands would be.

'I don't believe you,' he continued.

'It's true.'

'I don't care. I don't want you to talk to her again, understand?'

'You can't stop me.'

He walked up close to me. I could smell the sweat from his body.

'I'm not asking,' he said.

I was thirteen years old again. I was with my grandfather being reprimanded for answering a boy's question. I hadn't done anything wrong then, but I was treated like I had. The same here. And I knew I'd do the same as I had done back then. It was my lot to be told who I could or couldn't talk to. As much as I hated it, I knew I would obey, like I had when I was a kid. That was how I had been raised.

I think Sukhdave realised that, too.

I had to wonder what he thought I would tell his girlfriend, though. Did he think I would divulge everything I knew about India? Or was he worried I'd tell her about Surjit being treated like a slave, about being kept as if they were living in the nineteenth century, and the beatings if she tried to step out of it?

He needn't have worried. I was too scared to talk to anyone.

Unfortunately, his girlfriend didn't know that. I managed to keep out of her way in the playground, but then I happened to be walking one day and I saw her in the distance. From the way she was standing outside a house, I guessed she must live there. If I'd known I would have taken an alternative route.

I tried to avoid her but she saw me and called out. With Sukhdave's threats still fresh in my mind, I wanted to march past. But I couldn't. She'd done nothing wrong. She didn't deserve to be on the end of any rudeness from me. I had to explain.

'I'm sorry, I can't talk to you,' I said.

'What?'

'I'm not allowed to talk to you.'

'Says who?'

'Sukhdave.'

'Sukh—? He wouldn't.' She was confused. 'That's ridiculous.'

'It's nothing personal from me,' I said. 'I want you to know that. It's him. He says I shouldn't speak to you.'

She stared at me, disbelief in her eyes. I could see her weighing everything up. What I was saying was ludicrous. But why would I invent it?

'Do you know what happened to Sukhdave's wife?' she asked eventually.

I didn't expect that. 'I can't talk about her either,' I said.

'Only, I've heard rumours.'

'You'll have to ask Sukhdave. I'm sorry.'

She nodded and we parted.

The next afternoon I saw her again in the playground. Instinctively I turned my back but a few moments later she appeared next to me. I scanned the road, scared. What if Sukhdave was spying on us again?

'I just wanted to tell you I broke up with Sukhdave last night.'

'Oh,' I said. 'I'm sorry.'

'Don't be,' she replied. 'I should be thanking you.'

So he had been seeing her ...

***

I never admitted to Sukhdave that I'd spoken to his girlfriend but he seemed to know anyway. The day after the break-up he found me in my kitchen. I tried to keep calm but once again he came too close.

Get out!

I backed away from him but soon found myself wedged against a cupboard unit. If I could have willed myself to faint, I would have done. Anything to escape. My legs were trembling. Sukhdave hadn't said a word but my heart felt like it was going to burst out of my body.

He just stood there, staring at me like he was trying to read a book in a foreign language. Then he took another step closer.

'I've warned you before,' he hissed viciously into my face. 'Stay out of my business, OK?'

I didn't move.

'I said, "*OK*?"'

I nodded.

'Good.'

Then he left.

Terrified as I was, I felt I'd got off lightly. But then I discovered that Sukhdave and Mum probably had more pressing things to worry about. Surjit's father and brother had been pressing hard for police action, both in the UK and India. Mohinderpal Singh's local MP had forwarded his case to the Home Secretary and also agreed to speak to his equivalent in Delhi.

Probably as a direct result, Bachan Kaur's Indian contact rang the Athwal house one day. He'd been approached by local police and told that, as he was the last person to have seen her, he would be arrested soon as a suspect in the abduction of Surjit Kaur Athwal.

'So what,' he demanded of Sukhdave, 'are you going to do about it?'

'Don't worry. I'll fix this.'

For a few days there was a flurry of heated conversations in our house. I could only imagine what was going on next door. As usual I tried to keep my head down. I knew all I needed to about this family. The less I heard, the less they could threaten me about talking.

Ignorance is bliss.

Sukhdave only worked part-time and had Tuesdays, Wednesdays and Thursdays free. He devoted that time to writing letters and engaging a solicitor. On 26 April 1999, a letter from the firm A Dua & Co. was sent to the investigating police station in the Punjab. I saw the letter later and couldn't believe its audacious demands.

It read, 'Under no circumstances are you to conduct an investigation into the disappearance of Surjit Kaur, unless you have sought permission in the High Commission of India and British Embassy of India in Delhi.'

It also said, 'There's been an announcement on the local radio in London on 15 April 1999, that Surjit Kaur is back in England.'

Finally, it said, the Indian police 'should endeavour to contact the High Commissioner of India before arresting and detaining or charging [Bachan Kaur's contact, whom we cannot name in this book due to legal reasons].'

As if that weren't enough pressure to pile on the former colonial force, another letter arrived later on headed paper which purported to come from the London Metropolitan Police. It said that Surjit had been having an affair, and gave the name of her ex-lover and his address. It also listed another man she was supposedly dating, a man known only as 'Raj'.

'She had a number of boyfriends,' the letter said.

The letter concluded with a paragraph to make anyone think:

> She is terrified of her father, Mr Mohinderpal Singh, because Surjit's lifestyle is very modern. She cut her hair short, smokes and drinks alcohol. Her father does not approve of her lifestyle. He is a very violent man.

The letter, apparently from the senior investigator on Surjit's case, listed a dozen reasons why Surjit would want to run away from her old life in Hayes. It stopped just short of telling the Indian investigators to end their investigation because she had obviously planned it all from the start. But that was the implication – and an implication from the Met police carries a lot of weight in India, even now.

It might have been a coincidence, but the Indian investigation ground to a halt shortly afterwards.

* * *

On 15 November 1999, Sukhdave and Surjit's decree absolute was issued in her absence at Brentford County Court. Five months later the community learned why Sukhdave had been in such a hurry to acquire it as once again he walked down the aisle (actually a corridor in

Uxbridge Registry Office) on 14 April 2000 with his new bride, Manjit Kaur. I was not invited.

Manjit and her son were from Singapore and, as usual, she and Sukhdave had been brought together by their family connections. After the briefest of courtships, Sukhdave had proposed and his new family had flown over to begin their lives afresh in Willow Tree Lane. A cynic might say that by marrying a woman from out of the country there would be no chance of her hearing rumours or slander from locals like me that could threaten the burgeoning relationship. But they all seemed happy.

Once again, I was forbidden by Sukhdave from approaching his partner. As she didn't have a child at Taran's school, this was easily accomplished. But I did get invited to family celebrations next door. When I went, I couldn't help noticing one thing: there were no pictures of Surjit anywhere in the house.

In fact, every trace of my sister-in-law had been removed or thrown away. Her trinkets, ornaments, photographs, even some of the bits of furniture she'd chosen. All of them consigned to history. Even the children were being told to call Manjit 'Mum'. It was as if Surjit had never existed. As if she'd been airbrushed from Sukhdave's memory.

And now he wanted everyone else to forget her, too.

But someone hadn't forgotten Surjit. A few months later I was taking a shower one morning when I heard a hammering on the bathroom door. Having hurriedly dried and pulled on a robe, I opened the door to be met by a woman in police uniform.

'Sarbjit Athwal?' she asked.

'Yes,' I said.

'I'm arresting you for conspiracy to murder Surjit Kaur Athwal.'

CHAPTER FIFTEEN

DON'T SAY ANYTHING

It was 6.30 in the morning of 22 May 2000 and my life was about to come to an end. At least that's how it felt. Why was I being arrested? Why was I being read my rights?

I haven't done anything, I haven't done anything, I haven't done anything …

Those four words kept repeating in my head as the two female police officers escorted me to my bedroom and waited outside while I got dressed. When I was ready I managed to throw some clothes on a hysterical Balveen. Taran just sat on my bed in shock.

'It's OK,' I said.

One glance at my face told her I didn't believe it.

Downstairs I could hear Hardave already under caution.

When I caught my breath back, I spluttered, 'Why have you come here? We don't know anything.'

I wished I hadn't.

'Anything about what, Sarbjit?' one of the PCs said.

'I don't talk to them next door.'

I couldn't read their faces. Then I heard the unmistakable voice of my mother-in-law downstairs. They must have found her in the prayer room. If the police already knew that her bedroom was at No. 88 then I could see how my statement about not talking to them would seem suspicious. I decided not to say anything else on the subject.

Someone else agreed.

As soon as Hardave saw me coming down the stairs, he started yelling out in Punjabi, 'Don't say anything!'

An officer shouted at him to be quiet. Then, turning to me, she demanded, 'What did he say?'

'Nothing.'

'Tell me what he said.'

'He said, "Don't say anything".'

'What did he mean by that?'

'I don't know.'

I honestly didn't know who I was scared of more.

The officers told me I would be taken to Kingston police station.

'What about my children?'

'Is there someone who can look after them?' the second PC asked.

I racked my brains.

'My parents are away. I'll call my sister.'

Inder still lived with our parents so wasn't too far away – and she definitely wouldn't have set off for work yet.

'Inder, can you do me a favour and look after the children today?'

'Sarb? Do you know what time it is?'

'I'm sorry, but can you look after them?'

'No, I can't. I really have to go to work. Is everything OK? Sorry.'

'I can't talk about it right now.'

That didn't go well …

I was so nervous with the policewoman standing over my shoulder but, more importantly, with Hardave and Bachan Kaur in the room that I was terrified of explaining to my sister why I needed the emergency childcare in case I said the wrong thing. No wonder she said no.

I was also so ashamed.

'Is there anyone else?' the PC asked.

'I can try a neighbour. But she doesn't speak English,' I warned, 'so I'll have to speak Punjabi.'

'Fine. Let's go.'

***

There was a bed, grey walls, grey floor. A steel grey door blocked the way to freedom. Only a little square panel at the top where the police could peer in gave any glimpse of the outside world. It was the most depressing place I'd ever seen.

I thought only criminals were put in cells.

Then I realised that they thought I was one. I didn't know what they'd heard, or why they were acting now. Maybe they knew about Sukhdave and Bachan Kaur's plot or maybe they thought we all came up with it together. All I really knew is that I couldn't afford to tell them anything. The threats against me were as real now as they had been more than a year earlier when Sukhdave had first made them. What's more, he had already proved he would not be restrained by UK law. I didn't know anything about the workings of British justice – but I knew a lot about my family. Even if the police believed that I didn't have anything to do with Surjit's murder, would they be able to protect me from Sukhdave, Bachan Kaur and their contacts if I dared to speak out?

I knew the answer and it made me feel sick.

Dark thought after dark thought filled my head while I waited for something to happen. What was the point of arresting me at the crack of dawn and then leaving me to stew for hours in that grey hell? Then I realised: the longer I stayed in my cell, the more time I would have to imagine the worst, and the more desperate I would be to get out of there – by telling the police what they wanted to hear.

Just as my imagination was convincing me I was going to hang, I heard footsteps echoing down the corridor outside. A few seconds later the panel on my door slid back. A policeman's face appeared, framed by the door.

'I've got a message from your husband, Mrs Athwal. He wants to know if you're all right.'

My husband?

'Is he here as well?' I asked, shocked to realise he was so close by.

'Yes, further down.'

'Oh. Tell him I'm fine.'

A few minutes later the officer returned.

'Mr Athwal would like you to know he loves you.'

For some reason that made me wild. If he loved me I wouldn't be in a prison cell right now. If he loved me he would have rescued me from his diabolical family. He would have protected me against their threats and gone to the police with what he knew.

I realised the policeman was waiting, probably expecting an answer.

'Tell him I know,' I said sourly. 'And tell him to stop talking to me.'

However dark my thoughts, they got worse when I was finally called out. On my way to the interview room I passed a window. On the other side I glimpsed Bachan Kaur. She saw me and smiled – and waved! How on earth could she be so calm at a time like this?

Then it occurred to me. She might be happy because she's just blamed someone else. *Maybe me.*

The interview room was as glum, in its own way, as the cell. There was a table with chairs either side. Apart from a notice about what to do in the event of fire, the walls were bare.

I was provided with a solicitor then introduced to the two officers across from me. I recognised them as the pair who'd brought me in, WPCs Brunt and Jeffries. They were efficient

and professional. They smiled but not with their eyes. They
told me to relax, reminded me why I'd been arrested, then
turned on a tape machine. I know I must have looked guilty.
I was shaking with nerves. Whatever I said now would be on
tape for ever. If I lied to the police, they would have the
evidence to play back. But if I told the truth and Sukhdave
heard the recording ...

Again and again the officers asked me about what I knew
and again and again I replied, 'I don't know. I don't know.'

'Where is Surjit?'

'I don't know.'

'Do you know what happened to her?'

'I don't know.'

'Who—?'

'I don't know, I don't know, I don't know!'

I could see them getting frustrated.

Am I going to prison?

Eventually they decided they'd heard enough, and after a
full day of psychological torment in Kingston, and two
sessions of interviews, I was finally allowed to go home.
Now the real torture would begin.

* * *

I reached No. 90 just before Hardave. I think he must have
told them the same as me. But it wasn't his testimony he
wanted to talk about.

'What did you tell them?' he asked, sweat pouring from
him. He looked as petrified as I felt. 'You'd better not have
said anything.'

'I didn't say a word,' I promised. Even though it was true,
I'd spent so long lying it felt like another one.

'If Sukhdave finds out you've said anything ...'

He didn't need to finish. We both knew exactly what
Sukhdave would do.

'Where is he, anyway?' I asked.

'He and Mum haven't been released yet. Seriously, Sarb, if you've—'

I was saved by the telephone. I recognised Inder's number and said, 'It's my sister.'

Hardave nodded and left the room.

'Are you all right?' my sister said. She sounded panicked.

'I'm OK.' What else could I say with Hardave in the next room?

'I read about you in the *Evening Standard*. Oh my God, Sarb, why didn't you say that's why you wanted me to have the kids this morning?'

I felt myself burning up with anxiety.

'Look, I can't talk.'

'Can I come round?'

'No! No.'

'Well, come out and meet me.'

'OK.'

'Do you know the Grapes pub on the Uxbridge Road? There's a car park and a parade of shops. I'll meet you there in half an hour.'

I was grateful to Inder for doing the planning. But I still had to get out of the house.

'Where are you going?' Hardave demanded.

'I need to collect the kids,' I lied. 'I won't be long.'

'OK.'

As I left the house I thought, *I'm lying to everyone now.* How had it come to this?

* * *

I'd never been so happy to see anyone. As I pulled into the car park I saw Inder's blue Escort and her pretty face behind the window. She started talking the second I climbed into the car, at nineteen to the dozen. When she'd calmed down, she apologised for not helping me out that morning. Then she revealed how she had found a copy of the *Standard* that afternoon and realised, to her horror, 'Sarbjit's been arrested for murder!'

No one had been named in the article – it just said that four people had been arrested in connection with the murder of Surjit Athwal – but Inder had worked it out. And if she could, so could anyone else who knew us.

So much for protecting our honour in the community! Even if Bachan Kaur got away with Surjit's murder, her name was in ruins for ever. It had to be.

Inder had jumped into her car and tried to find me. When I wasn't at Hayes police station she'd driven to Harrow. Eventually someone there told her to try Kingston. She'd arrived just after I'd been released. I couldn't believe she'd gone to so much effort. That was the kind of love my life had been lacking for the last eleven years. That was the cue my tears were waiting for.

Inder might have been seven years younger than me, but she looked more grown-up than I felt right then. And she wanted to know what I'd been through that day. She asked me about the police station and what I'd said. When I replied, 'Nothing,' Inder said, 'Are you sure that's wise?'

'I can't. If the Athwals find out I've said anything, I'll go the same way as Surjit.'

It was a spring evening but the temperature inside the car felt like winter.

'You don't know that,' my sister said finally.

'I do.'

And she knew I did.

* * *

Sukhdave and his mother were released later the same night. Instead of going into No. 88 they came straight to our front door. Straight to me.

However panicked that Hardave had been in case I'd spoken out of turn, his brother was worse.

'If you say anything, you will regret it,' he snarled. 'Remember who you're dealing with.'

Then, after a while of repeating that, he changed tack.

'And just remember, even if you get clever and think that we can't get to you if we're in prison – you'll be coming with us, too.'

I'd taken his rant in silence until then. But I couldn't let that go.

'What are you talking about? It's got nothing to do with me.'

Sukhdave smiled. Not a pleasant sight in the circumstances. 'You were there at the meeting,' he said coolly. 'You're as guilty as anyone in this room. If any of us go down for Surjit, I'll make sure you go down with us too.'

I ran to the prayer room as soon as I'd put the children to bed. I needed to remind myself that I was innocent. That Sukhdave was bluffing. That the police had nothing on me.

And then I remembered the way WPC Jeffries had looked at me during the interview. It was precisely the same way she'd looked at Bachan Kaur and Hardave. In her eyes I was guilty – and during hours of questioning I'd done and said exactly nothing to change her mind.

4–0 to Sukhdave.

* * *

At the same time as we were arrested, Bachan Kaur's contact in India was also being interviewed – despite Sukhdave's earlier letter to the Indian police. Two officers from the Met travelled there to grill him. But after weeks of trying to put a case together, the police on both sides of the world admitted defeat. Charges against everyone were dropped due, they said, to lack of evidence. The Indian police did, however, put out a warrant for the arrest of

Bachan Kaur and her elder son. If nothing else, they would not be visiting the country for a while unless their names had been cleared.

But to all intents and purposes, it was over. The police would not be asking any more questions. I would not have to lie under interrogation again. There was no chance I could slip up and pay the ultimate price. Maybe I could stop looking over my shoulder for the first time in years.

Next door, they weren't just preparing to relax. Anyone watching could have been forgiven for thinking that Bachan Kaur and Sukhdave had won the Lotto. They'd done it. They'd got away with it.

They'd literally got away with murder.

5–0 to Sukhdave.

But I knew the truth. And, as soon as my relief at not being charged calmed down, that truth hurt. Because my freedom – and No. 88's celebrations – had come at a huge cost. Surjit had been murdered, but that story would never come out now. As far as the public at large and, more importantly, the *community* were concerned, she had run off with a lover and abandoned her family. Bachan Kaur could hold her head up high at the *gurdwara* without anyone criticising her. If anything, she seemed more respected than ever, as people rushed to offer commiserations for being the victim of a wicked, selfish daughter-in-law. It was sickening to watch my mother-in-law bask in the attention, but again I maintained the silence.

I may not have colluded in her murder, but I was colluding in that.

It was awful, as well, to think of what Surjit's brother Jagdeesh Singh and her parents had to be going through. The rumours about Surjit didn't tally with the sister and daughter they loved. How do loved ones get over something like that? And then there were the children. They were growing up believing their mother ran away to escape them. Looking back, why didn't I speak out for their sakes, even just to comfort them in private?

But I knew why. Because if they knew, it would put them at risk, too. And on top of that, I was scared. So, so scared. I felt it all around me like a second skin: a living, breathing, cloying fear I would never be rid of.

***

Night after night I cried myself to sleep knowing it was all so wrong, that Surjit had been dishonoured in the worst possible way and it was all a lie. Knowing, to my shame: *She will never get the justice she deserves.*

I couldn't take it any more.

I had to get away. I had to get my children away from their grandmother, their uncle and their house. Willow Tree Lane sounded an idyllic address but it was hell on earth. I was scared even to look at my mother- and brother-in-law and I didn't like the person I was becoming living there. But where to go – and how would Hardave ever agree?

It turned out that Hardave was as keen as I was – but only when I told him our destination.

Canada.

England, Singapore and India weren't the only countries to host members of our extended family. My eldest sister, Karmjit, had moved to Vancouver with her Canadian husband a few years after my own wedding. The second she heard how desperate I was to put distance between me and Hayes, she came up with an offer I couldn't refuse.

'Come over here, right now. You can all stay with us for a couple of months until you put down some roots.'

Hardave immediately started looking for jobs in the security industry in Vancouver. He'd taken it up recently in London and preferred it to electronics. That only left one hurdle.

I expected Bachan Kaur to have a say and she did.

'You can't go. This is your home. I won't let you take my granddaughters.'

For once Hardave supported me, which had an unexpected result. My mother-in-law started to be nice.

'Look, if you stay, I will sign the whole of No. 90 over to you. It will be yours, not mine, not your brother's.'

Hardave wavered at that. He even asked my opinion.

'I don't care about that house,' I said. 'I didn't choose it and nothing in it is mine. Apart from our daughters, it holds only bad memories.'

If he took that as an insult he didn't let on. But he did acknowledge how serious I was and reported back to Mum that it wasn't enough to change our minds.

Being stood up to by her weaker son was clearly a shock for Bachan Kaur and it prompted another U-turn. This time it was one I could understand.

'OK, then you go with my blessing,' she said. 'You deserve your own life away from everything here.'

She wants me as far away from the community as possible, I realised. *Who can I possibly talk to over there?*

Even though she was suddenly being so supportive, Bachan Kaur still had one more sting in her tail.

'There's just one thing,' she said. 'Before you go we will have to sell No. 90.'

'What? That makes no sense.' Even though we were hoping to make a new life for ourselves abroad, the security of owning the house was something we didn't want to give up. What if it didn't work out? Where would we live if we had to come back?

Now her true colours came out.

'That's not my problem. But I own a third of that house and I don't want it standing empty.'

'So rent it out,' I said. 'You can have all the rent, we won't take a penny. Then if we come back in a year or so we can move back in, and if we don't come back you've got an investment for life.'

Nothing made more sense. So obviously she said, 'No.'

I couldn't understand her motive. There had to be one. There always was with her. If Hardave knew it, he didn't let on. I didn't push him for once because, I realised, we'd never been closer. My husband and I were planning to run away together. It was almost romantic. Except for the baggage we would be taking with us ...

It was with great reluctance that we oversaw the sale of No. 90. But, even once we'd paid Sukhdave £25,000 and Bachan Kaur £45,000 as their share of the profits, we still had a nice sum to fund our new life. If we were lucky, however, we wouldn't need to draw on much of it – because Hardave had been invited to a job interview.

We couldn't believe that a company would expect an applicant to travel thousands of miles on the off-chance of a position – what was wrong with a phone interview? – but we needed a date to leave and this was it.

I just prayed he got the job!

One of my sisters sorted discounted tickets via a friend at United Airlines and then, before we knew it, I was sitting between Taran and Balveen on a 747 heading across the Atlantic. They were scared by the take-off and so would I have been just twelve months earlier. But after the year I'd had, nothing would scare me now.

I was finally putting distance between my family and my mother-in-law.

We're safe now, I thought. *She can't reach us here.*

Famous last words ...

CHAPTER SIXTEEN

NOT HERE AS WELL

A lot of Sikh houses are the same all over the world. But Karmjit's home in Vancouver was different. It was very large, set on a lovely plot, and beautifully decorated. I was so proud of my sister for having done so well for herself. But that in itself was telling.

She'd done it for herself – whereas I had no choice.

However pious they'd been during our childhood, my parents had not enjoyed watching me flounder in my arranged marriage. It had worked for them, the same as it had worked for millions of others around the world. But although they never mentioned it, I think they felt guilty having pushed me, with the encouragement of their family, into marriage with an unsuitable match. As a result, I was the last one to endure an arranged union.

It was great to see Karm again, and she and her husband Satwant and their two sons made us all welcome. They had so much land that Taran and Balveen could run around without any danger of traffic.

'There are more bears round here than cars,' Karm joked.

I happily slipped into a routine of helping out around the house. I was so grateful for my sister's generosity it was the least I could do. And, unlike at home where my mother-in-law had dominated my domestic arrangements, I actually enjoyed doing it here. When something is your own choice, it's amazing how much more tolerable it is.

Unfortunately for all of us, however, Hardave's interview didn't work out.

'Don't worry,' Karmjit said. 'You'll find one. There are plenty of jobs here.'

In between Hardave firing off applications, me settling the children in and sharing the running of the house and us trying to sort out immigration papers, we took the opportunity to sightsee. The idea of enjoying myself, knowing the Dhillon family was being torn apart by doubts and fears, was hard to accept. But then, pleasures as simple as enjoying a meal or watching TV filled me with guilt every day. Each moment that I was alive and Surjit's murderers were still at large was hard to bear but whatever issues I had, I couldn't let it impact on my children's lives. There were enough victims already. I had to protect them.

As a result, there wasn't a national park, stately home or funfair in British Columbia that we didn't visit. The kids loved it – especially as our permit situation meant they weren't enrolled in a school – and even Hardave and I grew quite close. After everything, all I'd ever wanted was to be a good wife, good mum and good daughter, and I'd never felt so close to achieving it. The amazing weather while we were there could have played a role in that. Who can be unhappy in sunshine?

It was all so perfect. And yet our reasons for being there weren't. I wasn't in Canada fulfilling a lifelong dream. I was running away. Every morning as I prayed before Guru Nanak, the guilt over Surjit returned. I could travel all I wanted, but I couldn't outrun my conscience.

Or my fear.

There were days when I contemplated calling Scotland Yard and confessing all. But then I'd remember Bachan Kaur and Sukhdave. *They'd find me*, I thought. *They'd always find me*.

Unfortunately, as the months passed and Hardave never came close to winning a position, I realised our ambition of a new beginning was close to being punctured. Whatever my sister said, I had to think of her husband and her family. There was a limit on how long I could call on their generosity.

Luckily, Hardave had relatives of his own that we could call on.

After an amazing five months, I wept as we packed our cases and headed for the airport. The Canadian experiment hadn't worked. Maybe we'd have better luck in San Jose.

Daler Singh was a cousin of Bachan Kaur. He was another extremely dedicated practitioner of the Sikh faith. I'm not sure how much notice he had from Hardave that we were arriving, but he was friendly and welcoming.

'However I can help you,' he said, 'I will.'

Sadly, work opportunities in California were just as scarce as north of the border. Fortunately, as in Canada, there was plenty to divert our attention during the day. I really could see myself settling there. I wasn't the only one who could see a life for us in America, however. And she wasn't happy about it at all.

I had no idea in advance that Bachan Kaur was flying into San Francisco Airport until I heard Daler Singh mention he was driving to pick her up. Almost instantaneously I felt that familiar sensation of bile rising in my stomach.

Not here, not here as well.

Why couldn't she leave me alone? I'd enjoyed half a year of bliss with my family, away from her toxic interference. And now, in one throwaway comment from my genial host, I'd had my peace shattered.

Hardave was delighted to see his mum and I suppose I was pleased to see my daughters happy as well. It meant I'd done a good job of protecting them from the poison in my life. But I could barely bring myself to smile as she kissed me hello. I knew what was coming. It took about a week before I was proved right.

'If you have no job here, you'll have to come home,' she announced one night.

'We're in no rush,' I said. 'We have enough money to see us through this patch.'

In truth, I was more worried about our visas running out than our cash. Without a job, we would be asked to leave anyway. But I didn't want my mother-in-law to know that.

Later that night I felt as though I'd gone back in time. As soon as we were alone, Hardave said, 'Do you think we should call it quits and go home?'

Your mother's only been here five minutes and you're under her thumb already!

But I said, 'No, we can make this work.'

He didn't disagree, but everything Bachan Kaur touched turned sour and the rot had set in. Arguments began. As I saw my hopes of a fresh start slipping away, I saw an ulterior motive behind everything my husband said or did.

'You never wanted to stay here.'

'Yes, I did.'

'I bet you never even applied for those jobs!'

'Well, you could have tried to get one,' Hardave snapped back.

'That wasn't the plan and you know it.'

It was ugly.

Whatever Hardave said, the moment my mother-in-law returned to London I knew we wouldn't be far behind. By the time our flight took off, I was convinced he'd never intended to settle in North America and had only come because he was dazzled by the idea of a grand trip with thousands of pounds of house profit burning a hole in our –

his – pockets. Hours later, on the tarmac at Heathrow,
I was certain.

I bet he told his mum to come and get him.

***

The saddest sight in the world is a kicked puppy that keeps
going back to its master. We'd only been back in the country
half an hour and Hardave became once again that kicked
puppy. And there was no guessing needed as to the identity
of his brutal master – or mistress.

We'd been through passport control, collected our luggage
and were in the arrivals hall. Obviously it should have been
sorted before then. I thought it had been. But that is when
my husband made a call to No. 88. His mother answered.

'We're back,' he said. 'We'll be at Willow Tree Lane in
about forty minutes.'

'Why are you coming here?' Bachan Kaur replied.

'Why? To sleep. We have nowhere else to go.'

'I don't know if that's a good idea.'

I almost felt for Hardave watching him being crushed so
expertly. And I couldn't hear what was being said at the
other end. But my rising anger was drowning out any pity.
What the hell was going on?

'Mum, you told us to come back, and we have. You told
us to sell the house, and we did. Now we're at Heathrow
and we have nowhere to go.'

'Well, I'll have to ask Sukhdave. It's his house. Call me
back.'

For ten minutes we stood there, all our worldly chattels in
canvas bags around us. Then Hardave steeled himself and
called the familiar number. He got an equally familiar voice.

'He says no.'

'What do you mean he says no?'

'His wife lives here with her son. I'm here as well. Your
brother says there's no room.'

'Tell him we'll sleep on the sofa. Just give us the lounge for the night. He won't know we're there.'

'I'm sorry, Hardave. That won't work.'

'But Mum, we've got nowhere else to go!'

'That's your problem, dear.'

And that was the end of that. Three years after Hardave had stood up for Surjit at that fateful meeting, was Sukhdave finally having his revenge?

I don't know if it was an epiphany for Hardave or whether he'd been kicked by his mother so many times that he was used to it. All I know is she'd made us come home and now wouldn't lend us a bed. And he'd just taken it. My biggest problem with my spineless husband in the past had been the fact that he was a mummy's boy. Now even his mummy wasn't helping him. So where did that leave us?

We spent that night in a Premier Inn a cab-ride away in Slough. We spent the following night there as well, and another two after that. The kids thought it was fun. But living out of suitcases in a budget hotel with no cooking facilities wasn't my idea of entertainment. Because I blamed Hardave for the mess, he was the one who had to fix it.

He sort of did. We moved on the fifth day into the house of a friend – also in Slough. I could tell from the start that the friend would have preferred a cold to having us there, but he wanted to be a good friend to Hardave.

In contrast to the welcome in Canada, staying in Slough reminded us each day what an imposition we were. Eventually, after a long fortnight for all of us, Hardave's friend had to say, 'I'm sorry, I have family coming this weekend. You'll have to go.'

I wanted us to find our own place. But when Hardave spoke to his mother next – whatever she did, it seemed he would never cut her out – she revealed that Sukhdave was moving to Singapore. His wife had not been able to settle in England and so the whole family was emigrating.

'So now you can live at No. 88,' she said. 'With me.'

That was the last thing I wanted. Hardave couldn't have been happier.

* * *

From the minute I was back in Willow Tree Lane, it was as though I'd never been away. I was that timid, nineteen-year-old again, cowed into waiting on my ferocious mother-in-law hand and foot. Twelve years later she was just as unpleasant up close and equally threatening. She made no concession to the fact that what I knew about her could send her to prison for ever. She ordered me around, she bossed me and she manipulated me. Even visits to see my own parents and siblings became, once again, treats that she would dole out when she saw fit.

But however mean she was to me in person, it was nothing to the things she said behind my back. On one of my first trips to the *gurdwara* in Southall I was stopped by one of the community elders.

'You should be ashamed of yourself,' he said, barely looking me in the eye.

'I'm sorry? Are you talking to me?'

'You know I am. And you know what you did.'

He must have mistaken me for someone else.

'90 Willow Tree Lane was your house, was it not?' he said.

'Er, yes. It was.'

'Then you sold the house and you ran off with the money to Canada.'

'I don't know what it has got to do with you, but we sold the house, yes, and took our share – our third – of it to Canada.'

'It's bad enough that you embezzle from the family that gave you a husband and a roof over your head. But now you lie about it as well. You know you sold the house, kept all the money and made your poor mother-in-law homeless. Have you no thought for others? Have you no shame?'

'Who told you this rubbish?'

'Bachan Kaur herself. And accusing her of untruths is just adding to your sins.'

There was nothing I could say. The poison had sunk too deep, its grip on this stranger too strong. It didn't matter to him that it was Bachan Kaur's name on the deeds, that she made us sell No. 90 or that we, in fact, were the homeless ones.

I couldn't work it out. Why would she say such wicked things, especially against her own son? Then I realised: she needed to be seen as a victim. There were so many unpleasant stories flying around the *gurdwara* about her involvement with Surjit's disappearance, she needed to claim back some ground. And being a victim of family greed achieved exactly that purpose. How could poor, frail, homeless Bachan Kaur be guilty of masterminding anything unpleasant? What's more, if you really wanted to see people who would stop at nothing for a few pounds, think about the woman who duped her mother-in-law out of what was rightfully hers ...

I wasn't the only person Bachan Kaur had spread rumours about. After Surjit's brother, Jagdeesh Singh, moved to west London in 2001 he began attending the local *gurdwaras*. He was in the car park one day when, again, a community elder approached him. Whether it was the same one who had spread Bachan Kaur's vitriol to me, I don't know. As I suspect she'd done her best to brainwash as many worshippers as possible, it could have been anyone.

The stranger confirmed Jagdeesh Singh's identity and then said, 'There is no way that the Athwals would be capable of killing Surjit. They are not that kind of people. The police have closed the case and they have realised that the Athwals are innocent. You should stop pushing this case, creating the fuss that you have. Surjit was a woman who frequently went off and disappeared with men. She was unreliable as a person and untrustworthy. She has disappeared by her own will.'

Jagdeesh Singh was stunned. Partly because it was an assault on his family out of the blue from a complete stranger, but mainly because the account was so one-sided it could only have come from one source.

He had already started to pursue justice for Surjit through the media. If the police wouldn't do it, it was his duty, he felt, as a brother. Despite the warning, this encounter only made him more determined.

I had my own encounter with Jagdeesh Singh and his wife not long after that. Ironically it was in the same place: the car park at the Southall *gurdwara*. My instinct when I saw them, I'm sad to admit, was to run away in the hope that they didn't see me. There were so many eyes around us, all potential spies for my mother-in-law, that I shook at the idea of being spotted with this enemy of 'the family'. But I was too old for that. Jagdeesh Singh and I had both suffered a loss, him much more than me. As scared as I was of repercussions, I owed it to him not to run away.

'Hello, Sarbjit,' he said, as warmly as anyone has ever said it. 'How are you?'

I told him briefly about Canada and the children. Hard as I tried to be relaxed, I'm sure it showed that I wasn't at all. Jagdeesh Singh, always the perfect judge of a mood, decided to cut the encounter short for my benefit. But as we parted he said something that I will never, ever forget.

'You don't have to speak if you don't want to. I understand you're living in the same family and how hard it must be for you living under the same conditions that my sister had to.' He paused, selecting his words carefully. 'I don't want to put you in any danger. All I'll say to you now, Sarbjit, is when the time is right, don't hesitate to go forward.'

He was a generous man but a bad judge of character. I could not envisage a scenario where I would ever, ever go forward. And for that, I wasn't very proud of myself at all.

***

The venom on hand from other quarters at the *gurdwara* was unpleasant, but nothing like the brutality of life under the same roof as Bachan Kaur. I knew I'd go mad if we didn't escape her soon. Then finally our purchase of a new home in Crown Meadow, Colnbrook – just outside the M25 motorway, between Windsor and Heathrow – went through. For the first time in my life I was getting a home of my own. One that I'd paid for, that belonged to me – and that was out of the clutches of my mother-in-law.

Or so I thought. Hardave had other ideas.

'I want to put Mum's name on the deeds,' he announced.

'Why? She hasn't paid a penny.'

'Because she has no home with her name on.'

'No, absolutely not. Out of the question.'

Hardave sighed. 'I order you,' he demanded.

And that was, of course, the end of it.

***

Settling in, I should have been happy. Although Bachan Kaur's name was on the deeds, she didn't move in with us and it was too far from Hayes for her to pop by as she used to when we lived right next door, although she was still there more often than I liked. I had my own space, my own garden, my own chance to build a real home for my ten- and four-year-old girls, and even a little area I converted to a prayer room. Yet, in my heart, I knew I was just trying to make the best of a bad lot. I thought back to my idyllic time in Vancouver and my sister's life of luxury. She'd chosen that life for herself. It wasn't arranged or forced upon her. She had something I'd never had: freedom.

I thought of how Inder had enjoyed her time as a single girl at university. When I'd visited her on campus at Leicester, I couldn't believe she'd come from the same family as me. I hadn't been allowed to talk to a thirteen-year-old boy in a school playground. She had been living in a shared house where girls had boyfriends staying with them.

Looking back, maybe it was that independence at university that helped Inder become a pillar of strength that I would so often lean on. I'm lucky to have her as a sister.

I had always determined to make the best of my life. But these moments of realisation – of what I'd missed out on, of what could have been – were so powerful I even found myself not wanting to see my parents. When they called and suggested meeting up at weekends I realised I wasn't that unhappy if Bachan Kaur had made a prior claim on my time. I guess it was resentment on some level, and I assumed the feeling would pass. Unfortunately for Dad, he phoned one day before it had.

'You never talk to us, Sarbjit. Is something wrong?'

'No, Dad,' I lied. 'I'm talking to you now, aren't I?'

'Yes, but it's been weeks since you called us.'

The touch paper was lit …

'That's not true.'

'And if we ask to see you, you say you're busy with your husband's family.'

Bang!

'What do you expect?' I exploded. 'You made me get married. You stuck me with this family! It's all your fault!'

I had never shouted at my father in my entire life. He didn't expect it either, but then he had no idea of the stress and the fear I had been living under for three years. Despite my attempts to rebuild some sort of life and give my children the home they deserved, there hadn't been a day that Surjit wasn't in my thoughts. She was there when I woke up, when I prayed and when I went to bed. Just looking at Taran often reminded me of her cousin Pav, and the happy life denied that poor girl and her brother. And then there were the nightmares as well …

No, Surjit was with me all the time. And where she was, fear of her murderers was never far behind.

None of which my father knew. Which is why I had erupted.

As a result, we didn't speak again for six months. And I felt more alone than ever.

* * *

Despite moving house, the shadow of my mother-in-law never went away. More often than not, she was there in person as well. Even worse, as we entered 2002, so was her elder son. Sukhdave was back.

His marriage to Manjit Kaur had fizzled out once they'd reached Singapore and he realised he wasn't the dominant one in the relationship. As much as he attempted to assert himself, Manjit was the one with the family all around them. Yes, Sukhdave had relatives in the island city-state, but not as many. And none so close.

Now he felt a little of what it was like for Surjit and me moving into Willow Tree Lane. And he didn't like it one bit.

Back in England – alone – he was soon back to his old self. I hadn't had a conversation about Surjit with anyone apart from God for more than a year, but that didn't stop Sukhdave getting my husband to remind me of the consequences of talking out of turn.

'Why do you want to say that?' I cried at him. 'His threats ruined my life at Willow Tree Lane and now you want me to be scared in this house as well? Well, guess what – I am. Satisfied?'

I already hated my brother-in-law, but seeing how quickly my own husband would dance to Sukhdave's tune turned my stomach.

How I wished I wasn't carrying his baby.

I'd fallen pregnant during one of our happier periods together. But as summer 2002 arrived I was seriously struggling to look at my husband without scowling. He was spineless next to his family. It wasn't just his mum and brother he did the bidding of, either. His sisters only had to comment on my clothes or something I'd said and he would come down on me like a ton of bricks. Someone must have told him to assert himself. His idea of assertion was doing whatever they suggested.

I don't know if it was the reappearance in my life of Sukhdave and his threats, or if it was the chemicals mixing in my brain as a result of six months of pregnancy – or a combination of both – but I woke up one July morning and reached crisis point. I fed Hardave and the girls and packed them off to work and school. Then I struggled back upstairs and filled a case with whatever I thought I could squeeze into. I made my way back down and sat about four stairs from the bottom, case by my side. I picked up my mobile and dialled a freephone number. Four years earlier I'd called a similar helpline and nothing had happened. My plea to Crimestoppers had gone ignored.

As the tears flowed down my cheeks, I prayed the Samaritans would do more than listen.

My life depended on it.

CHAPTER SEVENTEEN

MY NAME'S CLIVE

'I need help. I'm six months pregnant. I'm living in an abusive family. And I have to get away.'

The lady on the Samaritans switchboard could not have been nicer. I didn't need to give her my name if I didn't want to, but to help her help me she had to ask where I was.

'OK, we have nothing available in your area,' she said. 'Give me a moment, let me see what I can do.'

After a few minutes her bright voice came back on the line. She'd found a place with emergency accommodation about half an hour from Slough.

'It's important that you get out now,' she said. 'Do you have a car?'

'Yes, but my husband's taken it today.'

'Can someone drive you?'

'No. I'll have to come by bus.'

'OK, the main thing is to leave now before your husband gets in.'

'I've got other kids at school.'

'You can't wait for them. It's one step at a time. Right now you just need to get out of the house.'

'Leave my kids?'

How could I abandon my kids? But, I realised, they weren't the ones being threatened by Sukhdave. Hardave would never let his brother harm a hair on their heads. Not the two at school, anyway. But the one in my tummy needed me to be safe.

I saw what the counsellor meant. It was a psychological move as much as a physical one. I just had to get out and close the door behind me. I needed to free myself of the abusive environment and work from there.

'OK,' I said. 'I'll do it.'

I had the case in my hand and the front door within reach. Then conscience got the better of me. Practicalities overwhelmed me. What was I thinking? I couldn't leave without telling *someone*.

I steeled myself and rang my parents' house. The last six months of frostiness thawed in an instant as soon as I heard my mother's voice.

'I can't take this any more, Mum. I called the Samaritans. I'm going to leave.'

I heard the concern in her voice.

'Where are you going to go? You're pregnant.'

'They've found me emergency accommodation. I'm going to go and see where it leads.'

'Don't do it. Come over here instead. You'll be safe with us. Shall we send Inder to pick you up?'

I knew she'd say that. That's why I should never have rung. That's why the Samaritans lady told me to get out there and then – so I couldn't be persuaded by anyone to stay.

'No, Mum, if I come there that's the first place they'll look. You don't know what this family's like.'

'Then tell me.'

'I can't.'

'OK, Sarbjit, as long as you know what you're doing. Call us as soon as you can.'

I'd been emotional before that call. Now I could barely see through the tears. Mum hadn't thought about the community or the family name, just me. Maybe I should go to her instead?

No, there was a plan, and I had to stick to it. I had to keep going. I couldn't let anything stop me. But, as I reached the door, the phone began to ring.

Ignore it, I told myself. *Keep walking.*

It seemed to be getting louder and louder. What if it was important? What if it was the school calling about the girls?

Ignore it and I'll be free ...

But I answered. It was my father.

'Don't go,' he pleaded. 'You can't leave that house.'

'Dad, I have to. You don't know what they do to me. You don't know what's happening. I can't live like this.'

'Sarbjit, I love you, but if you leave that house you'll put a lot of shame on that family and they will never forgive you. In fact, they'll pile it back on you. Do you want Bachan Kaur to say, "This daughter-in-law has run away with another man just like my other one did"?'

I didn't care. But my father wasn't finished.

'Think about it, look at what they've done to Surjit's name. And she's missing, or worse. Imagine people talking like that about you – and you have to share the same temple!'

'But, Dad—'

'Think of your honour, Sarbjit. Think of your family's honour. Don't go anywhere, we'll come and support you.'

Shame, honour, shame, honour. Those words were everywhere I went. They governed everything I did. But wherever I heard them, at the end of the day, I was the one who always suffered.

Nevertheless, a lifetime's culture is hard to walk away from.

'OK, Dad,' I relented. 'You win. I'll stay.'

**

My first son, Manvinder Singh Athwal, was born on 4 October 2002. The whole family descended as usual to pay their respects, led by a jubilant Bachan Kaur. To the outside world she had never been anything but loving to her first grandson, but he would always, in her opinion, be tainted in the eyes of the community by his mother's behaviour. Now she had the chance to start again.

Despite just giving birth, as usual I was expected to cater for their arrival. I really thought that being away from my mother-in-law 24/7 would have changed her hold on me. But with her daughters and sons and grandchildren arriving, I knew I had no choice. If I didn't prepare for her guests, no one else would.

Sukhdave very rarely came to our house, which suited me fine. The less I saw of him the better. When he finally decided to end four years of benefits by applying for a minibus licence in 2003, I was aware, but not interested. I didn't even care when he found a new girlfriend – twelve years his junior – called Rishi. If he didn't care what the community thought about yet another new partner, I certainly didn't. Maybe he assumed his behaviour would be forgiven after what Surjit had put him through? Either way, when I recognised Rishi as another parent from school I could foresee problems.

According to Hardave, Rishi started attending family dinners, religious ceremonies, traditional events – none of which I was ever invited to. Sukhdave knew that one word from me could ruin everything. After all, as far as he was concerned, I'd done it before …

On the other hand, I had my own consequences to face if I stepped out of line, and Hardave was ordered to pass on a reminder of just how I'd be treated if I whispered into the wrong ear. I know my husband took no pleasure from passing on his elder brother's thinly veiled threats, but he still did it. That said, I would rather have heard from anyone than Sukhdave himself.

Unfortunately, our paths were destined to cross yet again. As with his first partner after Surjit, Sukhdave caught a glimpse of me making small-talk with Rishi outside the school premises and couldn't get over fast enough to lead her away. The following day, Crown Meadow received an early morning visitor. For a few minutes Bachan Kaur sat silently in a chair. Eventually Hardave asked, 'What's wrong, Mum?'

'Nothing,' she said. Then, as if suddenly inspired, she turned to me. 'Sarbjit, what happened yesterday?'

'Yesterday?' Nothing happened to me any day. 'I can't think of anything. Why?'

'You know why,' Bachan Kaur said. 'What did you say to Rishi yesterday?' *Not this again . . .*

'Rishi? Oh, her.'

'Well? What did you say?'

'Seriously? I just said hello and asked how her family was. That was it.'

Mum had heard enough. 'Right,' she said, puffing herself up, 'you are not to talk to her any more, understood? Stay away from her.'

'Oh, for goodness' sake, what do you think I'm going to say to her? Do you think I'm going to try to split them up by mentioning Surjit? Whether they get married or not has nothing to do with me.'

My voice was getting louder and for once I didn't care. Hardave did, though.

'Keep it down,' he lectured. 'Don't you dare speak to Mum like that.'

I hated Bachan Kaur for what she'd done to Surjit and more. But Hardave never ceased to disappoint me in new ways. Why on earth was he siding against his wife when he didn't even know half the story?

Coward.

Enraged by the interference from two of my closest family members, when I saw Sukhdave hovering outside the school in his work minibus the next afternoon, I marched straight over. I slid the side door open and said, 'I hear you've got a problem with me speaking to Rishi?'

'I've got no problem. I just don't want you to talk to her.'

'But why?'

'She's my wife. I will choose who she speaks to.'

'You're not even married.'

That wasn't the right thing to say. The sound of the noisy Toyota engine being over-revved made me stand back. Sukhdave was staring at me like he hated me.

Well, let him hate, I thought. *The feeling's mutual.*

As I walked back towards the school I was aware of the minibus's engine being gunned even louder. Then there was a squeal of wheelspin as it took off at speed. I turned round to see what Sukhdave was up to. I was lucky I did.

The van was coming straight at me.

I dived for cover and felt the slam of tarmac on my hands and knees as I fell between two parked cars. Barely a second later, I glimpsed the van swerve past the spot where I had been standing. As I pulled myself up I realised I was shaking, desperately trying not to vomit in shock.

He tried to hit me …

I was still leaning against another car when the school caretaker came dashing over.

'Did he try to run you over?'

I nodded, still out of breath.

'Did you get a look at his face?'

'Yes. It was my brother-in-law. Sukhdave Athwal.'

'Oh, him.' The caretaker said he'd heard reports of Sukhdave being rude, bullying and obnoxious with other parents and members of staff. But he'd never tried to mow anyone down before.

'If you want to press charges,' he said, 'I saw it all.'

I thanked him. I wouldn't be doing that. I knew it was a warning. But I also knew what it was a warning for.

If I hadn't been convinced already, this showed Sukhdave wouldn't hesitate to kill me the same way he killed his wife. Except this time he probably wouldn't even wait to send me to India.

There was something else I didn't need to have repeated, either. When Hardave came home that night he was furious.

'Mum told you to stay away,' he said.

'Your brother is the one who tried to run me over and you're telling me off?'

'Why do you always want to keep making problems? Just forget about it, OK?'

Yet again, taking anyone else's side other than mine. He hadn't even asked for my version of events. And he certainly hadn't checked to see if I was all right.

Why didn't I run when I had the chance?

* * *

While I was cowering from the threats in Colnbrook, further west in Slough, where he had now moved, Jagdeesh Singh was proving harder for the Athwals to shake off. Not only had he ignored the barely disguised warning from the stranger in the *gurdwara* car park, he'd actually stepped up his campaign to achieve justice for his sister. Whether he truly believed Bachan Kaur and Sukhdave had murdered Surjit I couldn't at that time say. But in June 2002 he told the *Coventry Evening Telegraph*, 'We accept that Surjit is dead and it is very difficult for us.' He knew she had never been found, alive or dead. He knew that the truth was out there. And he knew he would not rest until he found it.

He wasn't alone. Coventry North East MP Bob Ainsworth had been an early supporter and, with John McDonnell (MP for Hayes and Harlington), he'd put pressure on the British

Foreign Office to pursue an investigation in India. In the meantime, Jagdeesh Singh and his wife Paramjeet had presented a petition containing thousands of signatures to No. 10 Downing Street and Paramjeet had also flown to the Punjab to conduct her own investigation and distribute leaflets advertising their latest coup – a reward of £20,000 for information leading to the arrest of Surjit's killer.

In November 2003 Jagdeesh Singh's campaigning paid off when he finally achieved his goal of an audience with Jack Straw, the Foreign Secretary. Like everything else Jagdeesh achieved, it had been hard won by first securing the intervention of Baroness Symonds and representatives of the Slough Race Equality Council and Southall Black Sisters.

Just in case Mr Straw thought that Surjit's disappearance was too low-profile for his office to get involved, Jagdeesh Singh made a point of pushing his sister's story on to the desks of every major media outlet. He also tinged the debate with a hint of controversy, telling journalists, 'It was after five years of campaigning that the British Foreign Secretary, Jack Straw, agreed to push our case. The British Government never applied the kind of pressure it applied to solve other cases involving missing white people.'

Lucie Blackman, he said, was a case in point. The twenty-one-year-old vanished in Tokyo in July 2000.

'When Lucie Blackman disappeared in Japan, the British Prime Minister publicly criticised the Japanese for their failure to trace her. There was, however, no such urgency in our case. As if Surjit was less British than Lucie. She was serving Her Majesty's Customs in London.'

As well as appearing on numerous radio shows throughout the early 2000s and in many more local and national newspapers, Jagdeesh Singh also worked with BBC–TV's *Newsnight* programme to produce a report on what could have happened to Surjit. In 2003 he contributed to the documentary *Britain, My Britain*, which told her whole tragic story – as Jagdeesh Singh believed it could have happened.

I was only aware of some of this. Much of it I only heard about when my daughters caught something on TV or, more usually, Hardave reported his brother's and mother's fury at the latest piece of exposure. Sometimes I saw their anger first-hand.

'Why doesn't he just give up?' Sukhdave railed one day. 'He's bringing shame on all of us.'

As usual he spoke as though I weren't there. I wasn't even enough of a threat for him to bite his tongue in front of me.

'Don't worry, my son. He's just an irritation. As long as we all keep quiet there's nothing he can do.'

And that was the sorry truth of the matter. I knew that Jagdeesh Singh could get the Queen involved if he wanted, but still the killers of Surjit Athwal would never be brought to justice without cooperation from someone on the inside.

I just wish I had the strength for it to be me.

* * *

While I wasn't proud of my mental strength – or lack thereof – it was my physical strength that let me down in 2004.

It was a Saturday morning. The children were playing or watching TV. I had none of the objections to kids' programming that my parents had. The last thing I was going to do was deny them a childhood. Hardave had just popped out and I was enjoying a rare moment to myself. Out of nowhere I felt a massive lurch in my stomach, like it had suddenly launched into spin cycle. Something was wrong. Very wrong.

I started running.

It took me under a minute to get upstairs to the toilet and I just made it in time. As I fell against the sink it felt like a volcano erupting deep inside my stomach and I expelled a violent spray of crimson against the white enamel. Wave after wave came out in a powerful torrent that seemed to go on for ever.

I can't breathe.

I was choking on my own blood.

What's happening?

Outside of childbirth I'd never known such pain or confusion at my own body. Still coughing red phlegm down my front, I fell back on to the toilet. But it wasn't over and the next few seconds were the most terrifying of my life as blood poured out of me, from everywhere, all at the same time. It was as though everything in my body was determined to get out by any means possible.

I honestly felt I was going to die.

When the convulsions eventually stopped, I realised my eyes were closed. The sight that greeted me when I opened them nearly triggered another wave. But there was nothing left. I felt empty, deflated. Drained.

I tried to stand up and fell flat on the floor. I felt my eyes heavy again, too heavy to keep open.

Fight it. Stay awake. Get help.

The fear as my body began the process of shutting down was immense. Even if I had the energy to shout, the sound of the TV blasting from downstairs told me it would be a waste of time. But I had to do something. I managed to drag myself up alongside the bath, pulled down on the door handle then fell outside into the hall. Waiting for me was a desperate-looking Taran.

'Shall I call Dad?' she asked, eyes wide with fear.

'Yes.' My voice was tiny, my tongue still clogged by blood and sick. I coughed and once again felt my eyelids draw together.

I must have been in and out of consciousness half a dozen times by the time Hardave came bolting up the stairs.

'My God, what's wrong with you?' he said, panic cutting through his voice, as he tried to lift me on to a stool in the hallway. But my limbs weren't working. I couldn't even support my own head. On top of that, my vision was fading. I just wanted to sleep . . .

First there was something I had to say.

'A-a-ambulance.'

'Ambulance? Right.'

He darted downstairs and I heard the phone. But something was wrong. He wasn't talking to the emergency services. He was speaking to his mother!

Why has he called her? What good is she going to be?

I was passing in and out of consciousness. The next thing I remember is Hardave standing over me saying, 'Mum told me to dial 999. The ambulance will be here in a minute.'

I managed to ask him to call my sister Inder – not my parents; they would worry – and then that was it. Nothing. Everything went dark. I didn't see the paramedics arrive or hear them talk to me. How they transported me to the hospital and what they did to me I had no idea.

The next thing I remember was being surrounded by dozens of people in white lab coats rushing to and fro and talking, talking. Above the deafening noise one voice stood out.

'She needs blood, she needs blood!' it kept repeating again and again and . . .

And then I passed out again. When I woke up it was the following day. The first thing I noticed was the white hospital gown I was wearing. It took a few moments of coming around to spot the drip plugged into my arm.

What happened to me?

When they realised I was awake, one of the doctors came over and sat beside me. He gave me such a warm smile that I burst out crying. Instinctively he grabbed my hand and squeezed.

'It's OK,' he said, 'you're safe.'

I thought, *I'm not*. But he was talking medically. He didn't know about the rest of the mess that was my life. About the fear and the bullying and the threats and the hatred and the lies.

'You're lucky to be alive,' the doctor continued, and went on to explain that I'd suffered a ruptured stomach ulcer.

A common cause of ulcers, he said, was stress. He smiled kindly again. 'Is there anything you're worrying about that might have triggered this?'

He had such a comforting manner that I came close to telling him. But seriously, what could a doctor do?

'No,' I said. 'I can't think of anything.'

He seemed to accept that and went on to reveal that I had lost six pints of blood, most of it at home. 'Any more,' he said gravely, 'and you would have died.'

Left to my own thoughts later, part of me wished I had.

* * *

My husband arrived that afternoon. Obviously he did not come alone. Bachan Kaur rushed over to give me a kiss. It was only the recollection that she'd given consent for the ambulance – and indirectly saved my life – that stopped me turning away.

After Hardave asked if I was OK, his mother gave him a look that, I realised, was his cue to launch into her own agenda. I was amazed that she had one in a hospital, but she never did anything without a reason.

'Your dad's been causing trouble,' Hardave said. 'He's been threatening my mum.'

'Really?' It sounded incredibly unlikely. 'What's happened?'

'He rang mum up and said, "If anything happens to my daughter you are going to be responsible." Isn't that rude?'

'Hardave, I don't want to know!'

'But isn't that rude?' he went on. 'Why is he behaving like that? You should tell him to stop.'

I said, 'Look, I nearly died yesterday. I only just made it, no thanks to you.' I heard my voice getting louder. 'I'm on a drip and the last thing I want to do is talk to you about this!'

'OK, OK,' Hardave hissed, nervously looking around. 'We'll discuss it when you come home.'

'No,' I said. 'I don't want to.'

'You don't want to discuss it?'

'No, I don't want to come home.'

I saw the panic on Hardave's face and the looks he exchanged with his mother. When he began to answer, she put a hand out and said, 'Let Sarbjit rest.'

After they left, I couldn't believe I'd been so forward. Maybe it was the euphoria of just defeating death. Maybe it was the comfort of being in a place of good. Or maybe it was the medicine in my blood. Whatever the reason, I'd just talked myself out of a home.

***

My parents came later. Unlike with Bachan Kaur, I had to prise their side of the argument out of them. It wasn't true that I didn't want to hear the story – I just didn't want to hear my mother-in-law's distorted version.

After the ambulance had taken me away, Hardave had indeed called my sister at my parents' house and left a message. As soon as my dad picked it up, he'd rung No. 88 and got hold of my mother-in-law.

'Hello, Bachan Kaur,' he'd said. 'Can you tell me where my daughter is?'

It was a simple, polite and straightforward question – to which she replied, 'I don't know. She's your daughter. You should know where she is, not me.'

That's when Dad had snapped, 'If anything happens to her …'

If I'd had any doubts about telling Hardave I wouldn't be coming home with him, this removed them.

'Can I stay with you, Mum?' I asked.

As much as my parents disliked some of the things I said Bachan Kaur got up to, they both knew that for a daughter-in-law to walk out on her marriage would bring down a whole world of shame on Bachan Kaur. Since the rice-giving ceremony on my wedding day when I had become more Athwal than Bath, that mattered to them. The community had seen them give me away. As much as it hurt, that's just the way it was. I, by contrast, couldn't agree. Not any more.

'I know how it will look,' I said. 'And I don't care.'

I could have added, 'You stopped me walking out once – and I'm not going to let you do it again.'

Predictably, Dad was against the idea. That wasn't how he'd been raised or how he'd raised me. But then he didn't know the half of it.

If he carries on like this, I'll have to tell him.

Eventually, against their better judgement, they caved in. When I was discharged from the hospital it was Dad's car that I got into and his house I arrived at.

I felt safe.

***

For all my bravado from the hospital bed, the hardest decision I ever made was leaving Crown Meadow. It was only when my medication had worn off that I realised running away didn't just mean saying goodbye to Hardave and his abusive family – it meant not waking up in the same house as my precious children.

The memory of Taran's troubled face as she watched, open-mouthed, while I crawled out of the bathroom was etched on my brain. How could I abandon her? For all I knew, Bachan Kaur had told them I'd died.

I finished my recuperation at my parents' house. As soon as I was strong enough I rang Hardave to arrange a time to visit. He agreed. I suppose he thought that he could woo me back once I was inside.

That didn't happen, although it didn't prevent him trying the next time and the time after that. I only had eyes for my children, and he knew it. Which is why he refused to let me take them with me.

As my time in Hounslow stretched from weeks to months, my parents could tell that the separation from my children was tearing me apart. Yes, I loved being with my parents, not being treated like a slave, not being in fear of my life in case I said the wrong thing, and seeing my lovely sisters and brother so much. But was I really such a bad mother that I would give up living with my own children? What reason could I possibly have for pursuing this road?

I just need to get on my feet and I can demand he hands them over.

I couldn't drag them out of school with nowhere permanent to live. So, within the space of three months, I made – after electing to keep Sukhdave's murderous secret – the second hardest decision of my life.

I told my parents everything.

Dad sat there in silence for ages. Questions kept half-forming in his mouth, then he changed his mind. Eventually he said, 'Why didn't you tell us, Sarbjit?'

'Because they said they'd kill me.'

'How long have they been threatening you?'

'Since day one.'

Mum, like me, was in tears. Dad was having trouble processing what they were hearing. 'All these years you've been suffering alone,' he said. 'Anything could have happened to you. Bachan Kaur could have done the same thing to you.'

I nodded. That much had been made perfectly clear over the years.

'Have you told the authorities?' Dad asked.

'No.'

'Well, you need to tell the police.'

'I can't. I'm too scared.'

'If you don't, I will.'

'Dad, I know you're just trying to do the right thing and protect your daughter, but I swear, if you tell anyone, I won't speak to you again.'

I was so scared, I meant it. Dad could see that, too.

'OK,' he agreed, 'as long as you're safe. That's all that matters.'

'I'll be safe as long as you keep your word.'

* * *

It was such a relief to get everything off my chest. Over the next few weeks, however, I was put under daily pressure to tell the police. Then, after I'd been there about six months, a new pressure started coming from a different source.

Bachan Kaur had been ringing on and off for a while. But the longer I stayed away the more desperate she sounded – according to Dad, because I refused to speak to her.

'How would you like this shame on your family, Sewa Singh? You need to send your daughter back to me. The Athwal name in the community is being ruined and it's all your daughter's fault.'

How my dad bit his tongue during this exchange I do not know. He knew so much more than Bachan Kaur thought he did and he was dying to mention it. But he didn't. And when he reported what she'd said I actually began to consider it. After all, not only was I bringing shame on my mother-in-law, it would also reflect badly on my own parents – and my children.

My children.

'I can't leave them any longer,' I said.

Dad was beside himself. 'You can't go back to that house,' he begged. It was a complete reversal of his attitude of six months before.

I listened to his arguments and I wished I could obey him as I had all my life. Ironically, it was partly because of him and Mum that I found the strength not to. Just as confiding in my sister Inder in 1999 had lifted some of the burden from my shoulders, confessing my secret to Mum and Dad injected me with a new confidence.

I wasn't alone any more.

But my children were, and so I went back to Taran, Balveen and Manvinder. To the most important things in my life.

Within a few months, however, I would need to add another name to that list.

***

By returning to my marital home I was expected, as per our culture, to resume all marital duties. I did so reluctantly but the effect was the same, and as we entered 2005 I realised I was expecting my fourth child. My second son, Karaminder, was born on a beautiful summer's day, on 31 August.

But Karaminder wasn't the only new arrival to change my life that year. During the celebrations for my son, I saw and heard a lot more from my family than usual. So when my dad rang one afternoon and invited me to their house, I didn't give it a second thought.

I arrived the following day and went straight through to the lounge. I was surprised to see a smartly dressed man sitting on one of the two sofas. I couldn't remember the last time I'd seen a white face there. What possible reason could my parents have for stepping outside their culture like this? Their poor English usually stopped them even trying.

Then the man stood up and introduced himself.

'Hello, Sarbjit. My name's Clive – and I'm here to help you.'

CHAPTER EIGHTEEN

DON'T GO TO SLEEP

Detective Chief Inspector Clive Driscoll is today one of the Metropolitan Police Service's most distinguished members, having led the team that successfully brought prosecutions against two men in 2012 for the murder of south London schoolboy Stephen Lawrence. Such is his high profile and distinguished track record that in 2012 he was invited to give evidence to the Leveson Inquiry into the Culture, Practices and Ethics of the Press. Back in 2005, however, he was Senior Investigating Officer on the Met's Racial and Violent Crime Task Force. But I didn't know that. And it certainly didn't explain why he was sitting in my parents' lounge.

Luckily, the look on my father's face did.

'You told him?'

'I had to, Sarbjit. It's for your own good.'

Dad had sat on my information for a long time. Then, with each new visit or phone call when I had let slip some casual threat or insult Bachan Kaur had said, he had become more enraged. I never wanted to drag him further into my mess but from the moment he found out the truth, he couldn't let it lie. Eventually he'd called the police and been put through to Clive's desk.

'DCI Driscoll, my daughter is not safe. Her family are going to kill her.'

'What makes you say that?'

'Because they've already killed one woman.'

Clive had agreed to a meeting and at the end said, 'We need to speak to your daughter.'

'You can't,' Dad said. 'She's in fear of her life. If you go to her house she'll be punished – or worse.'

'Then invite her here.'

Which is where I met him. And which is where I was convinced my father had signed my death warrant. And I told him so in no uncertain terms.

I was just letting off steam because I was scared. But Clive calmed me down and put me at ease. He really was unlike any of the other officers I'd met at Kingston police station five years earlier. From the way he spoke to me, I trusted him immediately. He made it absolutely clear to me that he really wanted to bring Bachan Kaur and Sukhdave to justice – but, just as much, he wanted to protect me and my children.

'You have to help me here, Mrs A,' he said in his strong south London accent. 'You've got your kids to think about. Do you want them to lose their mum as well? Because let me tell you something, if these people are capable of murdering once then they're capable of doing it again. The second one is easier, in some ways. They know they can do it. They've already got away with it.'

He was trying to help but he terrified the life out of me. Gradually, though, I understood where he was coming from. And he was right. What on earth had I been doing living under the same roof as that family for so long?

Even with Clive so comforting, when he asked me to tell him my story, I wasn't sure I could go through with it.

Then I remembered the earnest face of Jagdeesh Singh Dhillon on the day we'd met in the car park at the *gurdwara*.

'Don't hesitate to go forward,' he'd urged, 'when the time is right.'

I knew that time was now.

Clive smiled at me. 'Whenever you're ready,' he said. 'Just tell me what you want to tell me.'

I clenched my hands hard in my lap and picked a point on the floor and focused on that. Then I started talking. I told him about Surjit not getting on with her husband and her going to India in December 1998, and how she was murdered.

A long pause. Then Clive said, 'Can you repeat what you just said.'

I said, 'Surjit's been murdered. Mother took her to India and only came back when it was done.'

'Who knows about this?'

'Everyone knows about it.'

I made the mistake of looking up and catching Clive's eye. He was trying to be so gentle but all I could think about was Surjit. I got really upset, and couldn't speak for ages. Eventually I managed to cry out, 'I'm really sorry I haven't come forward before.'

'Why didn't you? You were arrested in 2000. You could have told us then.'

'I was scared. They threatened me. They said, "If you tell anyone, the same will happen to you."'

'And you believed them?'

'One hundred per cent.' I was trying to pull myself together. 'But I did call Crimestoppers,' I said. 'And I wrote a letter to Hayes police station after they left for India.' If I'd known then about my sister reporting it to Charing Cross police station, I would have mentioned that as well.

Clive had the good grace to look disappointed that neither of my anonymous attempts at tipping off the authorities had been followed up.

'But we're going to make amends for that and follow it up all the way this time,' he said. 'I'll need you to make an official statement.'

No, no, no, no, no!

'I can't do it. I've told you what I know. It's up to you if you take my word or not. I don't want to get further involved.'

'I'm sorry, Mrs A,' Clive said softly, 'but you really have no choice.'

***

As Clive got up to leave, my dad stood in front of him with both hands together, like he was praying, and said, 'Mr Clive, I'm begging you. Please save my daughter.'

The DCI was not a man given to emotion or making empty promises. 'I wasn't able to save Surjit, Mr B, but I give you my word I will do everything I can to protect your daughter.'

Dad nodded. That's all he could ask for.

The meeting with Clive took place in January 2005. For ten long months his team combed over every piece of evidence gathered during the two previous investigations. Only when he was convinced he had enough to take a case to trial would he endanger my life by asking me to make an official statement. By 27 October 2005, he had it.

When the morning of my scheduled interview dawned, I could still hardly believe what I was about to do. I waited until Hardave left for work, and then made my way cautiously to the police station, riding in a relative's car and keeping my head down low. Getting out of the car, I was shaking. I walked slowly towards the police station. Three or four people were standing there, just outside the building. One of them was an Asian officer. I have to be honest, that really freaked me out. *No*, I thought, *I can't do this. That officer is Asian, he might know the Athwals, he might report back* ... I kept my head down and somehow found the strength to go inside, my heart racing as I walked past the policemen standing outside. But even once I was safely through the doors, I kept looking back over my shoulder, to see if anyone was there, if anyone had followed me. Had anyone seen me go inside?

On entering the police station, the first person I met was Clive. *Why do I trust him?* I thought to myself. *Can I?* The police hadn't helped me before – why would they this time? But I felt Clive was so understanding, and there was no pressure put on me at all. I remember Clive saying he was here to look after me. I'm not sure I could have gone through with it without his belief in me.

As we walked into the interview room and sat down, time seemed to slow. I knew exactly what I was about to do.

This step I was about to take could cost me my life.

I could end up losing everything.

As I sat in that bleak interview room at Feltham police station, contemplating the hellish double life I'd been living all year, I felt more dreadful than when I'd been arrested on conspiracy of murder. Back then, the worst thing I had to fear was the law. What I was about to do now would put me up against murderers.

Murderers who knew where I lived and had a key to my house.

My children kept coming to my mind and holding me back. I thought of Surjit and this gave me a push. I knew I had to do this. I had to do it for Surjit. I had to get justice for Surjit. I had to get justice for her family, her brother – and her precious children.

And so we began.

DS Angie Barton talked me through every stage of my statement. She didn't rush me or put words in my mouth. The only thing she pushed me on was the detail. Was I sure it was Bachan Kaur who did this, Sukhdave who did that?

I knew that my actions that day would have consequences that would last for ever. Yet, as I left the station, I felt a sense of great relief. I'd done the right thing. Whatever the consequences, I'd done what I should have done half a decade earlier.

I'm sorry, Surjit, that it took me so long ...

But Clive had made it very clear that a statement was only any use if I backed it up by giving evidence if the case ever went to court.

I just hope I live long enough.

***

The sense of paranoia I'd felt after posting my letter to Hayes police station in 1998 was nothing compared to how on edge I felt heading home that afternoon. I rushed back, knowing I had to get home before Hardave returned from work. But as we turned into our road, I was shocked to see Hardave's car parked up outside our house. He should have been at work; he was always at work at this time in the afternoon. I immediately panicked, not knowing what to do. I knew that Hardave would ask me where I'd been. What on earth was I going to say?

My emotions were all over the place, and I couldn't think straight. But there was nothing I could do to put the moment off. The later I returned home, the more questions he would have. There was nothing else for it but to go in and pretend all was well, and that I hadn't just gone directly against my husband's family's wishes.

Hardave opened the door to me as I stood fussing with my keys on the doorstep. He asked me where I'd been. I was convinced he could see exactly what I'd been up to. Surely he had to notice how nervous I was? I had no choice but to pretend, so I told him I had been shopping with my sister. He asked where she was now, confused that she hadn't come back for some tea, so I replied that she'd had to rush off.

I couldn't keep up my forced breeziness for long. I pretended the baby needed changing and almost ran up the stairs, wanting nothing more than to be left alone.

But Hardave followed me.

'Are you OK?' he asked directly.

'Yes, I'm fine,' I managed to get out. I could barely speak, I was so afraid. I felt sick, my stomach churning as I rifled through the changing bag, trying to keep my hands busy so that Hardave wouldn't notice how much I was trembling.

Hardave looked at me quizzically. I swear we could both hear my heart pounding.

'Did something happen?' he said at last.

I could only shake my head, but – somehow – it seemed to be enough. He left me to it and I breathed a sigh of relief, my thoughts racing. But I still had the evening to get through. I felt certain Hardave was watching me, noticing how nervous I was preparing dinner, how quickly I ran up to look after the children afterwards so I didn't have to spend any more time than necessary in his company, how I jumped every time he spoke to me.

The stress of worrying whether he would pick up on my anxiety made me shudder even more. Somehow, though, I got through the evening, made a brief call to my sister to let her know that everything was OK, and escaped to bed early. My stomach was churning so much I didn't have to pretend to be ill. It felt like another ulcer poised to erupt. As I lay there, scrunching my eyes tight shut, willing the anaesthetic of sleep to put me out of my misery, all I could think was, *What have I done?*

The next morning I woke more relaxed. I'd been silly. There was no reason why Hardave should have suspected anything the day before. He hadn't known where I'd been, who I'd been with or what I'd said. The only time I needed to be alert, Clive had said, was when his team was ready to act.

'You'll know when that is because your family will all be under arrest.'

Unfortunately, it didn't work out like that.

I was feeding Karaminder that same afternoon when a fierce banging on the front door made me nearly drop the spoon. I could hear from the angry voice calling my name through the letterbox that it was Sukhdave.

What on earth does he want?

My blood froze.

He knows something.

When I opened the door he pushed past me and straight into the lounge. I hurriedly put Karaminder in another room and closed the door. Sukhdave in this mood was no sight even for a baby. He waited till I returned before he launched into a tirade of abuse.

'You've spoken to someone, haven't you?'

How did he find out?

'What about? What do you mean?' I said, amazed at how my nerves had vanished at just the right time.

'You know what. Have you told your dad?'

'About you murdering Surjit? No, I haven't.'

'Then how do you explain this?'

He thrust an open copy of the *Evening Standard* in my face. He was too angry to hold it still but I caught the gist of the headline.

'The police are saying they've received new information about Surjit's disappearance,' Sukhdave shouted, in case I'd missed it. 'Where have they got that from, hey? It can only be you.'

I studied the article. It was there, in black and white: Surjit's case was being reopened by the Metropolitan Police because new leads had come to light. Why hadn't Clive warned me? Of course the family was going to think it was me!

I could feel Sukhdave's eyes searing into me as I read. The words began to blur as I struggled to keep my composure.

'Why would I do this now?' I said finally. 'Why would I wait until now to tell someone? I've kept your secret for seven years. Why would I change now?'

'I don't know,' he grunted. 'But remember this. It's *our* secret. You're in this up to your neck.'

'I'm not! I didn't do anything.'

Sukhdave's mouth twisted into an unpleasant smile. 'That's not what the police are going to think if they come near me.'

I burst into tears the second Sukhdave left. I don't know how I'd held it together. But when you've been lying for so long, it becomes easier.

Even though Sukhdave had gone, I didn't dare use the house phone or even my mobile. Not for the call I needed to make. With Hardave due home any minute, I grabbed Karam and ran out to the nearest phone box. Then I called DCI Driscoll and asked, as nicely as I could in my shaken state, why I hadn't been warned about the article.

'I'll hold my hands up, Mrs A, it was a mistake. That information should never have been released. But you have my word, that is the last mistake you will see from us.'

I hope you're right. I've got a bad feeling about this ...

* * *

Waiting for Hardave to come home that evening was worse than ever. Obviously his brother had got hold of him. The second Hardave marched through the door he launched into it.

'Was it you?' he asked.

'I've already told Sukhdave. No.'

'You know you'll be in trouble if you do tell anyone.'

'Yes, I know. I've known for seven years. Now leave me alone.'

He went to say something else but saw the futility of it. He didn't have the rage or as much to lose as Sukhdave. More importantly, he could see I was trying to look after the children. I was a mum of four. I should have been spending my energy looking after them, not worrying about their uncle and his mother. I think, on some level, Hardave knew this as well.

For my nightly update to my sister I had to be a lot more careful what I said in case Hardave became suspicious. She asked if I wanted some company, but I said that wouldn't be necessary. The following day, however, I would have no choice.

It was a Saturday so the house was heaving with the sounds of all six of us filling different rooms with noise and mess. These were the times I loved, even though for much of it I couldn't hear myself think. Perhaps it was because of that I loved them. When I was chasing Balveen or Manvinder from one room to another or trying to get to the end of Taran's bottomless laundry basket, my own troubles were the last thing on my mind.

Unfortunately, as busy as the house was, Hardave thought there was room for one more. I had about ten minutes' notice before his mother arrived for a visit. That was good – it meant I only had ten minutes to worry what her reaction to the newspaper article would be. But when she arrived I was pleasantly surprised. She didn't mention it once. No shouting, no accusations, no threats. And yet, everything I did, I could feel her watching me do it.

Why doesn't she just say something?

At least when she was shouting at me, I knew where I was. This was getting interminable. When my mobile rang at lunchtime I was so relieved to have an excuse to leave her.

'Are you OK?' Hearing my sister's voice was just what I needed.

'No, I'm not,' I said, then dropped to a whisper. 'Bachan Kaur's here.'

'Oh my God, are you safe?'

'Honestly, I don't know. I don't feel it.' I checked behind me for signs of prying ears then said, 'I'm scared.'

The second I admitted it I realised just how on edge I'd been all morning. The kids were a great distraction. But underneath I was terrified.

'I'm coming over,' my sister said.

'No, don't!' *That won't work.* 'It will look wrong if you suddenly arrive. She'll suspect something.'

'Why? I'm allowed to visit my sister.'

'But you never do if you know she's here.'

'OK, you win. But I'm going to check up on you. Let me know if anything happens.'

Walking back to the kitchen my legs felt like lead. When I saw my mother-in-law still sitting at the table my heart sounded like a machine gun. How could nobody else hear it?

Still, though, she didn't raise the subject of the Met's renewed investigation. Was it possible she didn't know about it? Was Sukhdave trying to protect her?

Not possible. No one in that family sneezed without her permission.

So what was she playing at? I was scared. Very scared. Jumping at shadows scared. Listening to Bachan Kaur speak to the kids, I heard an underlying meaning in everything she said. Even coo-cooing with the baby felt like she was doing it for my benefit. When she wandered over to speak to Hardave that just confirmed it in my imagination: she's talking about me. She's plotting something.

It was getting ridiculous. I was so uptight that when the phone rang again I nearly jumped out of my skin. I managed to hold myself together long enough to dissuade my sister again from coming over.

'You've got to stop calling,' I whispered urgently.

'No,' she said. 'I won't.'

Hardave was standing next to me by the time I hung up. 'Who was that?'

'My sister.'

'Why does she keep phoning?'

'She's just being silly.'

He wasn't convinced.

'What's going on?'

'Nothing. It's Saturday, she's bored.'

I didn't dare go back to where he and Mum were sitting after that. Not until I'd managed to regain what I could of my composure. Still, though, I saw an agenda in every little conversation they had. Every hour that passed was harder to cope with. By the time the phone rang for a third time, I was fit to burst.

'That had better not be your sister again,' Hardave called out grumpily.

It was. This time I must have sounded as weird as I felt, because my sister said she was coming over whether I liked it or not.

At least that will stop you calling ...

I returned to the lounge where the TV was blaring.

'Yes, it was her,' I said before my husband had a chance to ask. 'She wants me to go out with her.'

'You can't go anywhere. Mum's here.'

'I know, I know. So she's popping over here instead.'

I hoped that sounded casual. I didn't feel it. There wasn't enough air in the room for all of us. If I didn't sit down soon I was going to faint.

***

I couldn't remember the last time I'd been so happy to see anyone. My sister's smiling face turned serious the second she stepped inside the house. Could she sense the atmosphere or was I imagining that, too?

The children all managed to look up from the TV long enough to say hello to their aunt. Then the two of us went into the kitchen so we could cook as we talked. *Bachan Kaur followed.* She didn't help and she didn't really want to speak either. While she was there, though, no one else felt like chatting either.

That's her plan.

I've always been able to talk freely to my siblings, but everything we said that day felt so stilted and false. The poison in the house was infecting my sister too. But she wasn't as far gone as me. I watched my hand shake as I tried to hold an onion in place to cut it. My sister saw that and gently pressed her own hand over mine.

It's all right, her eyes were saying. But we both knew it wasn't.

She lasted about an hour before she made her excuses and left. As safe as I'd felt when she'd been there, it was actually a relief to see her go. On my own there was less chance of me making a slip-up.

With my sister going, I assumed my mother-in-law wouldn't be far behind. That turned out not to be the case. I was clearing up the dishes when Hardave announced, 'Mum's staying over tonight.'

I don't know how I didn't drop the plates.

'OK,' I managed to say. But Hardave hadn't finished.

'I'll sleep on the sofa. You and Mum can have our room.'

What?

'No, that's all right,' I said hurriedly. 'You have the couch, I'll go in with the kids and Mum can have our bed to herself.'

Hardave was shaking his head. 'No, no, Mum can't sleep on her own. That would be disrespectful.'

She always sleeps on her own!

He wouldn't be budged. Events were happening and I couldn't stop them. Was this their plan all along? Were they just toying with me during the day and then intending to do who-knew-what at night? Everything was falling into place – a place I didn't want to think about.

I stole a glance at the imposing frame of my mother-in-law. She could easily overpower me in my sleep without a second thought. At that moment I knew that she'd read the newspaper article. I also knew something else.

This is it. This is the night I die.

* * *

By the time the telephone rang again, I was almost resigned to my fate.

'Are you OK?' my sister's voice asked. 'Has she gone yet?'

'No. She's staying over.'

I couldn't have been calmer. It was as though I were numb with fear.

'She's staying?' my sister repeated. 'This isn't good.'

'And she's sleeping with me in my bed.'

'Oh, Sarb, you have to get out.'

'I can't. Don't you see that? I can't.'

'I'm telling Dad to get the police then.'

'Just leave me alone. You're not helping calling all the time.'

Both Bachan Kaur and Hardave were staring at me when I went back into the kitchen. I couldn't even be bothered lying so I just shrugged and carried on tidying. I looked at the clock. Three hours before bed. Three hours to think.

Three hours to live.

* * *

Don't go to sleep.

If I kept my eyes closed I could imagine I was lying next to Hardave. The size seemed the same, she even smelled like him. I tried to make myself as small as possible, curling up on the edge of the bed. What she felt like, I didn't want to know.

Don't go to sleep.

The sounds of traffic up and down the street, car doors slamming, voices of Saturday night revellers on their way home, even a helicopter buzzing over the area, keeping an eye on the town below: I was aware of it all. But I was listening for sounds inside the house, not outside. I was listening for the sound of my door handle turning, of voices conspiring in whispers, of the rustle of nightclothes, the creak of floorboards.

I was listening for the sound of my murderers.

Don't go to sleep.

If I did, I knew I would never wake up.

CHAPTER NINETEEN

ARE YOU *ARRESTING* ARRESTING ME?

The first day of the rest of my life.

That's how it felt as I locked the bathroom door the following morning. Everything was different now. The shower water felt more relaxing, the weather seemed warmer and the children were all playing as though they liked each other.

I was embarrassed at my paranoia the day before. What had I been thinking, getting my sister involved? And what if she had phoned the police? That would be humiliating. There was nothing else to say. I'd overreacted, let my imagination run riot. If my mother-in-law truly thought the police were on to her, it was ludicrous to think she'd be so stupid as to try anything now.

Nothing's going to happen.

Even without any sleep, I couldn't help relaxing and allowing myself an inward smile. For whatever reason, Bachan Kaur hadn't gone through with her plan – if she'd even had one. I felt almost giddy.

And I wasn't the only one in a good mood. I'd just finished changing Karaminder when I noticed Bachan Kaur watching from the bathroom doorway, a cup of tea in her hands. She rarely looked so content.

'He's a lovely boy,' she said, pride in her voice.

I wasn't particularly interested in making small talk but I had to agree. Bachan Kaur was clearly in a reflective mood.

'You know, Sarbjit,' she continued, 'I've been thinking. You have never met our family in India.'

'No,' I said.

And nor do I want to.

'So I'm going to do something about that. I've decided I'm going to take you on a trip. You and me, we'll visit everyone. Don't worry about the cost, I'll see to everything.'

I'll see to everything.

My blood froze. Did she really just say those words? Did she really just invite me to India? Did she really just say she was taking me on the same journey that she'd taken Surjit?

Did she really think I was so stupid?

One thing was sure. *She definitely knows about the investigation.*

* * *

'I'm going to the temple now.'

As suddenly as she'd arrived the previous day, Bachan Kaur had decided to leave.

'OK,' I said. 'We'll see you soon.'

The second she and Hardave set off, I picked up the phone. My sister answered.

'Thank God!' she said. 'What happened?'

'Nothing,' I replied. 'Nothing at all. But it was weird.'

'Do you want me to come over?'

'Please.'

Half an hour later, with the children happily enjoying themselves in other rooms, my sister and I sat down with tea. She wanted to know exactly what had happened last night, so I told her.

'We were so worried,' she said. 'Clive was close to breaking down the door and getting you out.'

'What?'

'When I rang him last night he told me to tell you to come out. I said you'd already refused. So he said if he can't get you out, he'd make sure nobody else got in.'

'What do you mean?'

'Did you know there was a police car outside your house all last night?'

Is she making this up?

'What was it doing?'

'It was watching your front door,' my sister said. 'Clive sent it there. Your mother-in-law didn't get her hands dirty in India, so he was worried that she'd ordered someone to come and pay you a visit.'

I was speechless. Had there really been a car there all night? Just for me?

'That's not all,' my sister said. 'Did you hear a helicopter last night?'

'Helicopter? I think I did actually.'

'That was Clive again.'

'No way!'

She told me how the police were worried about access to the back of the house. If Bachan Kaur's contacts had spotted the patrol vehicle out the front, they might have tried to get in across the series of linked gardens. As it was inaccessible by car or path, Clive had planted a helicopter directly above to monitor the back door.

I could not believe what I was hearing. I was flabbergasted. Words formed and died on my lips as I struggled to make sense of it all. With everything that's wrong in the world, all the people crying out for help, someone would choose to do all this to protect me?

Am I really that important?

My emotions were all over the place anyway. Fear had already been replaced by relief that morning. Now I was experiencing something else. What was it? Gratitude?

I hadn't felt that for a long time. Knowing someone cared, that someone believed me enough to spend valuable resources on my safety, was almost too much to take in. My eyes filled quickly but for once not out of horror.

Then the chilling realisation occurred.

Clive going to so much trouble was a massive boost to my confidence. It was proof that he believed in me. But it also showed how deadly seriously he'd taken my fears. The police truly believed I had been in danger.

And that I still was.

* * *

Over the next few days I juggled the school run and looking after my baby with stealing furtive minutes to speak to my guardian angel at Scotland Yard. It was only when I told Clive about my mother-in-law's proposition that I go with her to India – to retrace Surjit's final days – that I wondered whether there had been another family meeting.

Had the brothers sat alongside their mother at No. 88 Willow Tree Lane, just feet from where they'd all gathered nearly seven years earlier, and agreed that I too had brought shame on the family? That I too had destroyed the honour of the Athwal name? And that I too needed to be sorted out? Had Bachan Kaur uttered the same words?

'We have to get rid of her.'

I was confident my husband would not have been party to this. He had been against the original crime. But under the thumb of his mother, could I be sure?

* * *

Perhaps I wouldn't have to worry. On 2 November, nearly a week after I'd given my statement, Clive announced that the next phase of 'Operation Yewlands' – as the investigation was called – was ready to go.

'We're arresting your family tomorrow,' he warned. 'You might want to make yourself scarce.'

'Will it be as early as it was last time?' I asked, remembering the six o'clock rude awakening of 2000.

He laughed. 'Probably. That's the best time to catch people at home. "Catch" being the operative word.'

The DCI went on to explain again the legal process. It was a job to him but he realised that everything was new to me. Since I'd first spoken to Clive in January, his team had been trying to assemble enough evidence for the Criminal Prosecution Service to agree that the family or any individuals had a case to answer. It could still, he admitted, be tricky. The last murder enquiry in 2000 had fallen down through lack of evidence – and apart from me coming forward, not much had changed since then.

'If you think about it,' Clive said, 'we have a murder that took place in another country, carried out by another person or persons, and no body has ever been found.'

It didn't sound watertight. All my doubts about speaking rushed back.

'Do you really think you can win this case?' I asked.

'With your testimony in court, I think we've got a very good chance.'

A good *chance*? Was that enough to justify the risk I was taking?

Shall we just flip a coin?

All kinds of hasty, stupid, panicked thoughts flashed through my mind. They didn't last. After everything I'd been through, the DCI was the only person who had ever shown any faith in me. I had to believe him. I had to believe I wasn't beating myself up inside for nothing.

But I realised I had to brace myself for living in a world where the CPS refused to proceed with the case. What would happen if my mother- and brother-in-law didn't get sent to prison? If Clive didn't get a conviction? After all, how can you charge someone with murder if you can't find a body? Even to me that sounded weird.

I knew all too well what would happen. I also knew what I had to do to avoid it.

'I need you to do something for me,' I told Clive.

'Name it,' he said, with a laugh. I think Clive was amused at my unusual display of bossiness.

'When you arrest everyone tomorrow, you have to take me as well.'

Clive stopped laughing.

'I can't arrest you. You're my witness!'

'Look, if you don't arrest me then they're going to know that it was me who spoke out. I have to think about myself. If you don't manage to put these people away, I've still got to live with them.'

Getting past the fact that Clive didn't understand why I felt I needed to live with them in the first place – he had a lot, he admitted, to learn about Sikhs – he agreed.

'Tomorrow morning, Mrs A. Be prepared.'

* * *

By the time six o'clock came and went I'd been awake for hours. How could anyone sleep knowing what was going to happen? But nothing did. Then came seven, then eight, with still no noise or movement outside. Even busying myself with getting the kids ready for school, the waiting was killing me.

Come on, Clive, where are you?

At half past eight it was time to drop Balveen and Manvinder off. Taran preferred to walk to her school. Karam stayed indoors with Hardave. By the time I got home, my husband and son weren't alone in the house. I was greeted inside the door by a female officer. Even though I was expecting it, my knees gave way.

'Are you Sarbjit Athwal?' the officer asked.

It's happening.

'Yes.'

'I'm arresting you on suspicion of conspiracy to murder Surjit Athwal.'

I feel faint.

'No! I don't know anything!'

Panic surged through me. Flashbacks to the last time this had happened filled my brain. I don't know if it was the stress of the last week coming back to me or if I was going mad. I couldn't think of anything other than not wanting to get into another police car as long as I lived. I didn't think of Clive, of Operation Yewlands, or that being arrested was my idea in the first place. For that minute I was irrational, out of control and absolutely certain I was going to prison.

The WPC let me howl for a few seconds and then, after checking the stairs for footsteps, she leaned into me.

'Don't say anything,' she hissed. 'Just keep quiet.'

I stared at her blankly.

'Are you *arresting* arresting me?' I asked. It sounds so silly now.

'Just leave it at that,' she whispered firmly. But if she could have winked I think she would have done.

Thank you, Clive.

Hardave wasn't so lucky. Two officers escorted him downstairs and we were both led out, along with baby Karam, into separate cars. Hardave didn't take his eyes off me once.

He knows ...

At the same time, on the other side of the M25, a sixty-eight-year-old woman and her son were being escorted to police cars as well. Operation Yewlands was in motion.

***

En route to Sutton police station, our two-vehicle cavalcade conveniently became separated. Hardave would not have seen that my car didn't go anywhere near the station but instead took me directly to my sister's house. There was no way I could go home now.

The police were obviously busy enough with their real prisoners without worrying about me. There was only so much I could eat and drink during the day to distract me. In the afternoon my sister picked up the children from school and we all went to my father's. I wished I knew what was going on at Sutton. Then at about five o'clock I was called by a member of Clive's team, who told me that Hardave would be released on bail within the hour. He reiterated the advice that Clive had already given me.

'Do not go back to the house. We can't guarantee your safety.'

Clive had, in fact, asked me to consider the witness protection programme. Under that, I would be given a new home, a new identity, a new life. But the repercussions would be huge. I'd have to end contact with my family and my children would have to endure the same upheaval. I didn't want to spend my whole life looking over my shoulder, wondering if I'd been recognised, so I said no.

I hung up and looked at the audience of expectant but anxious faces in my parents' lounge.

'It's time to face the music,' I said.

A chorus of parents and siblings begging me not to go back fell on deaf ears. If I wasn't going to listen to DCI Driscoll, their pleas wouldn't work either.

'It's my home. It's where our children live. And besides,' I added, 'I've done nothing wrong.'

* * *

Hardave looked a broken man when he came in.

'When did you get out?' he asked.

'This afternoon.' I hated lying, but this family had trained me well.

'Mum and Sukhdave are still being held at Heathrow police station. Please, Sarbjit, what did you tell them?'

'I didn't tell anyone anything. I've never told anyone anything.'

I don't know if Hardave believed me or not.

I wasn't even sure if he could hear me.

He was pacing up and down like a man possessed.

* * *

Night fell and there was still no news from Heathrow. I couldn't relax and busied myself with the children or in the kitchen. Hardave had stopped making sense a long time ago. He was still marching up and down, muttering to himself.

'Where are they? Why aren't they home yet?'

'Someone must have talked? Who's talked?'

'What's going on? Where are they?'

I stayed out of his way as much as possible. My children, though, were worried.

'What's wrong with Dad?' Taran asked.

'He's worried about his mum,' I said. I told her where they were. She was shocked.

'Why do the police want them?'

'They think they did something to your aunt.'

'But she's run away. Mum said she had. Pav said. Everyone knows that.'

I wish I could tell you the truth ...

In a way, I was glad she didn't know what had really happened. But that day was coming and I just hoped she would be able to forgive me for what I'd done.

Hardave wasn't the only one suffering. The waiting was eating me up as well. What if Bachan Kaur and Sukhdave had been told by their interviewers about me talking? What if they were released and nobody let me know in time? I looked at the front door.

They could walk through there at any moment.

I locked and bolted it the second the thought entered my mind.

And then, the following morning, a month shy of seven years since Surjit left for India, Bachan Kaur and Sukhdave were formally charged with her murder.

Thank God!

But this was only the start. I learned later that Sukhdave and Bachan Kaur had refused to answer questions while their solicitors attempted to get the charges dropped. When that failed they campaigned strongly for bail.

They could still be released.

I prayed and prayed that the magistrate would see how dangerous they were and lock them up, for my sake. But there was no guarantee. Not even Clive could give me that.

They were kept in custody while the lawyers argued. On one side the police were saying they were killers. On the other the solicitors acting for the Athwals were saying their hands were clean, they were no threat to society.

I knew this was going on. Every chance I got, I dialled Clive's number on my mobile and he kept me informed. There was a danger Hardave would catch me but I needed to know. If Bachan Kaur and Sukhdave were awarded bail they would both be free to come home and continue their lives.

And continue to threaten mine.

The DCI tried to keep me upbeat. The police had a strong case, he insisted. But it wasn't watertight and the magistrates would make their own decision. All we could do was wait. And wait. And …

They were both denied bail by the magistrate.

What is that feeling?

So many of my emotions for years had been so negative. I realised I was experiencing something different. Something good.

Relief!

Utter relief. It would only get better when Clive said his best guess was that a trial could be anything up to two years away. Two years! I could barely process it. I wasn't going to see Bachan Kaur and Sukhdave for a very long time.

Neither, of course, was Hardave. He was shell-shocked, vacant, a wounded animal. His conspiracy theories spread out to blame just about everyone he could think of. They were all responsible for his beloved mother's and brother's incarceration. At the end of each rant, however, the spotlight usually fell back on me.

'Are you sure you didn't say anything?'

'Hardave, I swear I didn't. I don't know any more than you do.'

'OK.' Then an hour later he'd ask me again. He wanted so much to believe me but his brain wouldn't let him think of anyone else. The not knowing was tearing him apart.

He was in pain, I could see that. The children were horrified by his transformation. Hardave tried to put on a brave face but it was hard. He hated the idea of them going to school and saying, 'My gran has been arrested for murder,' bringing shame on the family. On the other hand, he also couldn't bring himself to lie to them. In the end he just kept repeating, 'It's nothing. You'll see Gran soon.'

Each day – each hour – that passed felt like an ordeal I wouldn't get through. The constant scrutiny, feeling my husband staring at me even when we were in different rooms, was insufferable. Even if Hardave couldn't read from my face and body language what I'd done, I was so worried I might say the wrong thing. He was challenging me every second, it seemed. There was only so much of it that I could take.

I'm not an actor. I can't do this.

I realised I wasn't making much sense to my children. They were worried about me, too. If I was lucky, Hardave would think I was as worried as him about his family. If I was less lucky, he'd put two and two together.

I was nauseous, faint and on the edge of tears for the entire day. I couldn't relax around my husband for a second. Was it going to be like this for two whole years? *Not for me,* I decided. *I can't do it. Not any more.*

That night I only had one thought.

I need to make a will.

Somehow, despite all the noise in my head, I thought of practicalities. If anything happens to me, my share of the house couldn't go to Hardave or his family. It had to go to my children.

For once, however, I wasn't thinking that Bachan Kaur or her friends in the community were going to claim my life. It was me. I'd reached that stage where I couldn't see any alternative. I was waking in the morning and feeling sick with fear, then going to bed in the same state. My hands had been shaking for days, my heart beating like a drum machine. I was at my wits' end. As low as I could go.

It will be better for everyone if I end this now.

Maybe not everyone. Only the thought of my children prompted me to reconsider. Even then I knew I had to do something – even if it hurt the ones I loved most.

On the morning of 6 November, after a third sleepless night, I sneaked into the bathroom and dialled the number I'd memorised.

'Clive? I'm so glad you picked up. I can't take this any more. Come and get me. Whatever you have to do, get me out of here.'

Within the hour there was a knock at the door. Two uniformed officers introduced themselves and asked me to accompany them.

'Where are you taking her?' Hardave demanded.

'Mrs Athwal is needed to help with our enquiries,' one of them said.

I felt dead behind the eyes as I watched my husband's face. To my mind there was no way he could suspect me now. But looking at him I had no idea what was going on inside his mind. He just looked empty.

I already felt sick about what I was poised to do. I couldn't let my plan get derailed by worrying any more about him.

'Can I say goodbye to my children?' I asked.

'Of course.'

I hugged Taran, Balveen and Manvinder, then scooped up baby Karam to take him with me. I was still breastfeeding him. We couldn't be separated. 'Bye,' I said, then turned and walked towards the unmarked car parked across the road.

And so it was that on the morning of my thirty-sixth birthday, I finally took the Samaritans' advice and walked out of my marriage for good.

* * *

Clive was waiting in the car.

'Are you all right, Mrs A?'

'No.'

'I'll take you to your parents.'

'I don't want to go there.'

'Where do you want to go? You can't go back home now.'

'I know, I know.'

How could I tell him I just wanted to be alone? And not for any reason he would understand.

As the car sped east towards Hounslow, I couldn't bring myself to talk. I should have been happy, relieved to escape. But as I sat holding my baby in the back of that car, my heart was aching and I just wanted to scream as loud as I could. I was so scared of what Hardave might do when he realised who the police's main witness was. He was already a man on the edge. And if it wasn't him, the whole community was on Bachan Kaur's side. How could I trust anyone?

The DCI was speaking but I didn't hear what he said. All I could think of was the consequences.

It's happening again, I thought. Twice I'd reported Surjit's death. Twice I'd been ignored. This time they'd promised I'd be OK, but I'd never felt worse.

I looked at the door handle. I knew it couldn't be opened from inside but I was tempted to try. I remembered how safe I'd felt in hospital after my ulcer. But this time I wanted to feel nothing at all.

We arrived at my parents' house before I could do anything rash. I felt apprehensive as I approached their door. Not so long ago, a daughter leaving her marriage would have been the most shameful event to them. Even now, I feared what the community would say, and how my parents – and I – would be able to cope with the sidelong glances and shocked rebukes. After all, even without the Athwals' influence in our community, a wife living apart from her husband would be frowned upon by the most liberated Sikhs. I feared I had brought shame on them by leaving.

But I needn't have worried. They were overjoyed to see I'd come to my senses, finally. Their only disappointment was the fact I hadn't been able to bring my older children. That annoyed me, to be frank. We'd had to pretend to take me into custody to get me out. You could hardly arrest children, could you?

You think I wanted to leave them behind?

Clive and his officers stayed with me until I was settled. Then as he went to leave I realised it was all wrong.

'I can't stay here.' I was sitting on the same sofa I'd been on when I'd first met Clive.

'Pardon?' my mother said. She rushed over to sit next to me. 'Of course you can, for as long as you like.'

'No, I have to go.'

'Sarbjit, what's wrong?' The tone of his voice told me Dad was scared.

'Nothing,' I said. 'I just have to get away.'

I looked at DCI Driscoll. 'Clive, please, get me out of here.' I was sobbing, distraught, confused and so, so scared. 'I just have to be on my own.'

My poor parents looked like I'd accused them of murder. I was so sorry to cause them pain, it wasn't their fault. But I just had to get away. I couldn't explain it. I just wanted to be alone.

Clive made a call. A few minutes later he said, 'It's sorted. Come with me, Mrs A.'

To this day I do not know what was going through my mind. I was short of breath and just so desperate to be with my own thoughts that I didn't seem to care if I offended my own parents. In the end, though, I agreed that Mum could come with me. At the time I fought it. In hindsight, however, I'm glad she did.

I remember looking out of the window as we drove across west London, and thinking, *Nobody will miss me. I've given my statement to the police. They'll get their murderers. And, finally, I'll get to sleep without the nightmares.*

I was lower than I'd ever been. Capable of anything, it seemed, and not in a good way. Only my mother being next to me in the car held me back. The way she held Karam reminded me of what I would be giving up. I'd forgotten what a real family was.

We drove for about forty-five minutes to a hotel in Epsom.

'No one will find you here,' Clive said.

It wasn't the Ritz. We had a box room with a window that barely opened, two single beds and a toilet in the same space for my mother, my son and me. But for a few precious hours, it was ours and nobody else's.

I lay with Karam until he fell asleep on my bed. Then I moved over to Mum's little space and together we spent most of the night crying.

'Don't worry, Sarbjit,' she croaked mid-sob, 'you'll get

through this. It will all get better in no time. Mark my words.'

As I listened to the sirens rushing by outside I had every reason to doubt her. But she was my mother. And, what's more, I was so tired ...

I felt that if I got through the night, I'd feel different in the morning. But that wasn't looking likely as my head hit the pillow and a kaleidoscope of images and fears and regrets filled my mind. I was thirty-six years old, I had four children and I'd just walked out on their father. What was I thinking of? I was a Sikh. I was raised to honour and respect the institution of marriage. To respect my husband and my family. So what was I playing at? My whole life had been turned upside down and at that moment I was convinced I had no one to blame but myself.

I knew I was looking for a way out. I knew in my heart that my life was over.

Then the next thing I realised it was a new day and my son was laughing.

Maybe, just maybe, I'm going to be all right.

* * *

Surjit was the victim in this story – but she wasn't the only one. Her children, already brainwashed into thinking they'd been abandoned by a mother who didn't love them, had now lost their father and grandmother – the two people they lived with. My testimony had made them homeless. With neither of them believing my story – they'd been told so often by Bachan Kaur and Sukhdave via letters and prison visits that I was lying – there was no way they wanted to stay with me or any of my family, so an aunt on the Athwal side took them in.

They weren't the only children affected. By leaving Hardave I not only humiliated him in the face of his family and his community, I had also walked out on three of my own kids. He wouldn't let them leave and I had nowhere to take them, not yet. Wherever I went, he told me he would find us and physically drag them back. He made that very clear. Karaminder, at least, never left my side.

After two nights in secure housing, I had to see them. Just phoning every day wasn't enough, for me or them. Dad was totally against me going to the house.

'Hardave is angry. You don't know what he'll do.'

I couldn't be sure, but I said, 'He's not like the other two. He was the one who tried to stop it all those years ago.'

'OK,' Dad said. 'I'm driving you. And if you're not out in fifteen minutes I'm coming in.'

'OK.'

'I also want you to call Clive.'

'I will.'

I was talking to Clive on my mobile when we pulled up in the little parking bay around the side of the house. He was still trying to stop me going in alone but getting nowhere.

'Just call me when you come out,' he said. 'And the first sign of trouble you get out of there fast.'

I promised and climbed out of the car.

'Fifteen minutes,' Dad reminded me.

Fifteen minutes.

The second I stepped through the door and saw Balveen, then Manvinder and Taran, the tears began to stream down my face.

'Mummy!'

I barely made it far enough inside to close the door before sinking to my knees under a sea of outstretched arms.

'Please don't go again,' Balveen begged.

'I'm sorry, darling, I have to.'

'Then take us with you!' They all chorused that. Even Taran, who tried so hard to be a grown-up at fourteen, was in unison with the others.

'I can't right now, I'm so sorry. But soon, I promise.'

Then another voice broke the spell.

'Taran, take your brother and sister in the lounge. Mum and I need to talk.'

No one budged.

'Go on,' I said. 'We won't be long.'

Eventually I struggled to my feet and followed Hardave upstairs to our room. The second I walked in he exploded. I'd never seen him so angry.

I should leave.

'Why did you do it? Why?' He was screaming, out of control. 'How could you do this? How could you rip this family apart?'

'Hardave – our children are downstairs.'

'I don't care.'

That was very out of character for him. However he treated me, he'd always tried to protect our children from family fall-outs.

He was shaking, absolutely fuming. He looked like he hadn't slept for a week.

'I know it was you,' he said, trying to keep control of his voice.

'What are you talking about?' I asked. I was too scared to think.

'I've spoken to Mum's solicitor,' he continued. 'They've seen your statement. They know it was you. And,' his voice was breaking, 'so do I. How could you do it, Sarb?'

He looked crushed, betrayed. Like his entire world had fallen in. How had it come to this? The suffocating shame of realising I had lied to him and given a statement against his family had sunk in.

In Hardave's mind, Sukhdave was the one who'd married badly. He was the one who'd chosen the wife who couldn't be tamed. He, Hardave, by contrast, had wed a traditional Sikh bride who would obey his every command. She would never lie to him. She would never betray him.

But I had.

And I didn't think he would ever get over it.

I knew I had to get away. Hardave wasn't thinking straight. I didn't know what else he was capable of. I brushed past and out of the room.

'Don't walk away when I'm talking to you!'

I felt the sting on my cheek before I even realised he'd hit me. As I pulled away from him, my foot slipped on the top step and I crashed back against the wall. By sheer luck I managed to fall on to the landing and not down the stairs. Another few inches and it would have been a different story.

Finally Hardave had stopped shouting.

'Do you know why I slapped you?' he asked, his voice breaking.

'No.'

I couldn't bring myself to look at him.

'Because I love you.'

'Well, I don't want that kind of love!'

As I pulled myself up, my mobile fell from my pocket. A moment later it began ringing. Hardave picked it up and read the caller ID.

'Your dad,' he said.

'How long are you going to be?' My father sounded worried.

'Sorry,' I said. 'Another five or ten minutes.'

'Are you OK?'

'I'll see you in ten minutes.'

Then I hung up.

Thirty seconds later it rang again. Hardave snatched it from my hand and read a new name.

'DCI Driscoll? Why are the police calling you?'

Stupidly I had saved the number under Clive's real name and title.

I was terrified of Hardave now.

'I don't know,' I said.

'Well, answer it then!'

He was scared, too. Scared that the police would think something was wrong. His honour was at stake.

The phone rang off then called back. I managed to control my voice and, still shivering with fear, pressed 'answer'.

'Sarbjit,' the big, familiar voice bellowed from the receiver. 'Are you all right?'

If I say no, I don't know what Hardave will do.

'No,' I said. 'I'm OK.'

'What? Mrs A, you're making no sense. Are you all right?'

The usually unflappable detective was anxious, I could tell. I tried to give my coded answer again – that 'no', I wasn't all right but I couldn't say. Clive picked up on it.

'OK, I want you to walk out of that house now. If you don't, we're coming in.'

'OK, I'm leaving now. I just need to kiss the children.'

'Call me when you're outside.'

Hardave watched open-mouthed as I gingerly pulled myself to my feet and edged warily down the stairs. The shouting had subsided. He was trying to process how his wife was taking orders from a white police officer and not him. That wasn't how he had been raised. And, he knew, it wasn't how I'd been raised either.

'Wash your face before you leave,' were his final words to me. He didn't want the community to see his wife leaving his house crying.

He had his honour to think of.

It was crushing to walk out without my children again. They wanted to come with me and I wanted them, but Hardave was the one with the house and he was not letting them out of it. Not without a fight.

I called Clive the second the cold winter air hit my face.

'I'm out,' I said.

'Good. Now don't go there again.'

CHAPTER TWENTY

TELL YOUR DAD
I'M COMING BACK

Don't go there again?

I didn't think about the house once for several days. But the people in it never left my thoughts. In my darkest moments I pictured Hardave scouring the capital and its suburbs for traces of me. The rest of the time I couldn't shake the guilt of leaving my three elder children behind.

I knew they were safe. That was never in doubt. The only question I did have was, 'What is Hardave telling them about me?' Taran and Balveen in particular were at an impressionable age. They looked up to their dad. And I'd heard how effortlessly his family had spun a lie about Surjit and extended it all the way over to India, where it was repeated again and again in another language. Outside of my family and hers, the world thought Surjit had run away with a series of other men. Even her own daughter believed those lies.

After three weeks I couldn't take it any more.

I've got to see them.

I called Clive for advice. He said Hardave should bring the children to a neutral place. Hardave refused. In that case, the DCI said, if I visited I had to take a chaperone.

'At no point are you to let Hardave speak to you alone.'

'You don't have to worry about that.'

* * *

I didn't use my key. I didn't want to give my husband any excuse to get annoyed. The second he opened the door, my children came bowling at me – just like they'd done the last time I visited. And, just like the last time, it was a blow to the ribs.

What am I doing living so far away from them?

Then I saw Hardave and I remembered why.

I was glad I wasn't alone. My aunt had volunteered. I was so grateful to her as I was desperate to see my children. She would be no match for my husband physically but I didn't fear Hardave like that, even after his roughness at the top of the stairs. It was his tongue I was afraid of. He had the Athwal gift for spitting poison like a cobra.

'Are you feeling better, Mum?' Taran asked.

'Were you scared in hospital?' Balveen's face looked so serious.

It took me a few seconds to work out what they were saying. Before I could answer, my husband spoke up.

'I told them how you hadn't been well and had to go into hospital,' he said.

I went to contradict him and thought better of it. How would they understand me choosing to walk away?

Let Hardave tell his lies if he wants. I know why he's doing it.

For the honour of the family. To protect their good name at the temple and in the community. The same reason his mother and brother killed Surjit.

I couldn't believe he was worried about shame in the eyes of his own children. But when you've been raised by a woman like Bachan Kaur to believe honour is all that matters, perhaps it's understandable. Shame, honour? A woman was dead because of those two words.

But I also thought of the kinder man I'd married. Maybe he deserved the benefit of the doubt. Was he protecting the children from the upset of knowing Mummy had left them? Was that his reason for lying? I found myself warming to him as I considered this.

But not much.

We went through to the lounge. For a glorious hour the children shared their news with me and I did my best not to sit there sobbing like a loon. I was so happy to be with them, it didn't matter to me what they said. Just seeing their faces was the tonic I'd needed so much but didn't know how to find. Taran seemed confused. I could see it written all over her face. Hadn't she swallowed her dad's lies about where I'd been? She must have remembered the police coming for me. I just wished I had taken her with me. Balveen also kept asking if she could come, too.

After a while there, Hardave came into the room and asked me for a private word.

My instincts said no. My aunt's face said the same. But the children's anxious looks made me crumble. Whatever was going on between their parents, they shouldn't have to see it played out.

'OK,' I said, and walked into the hall. I braced myself for a tirade or possibly tears. Hardave had looked permanently on the verge since 3 November when his mother was arrested. But he didn't scream, he didn't shout. He didn't look like he was going to threaten me in any way.

I was wrong.

He held his hand out. In it was a piece of paper. I picked it up and read the message scrawled on it in my husband's hand.

'Retract your evidence or you will never be safe.'

I stared at the paper. The words went from clear and angry to blurred and jumpy. I realised my eyes had filled with tears and I was shaking.

This is why I left in the first place.

I screwed up the paper and threw it at Hardave. Then I returned to my children and tried to concentrate on them. It was hard. I was seething.

I was also petrified.

Later that night, in my new accommodation in a Tolworth B&B, I realised I was crying. What did the note mean about me never being safe?

I immediately thought about my address. Had I been followed home? Was a member of the family keeping track of my movements? A shiver ran through me. The community. The Athwals' grip on certain parts of the *gurdwara* had been so tight, would any of them take action?

I didn't sleep well.

***

My time at the hotel and B&B was only ever meant to be a temporary measure. I was there for three nights in total. Without the kind support of the police I wouldn't have lasted that long. Angie Barton even gave me money for food. But it wasn't a home for the long term – and neither, sadly, was the next place we were moved to.

The YWCA was meant to be a step up, a haven after the emergency accommodation. It didn't feel like it. Our room was on the seventh floor – and the lift was out of order. I could carry Karam well enough, but Mum suffered very badly from arthritis, and the effort of going up when we arrived the first night made her cry in agony. I felt so sorry for her, and so guilty at putting her through it.

'Can't we go home?' she pleaded.

'You can, Mum, of course. But I can't. Not yet. I don't feel safe.'

If I felt bad for my mother that night, the following morning I could just about bear to look her in the eye. We trudged our way downstairs for breakfast and stood in the dining-room doorway, too shocked to go in.

'Are you sure this is a hotel?' Mum said.

'I think so.' But I wasn't convinced. The room was full, as far as first impressions go, of druggies, scrawny teens and dirty-looking people who stank of wee, or worse.

'Who are all these people?' Mum said.

'I think they live here, too.'

'Do you think it's safe for Karam here?'

'Well, I did till you said that. He's fine with me.'

She paced around further.

'This doesn't look like a B&B,' Mum said.

'I think you're right.'

She was. In fact, I learned, it was a hostel for the homeless. But again, I thought, *It's still better than where I was*.

After three nights, Mum's physical pain combating the stairs grew too much and she had to admit defeat. I was sad at the idea of letting her go, but not as sad as she was going. Then she said, 'Why don't you come with me?'

I considered it. No reason at all.

I'd tackled and beat my demons. Why shouldn't I enjoy the company of people who loved and cared for me?

* * *

I saw my children every weekend. And every weekend Hardave found a way to slip me a note of some description. I tried not to read them. Sometimes I couldn't help it. Each one contained a variation of the original message: *retract your evidence or suffer the consequences*. He even began to give me a piece of paper and a pen. Whatever questions he asked, he expected an answer. Of course he did. I was his to command – that's how he'd been raised to see marriage.

What the consequences for non-compliance were, however, he didn't elaborate.

He didn't need to.

After months of intimidation I crumbled. I'd spent every day I could inside my parents' house. When I left the building I was looking over my shoulder, assessing every person I passed as a potential member of the community. Even the people I recognised from the Southall or Havelock Road *gurdwara* made me jump. What if it was *them*? What if they were the ones who were going to protect the Athwals' honour?

I called my family liaison officer, the wonderful Angie Barton.

'Hi, Sarbjit, are you OK?'

'I need to see you and Clive.'

'What's it about?' Her voice switched from friendly to professional. 'Can I help you now?'

'I just need to see you.'

'OK. I'll call you back.'

She did. I met up with her and Clive the following morning. Normally I left any meeting with the DCI feeling like I could take on the world. This time I could barely make myself enter the same room. He didn't deserve what I was about to do. Not after the promise he'd made my dad to protect me. Not after everything he'd done.

'What's this about, Mrs A?' Clive asked.

'I've been thinking.' I'd rehearsed it in my head but the words wouldn't come out. I felt sick. Was I really going to go through with this? Was I really going to lie to the one man who could save me? 'I want to retract my statement,' I said.

Silence from the police officers.

'You want to retract your statement? Why would you want to do that?'

'I just do.' I stared at the floor, hoping for the strength to carry on.

'But why? Don't you want Surjit's murderers to be behind bars?'

'Of course I do. But I don't want to have anything to do with it.'

Clive leaned in. His usually friendly face was stern. 'Is someone putting pressure on you, Mrs A?'

I shook my head.

'You can tell me if they are. No one is allowed to speak to you about this case, do you understand? You are a court witness – you're our *main* witness, for goodness' sake – so if anyone tries to change your mind they're breaking the law and we can have 'em. Do you understand me? If anyone so much as suggests you change your mind about testifying in court, I will nick them. They won't trouble you again.'

He looked directly into my eyes. 'So I'm asking again, who is intimidating you?'

I clammed up. I couldn't trust myself to speak without caving in. I was so scared. Had I made a mistake in coming?

I thought of Hardave's face. I thought of how cut up he was about his mother being in prison. Then I thought about Surjit's unconscious body being thrown into the Ravi River and I realised the woman in my imagination had my face. I would never be safe.

'No one is intimidating me.'

'OK,' Clive said. 'We'll leave it at that.'

* * *

In March 2007, a few months after I'd pulled out of the case, Angie rang me to talk about my old house. In particular, some things the police had found there. She also mentioned why they'd entered the property in the first place.

'Clive wanted you to know that Hardave has been arrested for interfering with a witness and trying to pervert the course of justice.'

Wow. I was speechless. When did that happen?

Neither of them had believed me, it turned out, when I said that I had no reason to withdraw my statement. And if intimidation was likely to come from anywhere, it had to be my husband. Officers had arrested Hardave and then a team of experts had searched the house. The first sweep of upstairs and downstairs revealed nothing by way of proof. Then Clive had a brainwave. He asked DS Palpinder Singh, a very experienced Sikh officer, to search the prayer room.

Out of deference to our culture and beliefs, the officer removed his shoes. It was the only room that hadn't been searched. No one had dared, given its religious significance, and the Met's paranoia about offending minority cultures. Institutional racism was a hot potato in the media at the time.

The officer made a rudimentary search then looked at the one thing in the room that no one had considered. The Guru Granth Sahib. The Eleventh Guru. *The Holy Bible.*

Showing it the deference our religion demanded, the policeman flicked carefully through the large pages. Towards the end he stopped. There was something stuck near the spine of the book. He pulled the page open and a dozen pieces of paper fluttered to the floor.

Where I had been too scared to, Hardave had kept every note he ever gave me. As a result, he was arrested.

The bad news was Clive's reaction. I'd never seen him so angry before and never have since.

'Don't you dare lie to me again, Mrs A. We can't do anything if you're not honest. Can I trust you or not?'

I nodded.

'I'm sorry. You can trust me.'

Point made, Clive flashed me his customary wide smile. That was the face I was used to seeing.

'You've already been so strong, Mrs A, but you just need to keep it up until we get to court. We're here to help in any way we can but I promise you now, if you get through this, you will not only get justice for Surjit but you'll save the lives of hundreds of other girls like her.' He paused. 'Can you do this?'

'Yes,' I said.

And I meant it.

* * *

Hardave's run-in with the police coincided with me getting a new place to live. Moving was a huge effort but, looking back, it was also a sign that I was coming out of my dark place. A couple of months earlier I would never have been able to arrange anything so practical.

And there was an upside to the upheaval of the move as well. A magnificent, wonderful upside.

Because, rather than being a single room in a run-down hostel, my new home was a council house in Kingston. It was sparse and needed work but it had something I'd been dreaming of: three large bedrooms – enough for all my children.

The day I picked up the keys was the happiest I'd been in years. I collected the children an hour later. If I'd thought that was the start of good times, however, I was wrong. They'd only been in their new home a few minutes when Taran set the tone immediately by bursting into tears.

'What's wrong?'

'It's you!' she screamed.

'Me?'

'You got our dad arrested. You put my grandma in prison. You put our uncle in prison. What are you doing? When are you going to stop lying?'

I tried to hug her but she threw me off. Now I was crying as well. At sixteen Taran was a woman – the same age as Surjit when she married – but she would always be my little girl. I hated seeing her like this. Even more, I hated knowing what I was about to tell her.

'Taran, I'm not lying. Your gran and uncle killed Pawanpreet's mum. Whatever they tell you, that's what they did. Dad knows that.' I looked at her tear-stained, angry face. 'I'm not the one who's making things up.'

I could understand her being upset about her dad. I could understand she was angry with me, too. But what was the alternative?

Taran wasn't the only one Hardave managed to influence. From the moment he started seeing the children regularly at weekends, they all began repeating their father's words.

'Why did you tell the police lies about Mum and Uncle?' Balveen demanded one Sunday. As with Pav, Bachan Kaur had insisted my children call her 'Mum'.

My mouth fell open. *He's using you to get to me now?* Just when I thought Hardave couldn't go any lower.

'I haven't told any lies.'

'Dad says you have.'

'Dad just doesn't want to think anything bad about his family.' I refused to get into a slanging match. Hardave was their father, a good one once upon a time. No child deserves to be caught in the middle of a row between his or her parents. They certainly shouldn't be used as weapons.

I just wished Hardave felt the same. But any hope that he might have learned a lesson about his behaviour after the police had got involved vanished within months of weekend access to the children. Balveen couldn't wait to tell me her great news.

'Mum, Dad says we're all going to live as a family again.'

That was a blow I didn't see coming. Even after all we'd been through, after seventeen years of marriage, there was still a part of me that hoped a reconciliation wasn't out of the question. Now, I realised, that was never going to happen. *I can't be with a man who uses his kids like this.*

But I couldn't say that to an eight-year-old.

'What did Daddy say, darling?'

'He said if you tell the police you lied, then Mum and Uncle can come out of prison and we can all live as a family again. So can you do it? Can you phone them now?'

It's the hardest line to walk. Trying to tell your child that you're not a liar without saying their father is. One look at Balveen's face, crushed with disappointment, told me that whatever I said, I was to blame for everything that was wrong in her world.

And, for that moment, I felt I was, too.

'Can you do this?' Clive's words echoed in my brain.

Yes, I can. Whatever the cost, I will get through this.

But when I looked at my children's dejected faces, it was hard and it got worse. When Hardave drove them home one Sunday, Balveen came rushing into the kitchen.

'Mum, come and wave at Dad.'

'Wave at him? Why would I want to do that?'

'Mum, come on! Dad wants you to show him that you love him. He says he'll forgive you for lying. Then we can be a family again.'

'I'm not waving at him,' I said, as calmly as I could muster.

'Please!'

Even as my daughter exploded into tears, yelling at me how I was wrecking her life, I held my ground. Inside, however, I was crumbling. How could he do this? How could he sink so low that he'd get his own children to persuade me to drop my statement? Forget about notes on pieces of paper, this was intimidation that no police search could find.

And then things reached a new low. It was Balveen again who revealed gleefully, 'Dad's got a surprise for you!'

'What is it?'

'I can't tell you.'

Smiling, I said, 'OK.' *She's eight. I'll be surprised if her secret lasts another minute.*

When the pressure finally did get too much for her, I soon stopped smiling. Balveen revealed that every weekend the children saw Hardave he asked them to write notes about me. Things I'd said that they didn't like, lies they said I'd told, anything that was vaguely negative. It was so hurtful to hear. Worst of all was the pride Balveen seemed to have in telling me.

'My list is eight pages! Taran's is ten.'

How had Hardave distorted our children's reality like this? Remembering the childish glee in my daughter's voice when she told me about the notes, I couldn't remember feeling lower. In desperation I called an old family friend of the Athwals. As I knew from our conversations over the years, he was both an incredibly religious, virtuous man and someone Hardave respected. If anyone could talk some sense into my husband, it was him.

I found the number and waited till I was alone. I realised I was trembling as I dialled. But, I knew, if I got through this ordeal it could change my life.

It did. But not in the way I was hoping.

'Sarbjit, you must stop this campaign against your family!' the family elder ordered. 'You are bringing shame on everyone. How dare you go to the police.'

'But you don't understand,' I cried, 'they murdered Surjit. I have to tell the truth!'

'You have to honour your family. That is all. What have you got out of this? You've put your mother-in-law in prison and for what?'

'I've done it for Surjit.'

'Pah.'

I couldn't believe it. He didn't call me a liar like everyone else. In fact, he didn't speak about the murder at all. All he cared about was me damaging Hardave's name by walking out on him, and Bachan Kaur's and Sukhdave's names by putting them in prison. There was only one person to blame for the hell I was going through – and that, he said, was me.

* * *

It took me days to recover from the conversation with the family elder. Then, just as I'd managed to convince myself that he was wrong and that I was doing the right thing, I had an encounter at the temple that I will never forget. A man followed me out of the prayer room and into the car park. I recognised him as one of the temple elders, a highly respected man in the community.

'Sarbjit Kaur, I must speak with you.'

'Hello,' I said. 'What's on your mind?'

'You must stop these lies against Bachan Kaur.'

Not you as well!

I felt that familiar feeling of nausea. This man was meant to be a role model. Hundreds, if not thousands, of Sikhs looked up to him and they sought to lead their lives in his fashion. And he too was choosing to side with appearances over evidence. It didn't matter to him that an innocent girl had died.

'I am not lying,' I said, choosing my words as carefully as I could. 'Bachan Kaur had Surjit killed. She told me herself.'

'Lies!' His eyes bulged with rage. He was not a man used to being contradicted. 'She is a holy woman, she is a religious woman, she prays, she attends temple, she makes *langar* for our community. Tell the police you are mistaken. Let this poor woman have her life back.'

From the moment that man spoke to me, others in the community seemed to feel the urge to step forward too. None of them supported me. The nearer the trial date of April 2007 got, the comments from friends and strangers grew more frequent. The *gurdwara* is meant to be a haven, a place of sanctuary and sanctity for Sikhs. These people turned it into a place I dreaded to visit. I was a good Sikh. I lived the right way. But I was being ostracised by my own community. And for what? The honour of a murderer.

I began to dread Sunday afternoons and found myself driving further afield to worship at a place where I wouldn't be shunned.

Rows with strangers were one thing, however. The long nights of arguments with the people I loved most were what truly weakened me. There were times when I came close to saying, 'OK, Taran, OK, Balveen, OK, boys, I admit it, I lied. Tell your dad I'm coming back.' It would have meant so much to all of them.

It would also have got me out of the horror that was fast approaching – that day when I was going to have to stand in a court and confront the two people I'd been scared of my entire married life. That terrified me more than a lifetime playing happy families with a man I hated. As March turned into April, the anxious, sleepless nights when I thought of running away grew more frequent.

I just need to escape.

But I couldn't do it. Not to Surjit – and not to the hundreds of other girls that Clive said my testimony would save.

CHAPTER TWENTY-ONE

HAVE YOU REACHED
A VERDICT?

After two horrible years it was time.

As the trial date approached, the pressure from my children only increased. DCI Driscoll and DS Barton were there for me every step of the way. But the nerves I was experiencing weren't something the Metropolitan Police could help with.

The reason I'd kept silent about Surjit for so long was because I had been worried about my own safety. That fear, however, was nothing to the dread I had now that my children – and my community – would never forgive me.

Hardave didn't help. Despite everything we'd already been through, he called me one day, with the same plea he'd made for the past two years.

'You have to fix this,' he said. 'If my mother and brother are found guilty, they could go to prison for life. I'm begging you. You have to tell the police that you made it up.'

'I didn't make anything up! You know the truth. Why are you bullying me?'

He was a man on the edge. The last years without the cocoon of his family could have been the making of him. It seemed to me they'd snapped him instead.

'Just tell them, all right? I've spoken to my solicitor. You might get two years for perjury but it will get my family out. Then we can all start again.'

'Are you serious? You want me to lie and go to prison? To help those murderers?'

No answer.

'What about the children?' I asked.

'Mum will look after them.'

He had it all worked out. When I refused he actually seemed surprised.

***

I like to think that my daughter Taran didn't just choose to side with her dad because she loved him more than me – although I will always have to live with the fact that I was the one who'd left them in 2005, not him. Instead, I prefer to assume she just didn't want to think the worst of her grandma. Who would?

Knowing that was one thing, however. Dealing with it was another.

With the trial a week away, Hardave stepped up his negative PR campaign. Taran was filled with lie after lie about me and my motives. In his defence, I don't think it was ever Hardave's intention to turn his children against me for the sake of it. He was so wrapped up in trying to clear his mum and brother's name and save their honour, that he was desperate enough to try anything. And what was most likely to work, in his opinion? If my beloved children begged me to stop.

He told Taran that I was ill. That she should pity me. That I was losing my mind, rambling, making things up.

'You know your grandmother,' he said. 'She prays day and night. She could never murder anybody.'

Taran should have known me better. But she was confused and scared. She came home after her time with Dad in fighting form.

'Where's the body?' she demanded.

'Hello?'

'Dad says the reason he knows you're lying is because my aunt has never been found. If she's dead, where's the body?'

'The body's not been found.'

'How can you say she's been murdered then?'

I could have explained. I could have gone into the details Clive had shared of his investigation. He'd flown to India and learned that the Ravi River, which flows through the Punjab, leads straight to Pakistan. The Punjab, in fact, used to be part of that country, and relations these days are not good. According to local witnesses, Surjit's was just one of thousands of bodies disposed of in that river. There's nothing more satisfying to an Indian murderer, he gleaned, than knowing the corpse will be washed quickly across the border for their hated neighbours to deal with.

Instead, I said simply, 'It's not up to me. A jury's going to decide. All I can do is tell them honestly what I've heard and what I know.'

'Such as?'

'Such as: I know Surjit went to India. I know she was drugged, strangled and dumped in the river because your grandmother told me. And I was at the meeting when she planned it.' I promised myself I wouldn't get emotional, that I wouldn't let this subject come between me and my children. But the tears were coming. 'On top of that,' I continued, 'don't you think it's weird that nobody has heard from Surjit in nine years? Her credit cards have never been used, she's never contacted any of her friends and, even if you don't believe anything else, ask yourself: would the Auntie Surjit you knew and loved just leave her children behind? She adored her children like I adore you.'

Taran chewed over the idea. I could have continued but I wanted her to know the truth, not just believe me because

I was standing in front of her. That was Hardave's style, not mine.

'Look,' I said, 'don't take my word for it. Don't think you have to choose between your dad and me. You're nearly seventeen, you're an adult. Use your own judgement, your own common sense. Come to the Old Bailey next week. Sit in the gallery and listen to all the evidence. It's not just me going there. You'll hear things from both sides. The jury has to make its mind up. You can do the same.'

'OK,' she said. 'I'll do that.'

That night she called Hardave and told him she'd be going.

'OK, no problem. You'll hear the truth.'

I was surprised by that. But a few days later, after a visit to his mum in prison, Hardave called back, and Taran changed her mind.

'I'm not coming to court, Mum,' she said to me.

What?

'Of course you have to come. You're an adult now. You can make your own mind up about everything.'

I could see she wasn't sure.

'Look,' I said, 'I'm scared stiff of going. But you can sit with my mum. Knowing you two are up there watching will really help me go through with it.'

'OK, you win. I'll come.'

'Great,' I said.

Now I just have to convince myself to go.

* * *

Pawanpreet was forbidden from attending. Bachan Kaur and Sukhdave had sent the command from their cells. Knowing those two were still pulling the strings made me even more nervous than I already was about facing them in court. I began to fantasise. What if Bachan Kaur had arranged, through her son, for someone to make sure I never made it to the Old Bailey? Should I be looking over my shoulder?

There were only days to go. Clive and his team were finally showing some nerves of their own as they fussed around me, trying to act cool – to keep me cool – but desperate to make sure I was as prepared as I could be. We'd already gone over my evidence with the legal team. Now they described the process, the players, what the court physically looked like – everything they could think of to put my mind at rest. Finally, though, there was no more time for preparation. It was 25 April 2007. Judgement day. We were going to court.

The trial was actually in full swing for a few weeks before I was called to appear. In that time the defence and prosecution barristers had set out their cases and various witnesses had been called and cross-examined by both sides. For the defence, led by Kaly Kaul and Dafna Spiro for Bachan Kaur and Jonathan Rose and P Eastwood for Sukhdave, all of Hardave's sisters were called as well as a priest from the *gurdwara* and various friends who gave character references. Bachan Kaur and Sukhdave in the witness box obviously took the lion's share of court time. The prosecution, conducted by Michael Worsley QC and Bobbie Cheema, countered with appearances from my father and sisters, Jagdeesh Singh and his wife and father, several of Surjit's old colleagues, and even the alleged father of Surjit's little boy. DCI Driscoll was also called upon to give the results of his investigation.

During the course of the evidence given, so many things came to light that even I didn't know. Clive was able to produce all the phone records for 88 Willow Tree Lane showing the flurry of calls made to India in the run-up to when he suspected Surjit was killed. He also made known the fact that Sukhdave had been in contact with his second wife, Manjit Kaur, at least a month before Surjit disappeared

– her number and address appear in his diary in November 1998 – almost as though he were lining up her replacement. Most disturbing of all was the discovery of a diary written by Surjit in the run-up to her disappearance, as well as notes written for her impending divorce. In each she described being bullied and beaten, cowed and maltreated by her husband and mother-in-law. I was heartbroken to hear of her pain, knowing I had not been able to do anything about it.

The diaries and many other personal effects had been unearthed in an almost comical manner. Knowing they could be inflammatory, Sukhdave had boxed them up and taken them to the house of his sister Kalwant, to be stored in her loft. I don't believe Sukhdave ever told her what he was storing, but one day Kalwant's husband had discovered the collection and informed me and I told Clive. He was shocked at the treasure trove he discovered. Anyone else, he said, would have destroyed the lot. Sukhdave, for some reason, had kept it all safe and sound in his sister's house. For all the Athwals' scheming and deception, this, Clive reckoned, was such an amateur error he was amazed they'd evaded capture for as long as they had.

It was Sukhdave's evidence, however, that proved the most enlightening. In response to cross-examination about the meetings with Surjit's supposed friend 'Kate' at Heathrow Airport, he admitted, 'I made her up.' Put to him by Mr Worsley that this was the act of a guilty man trying to cover his tracks, Sukhdave said, 'I was under a lot of pressure at the time. I just wanted the questions to go away.'

Poor Clive. In his evidence he recalled how the police had found 156 Kates, Catherines, Katherines, Katies, Katys, some people who wanted to be called Kate and even one woman who was only Kate at weekends. It was a massive waste of manpower – and all because Sukhdave said he got bored of being bothered.

That pressure was also blamed for his trying to halt the Indian investigation. During his trip to the Punjab, DCI Driscoll had been confused why the police over there had done so little. It was at that point they produced the letter that was apparently from the London Metropolitan Police, telling them that Surjit was unhappy with her father – the implication being that she'd run away.

The original investigative team now explained that they had never sent any such letter to the Indian police, and closer examination of it showed it was actually a photocopy of the top and bottom of a letter from the police to Sukhdave, with new text added in the middle. No wonder the Indian police had hit the 'halt' button. London's mighty Metropolitan Police Service had told them to!

Sukhdave's forgery didn't end there. In 2004 the deeds of 88 Willow Tree Lane were transferred from him, Surjit, me and Hardave to Sukhdave and Bachan Kaur. My husband and I had signed. The crucial signature for Surjit had come from Sukhdave's shaking pen.

But there was another reason for the failure of the Indian side of the investigation. When Clive went over to pursue his own enquiries, he was met with many obstacles, some logistical, some cultural, some geographical and some seemingly designed to hinder his work. The suggestion that bribery was commonplace in certain areas of the Punjabi police was put to him and he was forced to take it seriously.

What he took even more seriously was an officer's throwaway comment to him.

'Why are the London police wasting so much resources on looking for this girl? This is family business. It is nothing to do with the police.'

And that, Clive said, was the exact problem he was facing in London – and the reason Bachan Kaur and Sukhdave were so convinced they could, quite literally, get away with murder.

There are areas of west London, Clive explained, that appear to operate more like villages in the Punjab than districts in Southall. If families have a problem they go to the elders of the temple. Everything is kept within the community. And I – 'Mrs A' – he said, had committed the crime in the community's eyes by forcing the rest of the world to take notice.

* * *

Knowing that the trial was going on didn't help my nerves one bit. I wasn't pleased, either, when on the very first day I was due to appear I got a message from Mr Worsley saying that he was holding me over until the following day. They'd decided to start with Jagdeesh Singh, followed by me.

The only good thing to come out of it was that Taran actually forced herself to go. Unfortunately she only lasted half a day.

At first I was angry with her for walking out. Then she explained and I became angry at someone else.

Having failed to get Hardave to ban his daughter from attending, Bachan Kaur had panicked. Spying Taran in the gallery she identified her companion: my mother. She called a court officer over and said, via an interpreter, 'There's a woman in the gallery pulling faces at me. I can't be expected to sit here and put up with that.'

A few minutes later two police officers appeared alongside my mum in the gallery.

'Would you come with me please, madam?' one of the PCs said. Taran translated.

Utterly perplexed and afraid, Mum had followed them out of the courtroom. The knock-on effect was Taran had no one to sit with and so couldn't go either. She shouldn't have to endure that alone.

Bachan Kaur's manipulative abilities hadn't been blunted in jail. She'd won yet again.

***

It wasn't the best omen.

Sitting in an anteroom along the corridor from the court chamber, I felt the air warming. I started to loosen my clothing. I was getting claustrophobic. Out of nowhere it felt like I was being strangled, suffocated.

Opposite me, my family liaison officer's mouth was moving. She was talking to me. *I need to listen ...*

Angie Barton was answering my question about giving evidence. I'd said I couldn't imagine speaking out of turn in front of my family. I'd been raised to respect my elders. So, remembering the statement I'd given in 2005, I asked to give my evidence via video.

'That's not going to be possible.'

'But I've read about it. You can do it now.'

'It's not a question of technology,' Angie said. 'It's a question of you connecting with the jury and the judge. And I know you, Sarbjit. Anyone who sees you speak will fall on your side. You have to do it in person. We can't leave anything to chance.'

We argued, between my palpitations, for three hours. Then a clerk of the court appeared in the doorway.

'Time,' he said.

Angie looked excited. 'Let's go,' she said. 'Let's go and get justice for Surjit.'

The walk along the long, windowless corridor to our courtroom seemed to go on for ever. With every step my legs got weaker and weaker. We reached a large wooden door and the court official guarding it checked to see if we were allowed to enter. Then he returned, nodded, and I nearly cried.

This is it. I'm going to do this!

In the sketch I'd been drawn of the courtroom I remembered seeing the judge and the jury. I thought I would walk through that door now and be in front of both of them. What I didn't take into account was the journey to my seat.

When the court official opened the door and I stepped through, I got the shock of my life. Sitting directly opposite the door and staring right at me were Sukhdave and Bachan Kaur Athwal. I hadn't seen them for nearly two years but my heart jumped like it was yesterday.

I wanted so much to turn back and tell everyone it was a mistake. Then I saw the official had stopped by my chair. I stopped, sat down and caught my breath. I was facing the judge, His Honour Giles Forrester, and the jury now. But when the judge asked me to swear my name, I stuttered in reply. Even though I was no longer facing them, all I could think about were the four unforgiving eyes glaring over my shoulders.

I felt like a new kid at school. Everyone else in the room had been there the day before. I was the one trying to find my way, to fit in. Everywhere I looked there were expressionless faces judging me before I'd even uttered a word.

And then there were the wigs. And the gowns. It was all so alien. Clive had told me that if I relaxed everything would be fine. How was that possible when I'd never felt so out of place?

Mr Worsley did his utmost to put me at my ease. He guided me through my statement of 27 October 2005 and later information I'd given the police. Nothing worked, though. The first few answers I gave were monosyllabic. The ones after that weren't much better. I'd never spoken in public before. I'd certainly never addressed a room like this in English. That in itself was intimidating. Hearing my own fragile voice drowned out by the silence of that grand hall proved too distracting. But that wasn't the real problem. The real reasons I stumbled and tripped over my words were sitting to my right. Even with the jury in front of me and

Judge Forrester and the barrister to my left, out of the corner of my eye I was aware at all times of the glowering faces of Bachan Kaur and Sukhdave Athwal.

I had only ever raised my voice once to my mother-in-law and never to Sukhdave. I was absolutely terrified of them and had lived in fear of them for my entire marriage. How on earth did anyone expect me to suddenly shake off a lifetime's training to obey my elders and speak out now?

With every answer I gave I felt more sick. Was I imagining it or could I hear them whispering at me to shut up? The more I thought about their venomous faces, the more stilted my answers became.

I just want to get out.

At the end of the day I was drained and sure of one thing. I did not want to do it again. Unfortunately, I was told I had to.

'This could take days,' Angie, my family liaison officer, said.

The more I dwelled on it, the more I convinced myself I couldn't go through that torture again.

'I'm sorry, Sarbjit,' Angie said. 'But you have to.'

'Well, can I be hidden then? I've seen programmes on TV where witnesses go behind a screen or they're even filmed from another room.'

'I'll check.'

It was an anxious half an hour before a reply came back. I could tell from Angie's face which way it had gone before she opened her mouth.

'I'm sorry. His Honour says you're doing brilliantly. He wouldn't be doing the prosecution justice if he allowed you to hide.'

Doing brilliantly? I thought I must have looked like an idiot. I was so nervous I even got one or two facts wrong and had to go back and correct them. That didn't sound brilliant to me.

* * *

But the next day, after a fitful night's sleep, something odd happened. Whether it was the judge's faith in me or just the fact I wasn't overawed by new surroundings this time I don't know, but I began to speak with conviction. It took a while, but the fear that had tied my tongue soon gave way to anger – at what they'd done to Surjit and the intimidation they'd used to cover it up – and that emotion was just crying out to be heard.

I could see from Mr Worsley's expression that he was pleased. Sadly, when he had finished holding my hand through his questions, it was time to be put under the grill by the defence team. For the next two days I was called a liar in new and inventive ways. One exchange summed it up.

On 16 May, Miss Kaul said, 'You, from the beginning, about this matter, have been telling lies.'

To which I replied, 'I haven't.'

It was Sukhdave and Bachan Kaur's defence that I'd concocted this vicious slur on their characters recently. Statements given by my sister Inder, where she revealed being told the truth in 1999, shot this down – as did the Met's discovery of my 1998 letter to Hayes police station sitting ignored on a shelf for nine years. But that didn't stop Miss Kaul and her colleagues raining punches on my integrity hour after hour.

Years ago they would have broken me. But as I stood in that witness box in May 2007, I realised, *I've been called a liar and threatened for nearly ten years now – and by people a lot scarier than you.*

The only people in the world I was afraid of were in the same room but they weren't the ones in wigs. It was the knowledge that my testimony would protect me from them that made me work even harder.

* * *

And then it was over. My moment in centre-stage had passed, the defence and prosecution concluded their arguments and the jury retired to consider their verdict.

'How long will this take?' I asked Clive.

'Could be half an hour, could be a month.' In his opinion it should have been the former but with juries you never knew.

As the first day with no answer turned into night, I realised how tense I'd become. *Remember to breathe, Sarbjit.* Any relief that I'd felt stepping down from the witness box was gone. The rest of my life depended on whatever decision those strangers I'd spent three-and-a-half days staring at came up with.

By day two I found the strength to leave the house. This wasn't easy. Since the trial had started, the news had been saturated with details. My name and testimony had been on the Internet almost as soon as I'd said it, with the radio, television and newspapers picking up on it immediately after. Walking down my own street I was convinced people were staring. Just when I thought I'd encountered all the unpleasantness I could, this was new.

By the time the jury had been out for nearly a week I was at my wits' end. How hard could it be? Hadn't they heard anything I said? All I wanted to hear was that the judge had said, 'Members of the jury – have you reached a verdict?' I was getting so twitchy leaving the house that I even found myself not caring if they came up with a 'not guilty' verdict, just to get it over with. My mother-in-law hadn't been able to kill me but it really felt like the suspense might.

When my sister Inder asked me to accompany her into Victoria to pick up a passport for her daughter, I said no. When she persuaded me into it I agreed, as long as we weren't too long. The idea of being so far from home, surrounded by peering strangers, made me short of breath.

I was outside the passport office when my mobile rang.
Clive's number.

My fingers were shaking too much to answer first time.
I managed to hit 'accept' and lift the phone to my ear
without dropping it. I was so tense I didn't actually take in
the first few things Clive said. But I made out one word.

'Guilty.'

Everything after that went straight over my head. My
mind went blank, I started to choke, my stomach felt like it
was going to empty itself and my legs folded. My sister
discovered me a few minutes later slumped against the wall.

'Sarb! Are you all right? What's happened?'

I could barely speak. But I managed to repeat the only
word I'd heard.

'Guilty.'

Inder's excited hug forced the air from my lungs.

'You did it, Sarb! You won.'

I didn't feel like a winner at that moment. But when
Bachan Kaur was sentenced to serve a minimum of twenty
years in prison and Sukhdave a minimum of twenty-seven, I
let myself begin to believe it.

It's over, I thought. *It's finally over.*

After nine long years, we'd done it. We'd beaten them.

We'd got justice for Surjit.

I smiled as the memory of my name's meaning flashed into
my head. Perhaps my dad knew something after all. Maybe,
just this once, I could be called 'all victorious'.

IF I HAD A KNIFE

Following an appeal in May 2009, the lawyers acting for Bachan Kaur and Sukhdave earned their clients a reduction in their minimum sentences, from twenty-seven to twenty years for Sukhdave and twenty to fifteen for his mother. After the trial was over, the CPS elected not to continue with the prosecution against Hardave for intimidating a witness as they said it was not in the public interest.

Responding to the discovery that Sukhdave had forged Surjit's signature to transfer the deeds of No. 88 Willow Tree Lane from her, me and Hardave, to just Sukhdave and his mother, Clive set in motion a Confiscation Order. By wiping Surjit off the house title, Sukhdave had effectively robbed his own children of their legal inheritance. Despite the money being dissipated via a series of bank accounts in different names, the police were able to get it back. Surjit's children were both awarded more than £40,000, to be held in trust until they are of a certain age.

I will never forgive Bachan Kaur Athwal for distorting the teachings of the Ten Gurus. Over the years I questioned many times whether it was my religion's fault that Surjit was murdered. But it wasn't. Bachan Kaur claimed to be acting in the name of the community, in the name of Sikhs' honour everywhere. She wasn't. She only ever acted in the name of evil, in the name of selfishness, greed and vanity.

To this day I try to avoid Southall temple. When I do go, it is rare that I am not accosted by someone who accuses me of bringing shame on my family by having my mother- and brother-in-law arrested. It's a warped logic that values a murderer's good name over the life of a young girl whose only crime was to be stuck in a loveless marriage.

In December 2012, after five long years of fighting, I finally won my divorce from Hardave. I'm pleased to say my children all live with me in a new home in Surrey, and I do my best to give them not only the childhood Hardave would not allow, but also the one I was denied. They go swimming, they watch television, they stay over at friends' houses, and have every support in their education that I can provide. But that is not to say there is no place for religion in our home. My children may not be able to speak Punjabi, but my paintings of the First Guru and the Golden Temple in Amritsar still look down from our walls, and we are all Sikhs. My faith, in all of this, has never wavered.

For the record, should any of my children ever ask for an arranged marriage – they will definitely not be getting one.

* * *

Inspired by the incredible, selfless work that DCI Driscoll and his team did in bringing Surjit's murderers to justice, in November 2008 I embarked on a new challenge: I began training to become a police community support officer. If it weren't for the police, and their patience and support, I don't think I would be here today. The way Clive understood the difficulties I was facing and gave me the courage and the confidence to fight back changed my life. I came out of the experience a new person. As a result I wanted to give something back. I wanted to become the support and encouragement for others in my position. If I can help just one person it will all have been worthwhile.

* * *

But my story nearly didn't have a happy ending. I was at my parents' house a few weeks after the sentencing in 2007 when my daughter, Taran, turned up. She surprised us all by saying, 'Pav's outside.'

'Well, invite her in to say hello then,' I said.

'You're the last person she wants to see.'

'Why?'

'Why do you think? You're the one who put her grandma and father in prison. The only people she had left in the world, and you put them away. She's got no one now, thanks to you.'

'If she thinks that,' I said, 'then I definitely need to see her.'

Taran disappeared out the front. When she returned she was followed by a beautiful young woman whom I'd last spoken to as a girl. After so many years of being kept apart by Sukhdave – Pav had been forbidden to speak to me since 2005 – I was so happy to see her. By contrast, she looked like she wanted to punch me.

Actually, it was worse.

'If I had a knife now I would stab you,' Pav said calmly and coldly.

Taken aback, I said, 'Well, what's stopping you?'

She didn't answer that, just rolled her eyes and said, 'Thanks to you I've got no one in my life. My mum's already run away and now you've lied and got my dad and gran imprisoned as well.'

I knew immediately that Hardave and his sisters, on Sukhdave and Bachan Kaur's orders, had found some way to prevent Pav from following the case on the news. I don't know how – it had been everywhere. They must have stopped her socialising as well, because the whole community was talking about the verdict.

'Pawanpreet, I would never lie to you and I will not start now.'

'OK,' she said, desperately fighting her own emotions, 'Then where's my mum?'

Oh, you poor child.

'Your mum's not here,' I said as flatly as I could manage.

'She left me though, didn't she? She ran away with someone.'

'That's not what happened,' I said. 'She would never leave you.'

'Don't lie. Grandma said you'd lie. She said you're our worst enemy.'

'Pav, look at me. The only time your mother left you was to go on holiday with your grandma. Just a holiday, do you understand? She thought she was coming back after a fortnight. She planned to. There was no way she could bear to be without you and your brother for more than that.'

The poor girl was confused now, her anger diluted by a desire to know what really happened to her mother.

'Do you want me to tell you?' I asked. 'Do you really want to know what happened?

'Yes.'

'I'm really sorry, Pav, but ...'

I can't do it. I can't be the one to tell her.

No one had been honest with this young girl in her entire life. How could I do it now, knowing that what I was about to say would break her heart? But someone had to. She couldn't go on living a lie that wasn't her making. I took a deep breath, fought back the tears and said, 'They did it. They killed your mum. I'm so sorry, there's no other way to say it.'

'No!' she shouted, her face flushed with rage. 'Dad loved her even though she was horrible to him. And Grandma brought me up. You know how religious she is.' She was shaking. I just wanted to hold her, but she would not let me near. 'They would never do that.'

'Well, the truth is, they did. But like I've said to Taran and my other children, don't take my word for it. Ask the police. They have all the information. They have your mum's divorce application and even her personal diary. Ask them for a transcript of the court case. I wasn't the only one who spoke out.'

'Dad said you were.'

I don't know which of us was hating this more. But I had to go on, even though with every word I uttered, I saw my niece crumble.

'Why do you think he stopped you going to the Old Bailey?' I asked as gently as I could. 'Why did he tell your aunt to stop you watching TV? From listening to the radio? From going out? He knows what he did and he knows you would have discovered it as well if you'd heard the news, bumped into one of your friends or sat in that court.'

Pav went silent for a few minutes. She was clearly shaken. Anyone would be, trying to process what I'd just told her.

'Dad said you just did it for money,' she said, eventually. *I'm sorry?*

'What money?' I asked. I could barely disguise my laughter.

'Well, Dad and Grandma are in prison and you're living in a mansion now, aren't you? Where did you get the money for that?'

'Are you serious? Who told you that?'

It was common knowledge, she said, at home and in the community. That didn't surprise me. Bachan Kaur's friends at the temple had been so quick to accuse me of stealing money from her before, when we'd flown to Canada. Pav also claimed I owned a fleet of brand-new cars, all bought with my ill-gotten gains from testifying against Bachan Kaur and Sukhdave.

'Why else would you do it?' Pav said. 'You had to get something out of it.'

'Is that what your grandmother said?'

She nodded. 'OK,' I said, 'this is silly. Do me a favour. I live about thirty minutes from here. Come to my house.'

'I don't want to come to your mansion.'

'Please, I'm begging you. Come and see the hole I live in.'

I had a new car at that time, paid for on HP – but it was only new to me. There couldn't have been a more rattly piece of engineering in London. But it got me from A to B. And it got me – and Pav – home. The only problem was, she didn't believe we'd arrived. Even as we walked down the side of the unassuming semi-detached house, even as I pulled the keys from my pocket and even as I put them in the Yale lock, my niece was still saying, 'Where do you live?'

I pushed the side door open and gestured to the plain home inside.

'Here.'

I explained to her the squalor I'd been living in for two years, how this was only meant to be temporary accommodation but that we'd been there for what seemed like forever. Pav didn't have to see much of the house to realise I was telling the truth.

'So they lied to me about the money, then,' she said. She went silent, taking in her surroundings, like she was double-checking that the peeled paintwork wasn't hiding gold.

'The thing is, Pav,' I said, 'if they lied to you about the money ...' The rest didn't need saying. She nodded, slowly, weighed down suddenly by the weight of the world. She had learned enough, I could tell.

'OK,' she announced, 'I want to speak to the police.'

A short while later, having studied the police's evidence, Pav wrote to her father and grandmother and explained that she would not be visiting them again – and she explained why.

I took no pleasure from this. A child should be able to believe in their parents. By telling Pav the truth, I'd denied her that bond. But, I had to keep reminding myself, it wasn't just Pav and her brother that I'd been looking out for. Everything I'd done had been for Surjit.

Years later, I'm proud to say that I have a very close relationship with Pav, her brother, her husband – and her daughter and son! I just wish her mother could be here to share the pleasure. In her absence, we do our best for each other.

In December 2012, Pav and I hosted a meeting in Surjit's name at the Houses of Parliament, designed to raise awareness of honour killings. Watching Pav speak to some of our country's leaders, including the Right Honourable Stephen Timms MP, about honour killings, I've never been more proud of my niece.

Also present at Parliament that day was Clive. He spoke eloquently and movingly about his determination to get justice for Surjit where two other investigations had failed. Unlike me and Pav, he didn't know and love her, but his dedication couldn't have been more powerful. Then, having impressed the audience of honour-based-violence workers, MPs and victims with the details of his investigation, Clive pointed to me and said, 'That woman over there, ladies and gentlemen, is my hero.'

I didn't know whether to blush or cry.

At least I was able to repay the compliment. Because there is only one hero in this terrible story and it is him. All I'd done was overcome my fear and eventually tell the truth. Clive was the person who'd achieved the impossible. He was the one who'd believed in me and got me to believe in myself. He was the one who managed to build a successful murder case in a different country to where the crime took place, against two people who didn't physically do it, and when no body was ever found. Nobody had ever managed that in the British courts before.

'He is, quite simply,' I said, choking back the tears, 'the man who saved my life.'

But he and his team did more than that. He'd kept a
promise he made to my father in January 2005. He'd rescued
me from a life of terror, he'd given closure to two children
who'd been convinced their mum had abandoned them.
He'd won justice for Surjit Athwal and cleared her name.

But more importantly than that, he'd shown the whole
world that murders in the name of so-called 'honour' and
'shame' would not go undetected. Not in England. Not any
more. Not on DCI Driscoll's watch.

Bachan Kaur and Sukhdave Athwal
are currently serving fifteen and twenty years
respectively in prison. They are scheduled for
release in 2022 and 2027.

The Indian murderers of Surjit Athwal
have never been brought to justice –
but the fight goes on.

Surjit's body has never been found.

ACKNOWLEDGEMENTS

I'm indebted to so many people, not only for their help on this book, but for their help in my life.

First, to my family, to whom I owe so much.

Mum and Dad, I am sorry for putting you through difficult times, insisting you drove me in the dark winter's snowy cold days when your health was down so I could see my children. I thank you endlessly for all the support you gave me and my children throughout it all; for being there, for being patient and understanding me. For the values and principles you taught me and for always being strong with me.

My daughter Taran – Taz – thank you for everything you have done, for your understanding, for the heart-to-hearts we had, the tears we've shed together, for your hugs, for staying strong and more importantly being there for me. I agree with you that we are now much closer than we ever have been over the past years, and I am so sorry for the times we spent apart and the precious moments we missed out on. Taz, I am so proud of you for everything you have achieved. You are beautiful, you are smart and loving and caring, and

I wish you every happiness and am sure you will fulfil all your dreams. And remember, as always you have been, you are and always will be Mummy's little princess.

My daughter Balveen, you were the little confused girl trying to make sense of everything, having all those questions but never finding the answers. I'm sorry for the precious times we missed out on and not being there as much as I should have been. It is hard to express my words for you. You were always there for me, giving me hugs, kisses, hope; you said the little things that meant the world to me, and your lovely smile always brightened up my dull days. You are a caring, gentle, loving daughter that every mother would wish for. Balveen, I am so proud of you and thank you for everything you have done, despite all that you've been through. I know you will achieve all your dreams. I wish you all the happiness in the world and more, and yes, I will always be your best friend. You will always be my petal.

My son Manvinder, there was never a day that passed without you saying, 'Mummy, I love you.' You were Mummy's little boy who has always been loving, caring, kind, smart and funny. It is so wonderful to see you growing into a handsome young boy. You have stayed strong through all the times you were upset, helped Mummy and told Mummy to be strong. Manvinder, you are amazing; the only thing that kept Mummy strong was your warm cuddles, kisses and smiles. You have so many dreams for when you grow up and I know you will make them come true. I wish you all the love and happiness in the world; keep smiling and never give up. You are my sunshine.

My son Karaminder, I often called you my lucky star, you were my saviour from the day you were born. Kam, you are a bright little boy who has so much to look forward to and are full of so many great ideas at such a young age. You are smart, clever, kind, loving and caring, and confident, and always came running to me when you saw me upset and asked me, 'Mummy, are you OK?' Learn all you can and be strong, find new ways to explore and make all your dreams come true.

My niece Pawanpreet, I am so sorry for everything you have been through and how difficult it was finding out the truth about your mum. Despite everything that has gone on in your life, you have come through as a stronger person. Thank you for all the times you supported me. I wish you all the happiness in life with your new family and I know you will give your beautiful little treasures all the love you can. I am so proud of you.

My sister Inder, to me you are an angel in disguise: full of intuition, intelligent and wise. Always giving and helping through good times and bad. You are the best friend I've ever had. If I had one wish it would surely be to give you as much as you've given to me. Though I've put our relationship through some cloudy days, you've been my strength in many ways. You gave me your hand whenever you could. And your husband, Pauljit, thank you so much for your support and being a great role model for my little ones.

My sister Dalvinder, I am so grateful for all your support during my difficult times. You were so young yet did so much. I appreciate the little things you did that made a huge difference to me and my children, and I knew I could count on you no matter what. Thank you for all those times you spent with me when I was alone, the chats we had and the smiles we shared. Most of all, thank you for being there for me.

Uncle Bobby, thank you for the support and under-standing, the chats we had and the time you took out for me and my children.

My sister Kamaljit and husband Sarbjit, thank you for all your support and encouragement you gave to me.

My sister Karmjit and husband Satwant, the generous support you gave to my family was much appreciated, thank you.

Jagdeesh Singh, you are a saint. I admire you so much for your strength, your courage and your determination. In the face of everything, you stayed strong, you had hope and you never gave up. I hope you can understand from this book just how much pressure I was under.

There are many other people who have done so much for me that they feel like family.

Top of the list has to be DCI Clive Driscoll. Clive, I am privileged and honoured to have met you. Words cannot express my gratitude towards you. I appreciate everything you have done for me and my children. I am grateful for all the support, the courage you gave me and for your understanding. Thank you for believing in me when others let me down. You are a great credit to the MPS, Clive, and please do not change. My gratitude for you has no end. Thank you for saving my life.

Special mention should go as well to DS Angie Barton, DS Allan Goodley, DI Shaun Keep, DI Pal Singh, DS Richard McGuiness and all those who worked with Clive on Operation Yewlands. Your hard work, your professionalism and support was much appreciated during the investigation.

I also wish to praise the jury at the murder trial, who sat through all those weeks of evidence. I can only imagine how difficult it must have been for them all. Thank you too to His Honour Giles Forrester, and to my barrister Mr Worsley QC, who was amazing.

For helping me bring Surjit's story to the world, I have to thank my literary agent, Robert Smith, my co-writer, Jeff Hudson, my editor, Kate Moore, and all her team at Virgin Books.

Thank you also to Stephen Timms MP, for inviting Pav and me to speak about Surjit and honour killings at the Houses of Parliament; to Dr Thacker and Dr Shah and all those at the medical centre for their constant help and support; to Slough Grammar School, Kingston College, King

Athelstan Primary, TGS for supporting my children; to PS Alastair Carlton for his support and being a great line manager and also his quick response to Kingston College to ensure the safety of my daughter.

To special friends I have come to know, Rohema Miah, Bal and Phil Howard, Harpreet, Preeya Kaur, Jatinder Khatkar; to Madhu Penji, for the courage, the strength, the support, the time, the understanding, and much more; to Jo Keogh for all her hard work and support; and to all those who are not mentioned, your valuable time was much appreciated.

For inviting me to speak on the BBC World Service and share my experience, Kristine Pommert and Michael Ford. For inviting me and my family to an event at New Scotland Yard – and for praising me for my bravery and integrity during my support in Operations Yewlands – AC Cressida Dick. Thanks also to Christine Boot of Grants Solicitors for all your hard work and support and understanding during my difficult times.

Norfolk Constabulary Eastern Regional's Amanda Murr; Essex Police's Sally Goldfinch and DC Darren Sibley; DI Stuart Hooper at Essex Police College HQ; Camberwell Child Protection Team; Paul at Hendon Police College; Suffolk Constabulary's Tonya Antonis; Suffolk HQ; Basildon Women's Aid; Nazir Afzal, Chief Crown Prosecutor; Donal Macintyre; and William Marx. Thank you all so much.